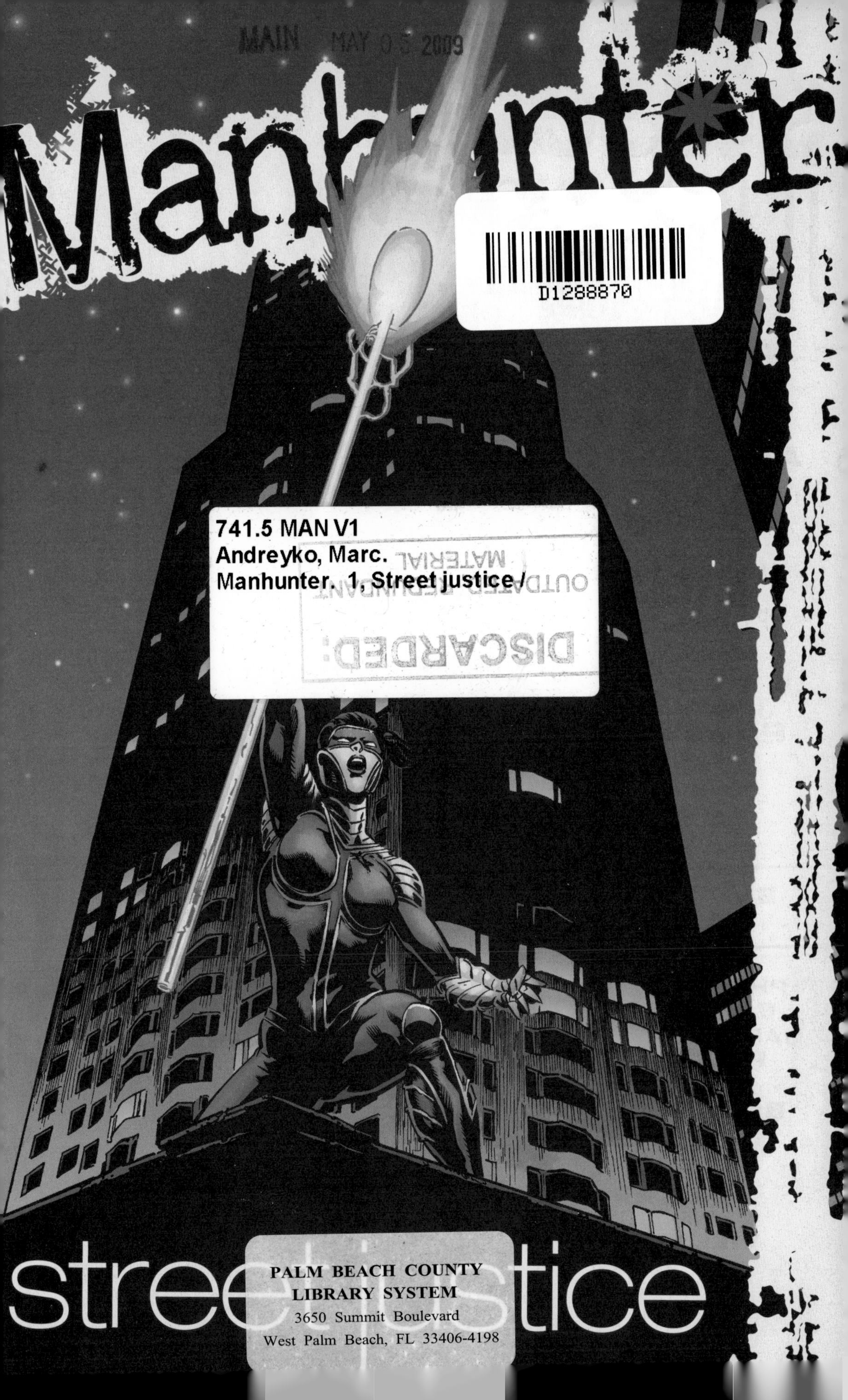
Manhunter
street justice

street justice

MARC
ANDREYKO
WRITER

JESUS
SAIZ
PENCILLER

JIMMY
PALMIOTTI
INKER

STEVE
BUCCELLATO
COLORIST

PHIL
BALSMAN
JARED K.
FLETCHER
PAT
BROSSEAU
LETTERERS

JAE **LEE**
WITH JOSE
VILLARRUBIA
& JUNE
CHUNG
ORIGINAL COVERS

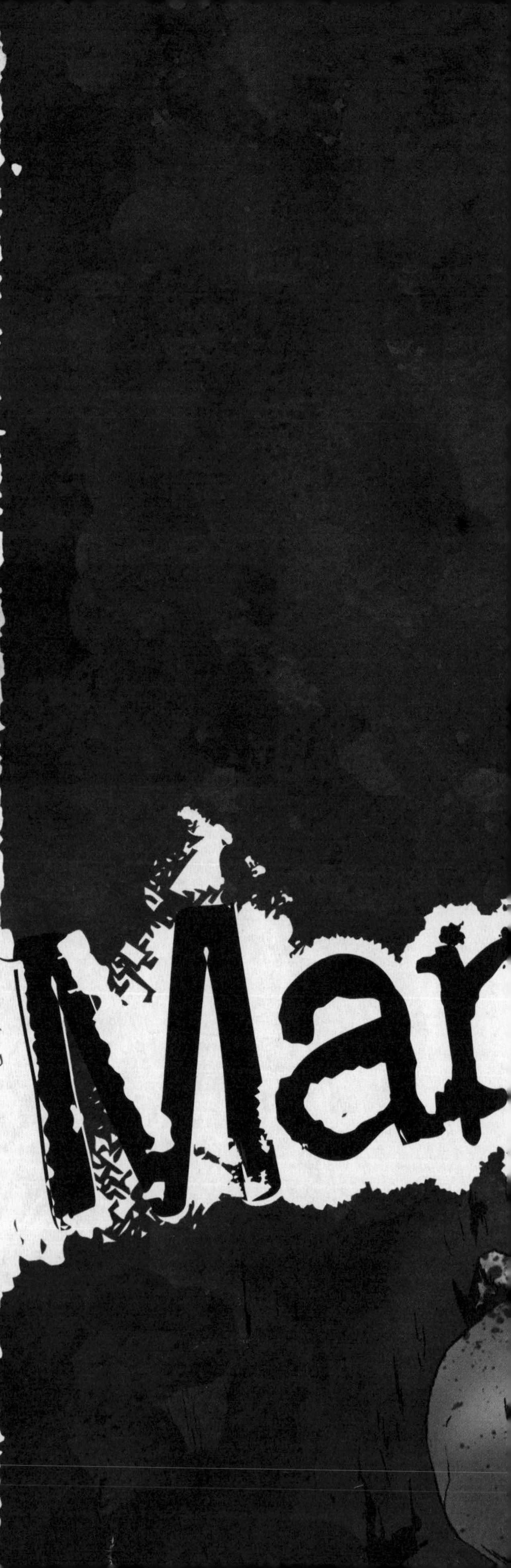

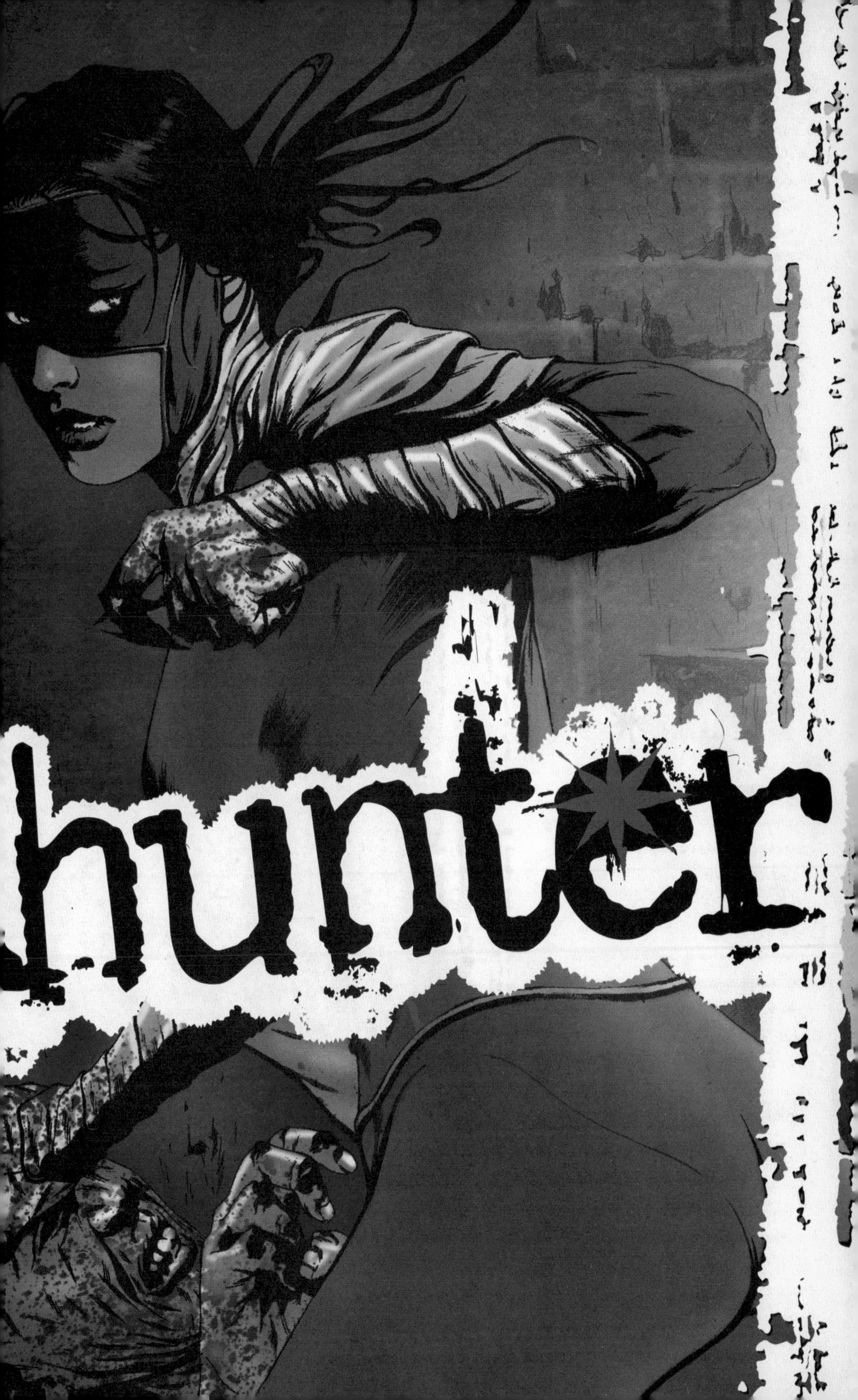
hunter

Dan DiDio VP-Executive Editor

Joan Hilty Editor-original series

Harvey Richards and Rachel Gluckstern

Assistant Editors-original series

Anton Kawasaki Editor-collected edition

Robbin Brosterman Senior Art Director

Paul Levitz President & Publisher

Georg Brewer VP-Design & DC Direct Creative

Richard Bruning Senior VP-Creative Director

Patrick Caldon Senior VP-Finance & Operations

Chris Caramalis VP-Finance

Terri Cunningham VP-Managing Editor

Stephanie Fierman Senior VP-Sales & Marketing

Alison Gill VP-Manufacturing

Rich Johnson VP-Book Trade Sales

Hank Kanalz VP-General Manager, WildStorm

Lillian Laserson Senior VP & General Counsel

Jim Lee Editorial Director-WildStorm

Paula Lowitt Senior VP-Business & Legal Affairs

David McKillips VP-Advertising & Custom Publishing

John Nee VP-Business Development

Gregory Noveck Senior VP-Creative Affairs

Cheryl Rubin Senior VP-Brand Management

Jeff Trojan VP-Business Development, DC Direct

Bob Wayne VP-Sales

MANHUNTER: STREET JUSTICE

DC Comics, 1700 Broadway, New York, NY 10019

A Warner Bros. Entertainment Company

Printed in Canada. Second Printing.

ISBN: 1-4012-0728-6

ISBN 13: 978-1-4012-0728-1

Cover art by Jae Lee with June Chung

Publication design by Amie Brockway-Metcalf

introduction

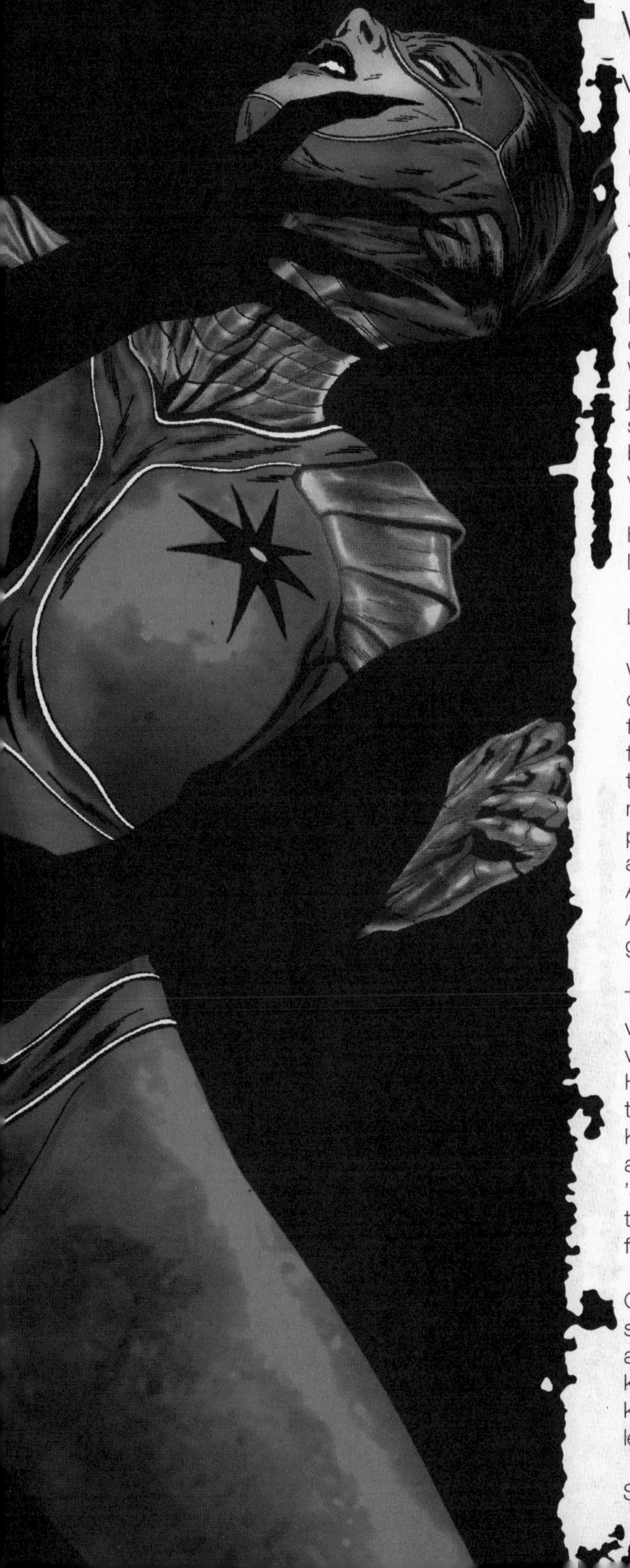

Wow, I *never* thought this would happen. Did you?

OK, let me elaborate (for those of you new to the MANHUNTER experience):

This book contains a female protagonist. Who smokes. Who is divorced. Who has slightly better maternal skills than Mrs. Bates. Who resides not in Gotham or Metropolis, but Los Angeles. Who isn't afraid to kill in the name of justice. And most shocking of all for a super-heroine, she doesn't wear a metal bra, stripper heels or a T-back thong while fighting crime.

How the hell did she get a series, let alone a trade paperback?

Let's backtrack, shall we?

When I was pitching the character of Kate Spencer/Manhunter to DC, I figured "what the hell? I'll pitch the female character I wanna see" (since up to this point I had, ahem, shall we say, many "missions scrubbed on the launch pad" in mainstream comics. But that's another introduction for another day. After a few drinks. And a few more. All right, one more. But somebody's gotta drive me home.)

The female characters who inspired me weren't the earth mothers, the devoted wives, or the sex kittens. Give me Helen Mirren's "Jane Tennison" (from the exquisite *Prime Suspect* series), Katharine Hepburn and Rosalind Russell and the classic "dames" of the '30s and '40s. Give me a woman who ain't afraid to be a "broad" and doesn't lose her femininity because of it.

OK, what do we have then? A flawed, somewhat unlikable, fully-clothed, average-busted woman? Oh yeah, for kicks, let's make her a lawyer. One who kills the bad guys who deserve it. And let's put her in the mainstream DCU.

See why I'm surprised to be here?

Luckily for Kate, and me (and hopefully, you'll think for *you* after reading these stories), DC has been in a bit of a renaissance lately. Perhaps you've heard of their intimate, drawing room successes — IDENTITY CRISIS (which has a tie-in in this very tome — the sold-out issue #5), COUNTDOWN, INFINITE CRISIS and the like.

So, DC, on all fronts, was not only supportive of this new "Manhunter" (for a peek into the elaborate history of the prior 'hunters see issues #10-14 of Kate's book — or, God willing, the next volume in this collection!), but they encouraged going further with the character. They gave me a shocking list of bad guys who were allowed to meet their maker at Kate's hands. They let her be integrated into the DCU with gusto. They let her male co-worker flirt with Hawkman (see chapter 5)!

I felt like it was all part of an elaborate ruse to dash my hope upon the rocks of comicdom. But I was wrong. Boy, was I wrong.

And I couldn't be more proud of the results or the reaction to Kate's adventures. See, to my surprise, people responded to Kate. The reviews are great. The devotion of fans to such a new character continues to humble me. We have been called a "sleeper," a "cult hit," and "the best new super-hero book out there." Understand why I was waiting for the punch line?

But, the punch line never came. And every day I get to sit down in front of my computer and work on the adventures of Kate Spencer. How lucky am I?

So, as I sign off, let me say a hearty thank-you to DC, to Jesus and Jimmy and Steve, to Dan and Joan, and to you, the wonderful fans — (Whoa. Stop channeling Joan Crawford, dude. It's waaaaaaay cliché.)

Anyway, I hope you dig these collected stories half as much as we did in telling them. Be careful around Kate though. She knows how to get under your skin. And once she's there...well, you'll see.

MARC ANDREYKO
Los Angeles
August 2005

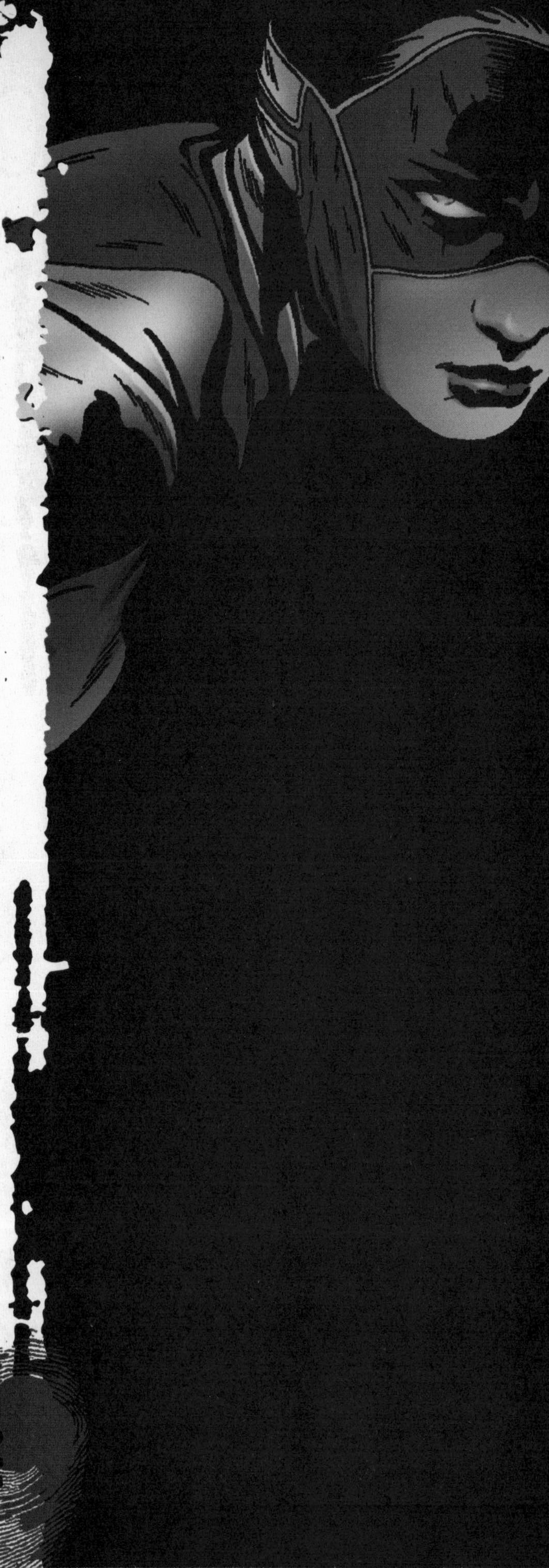

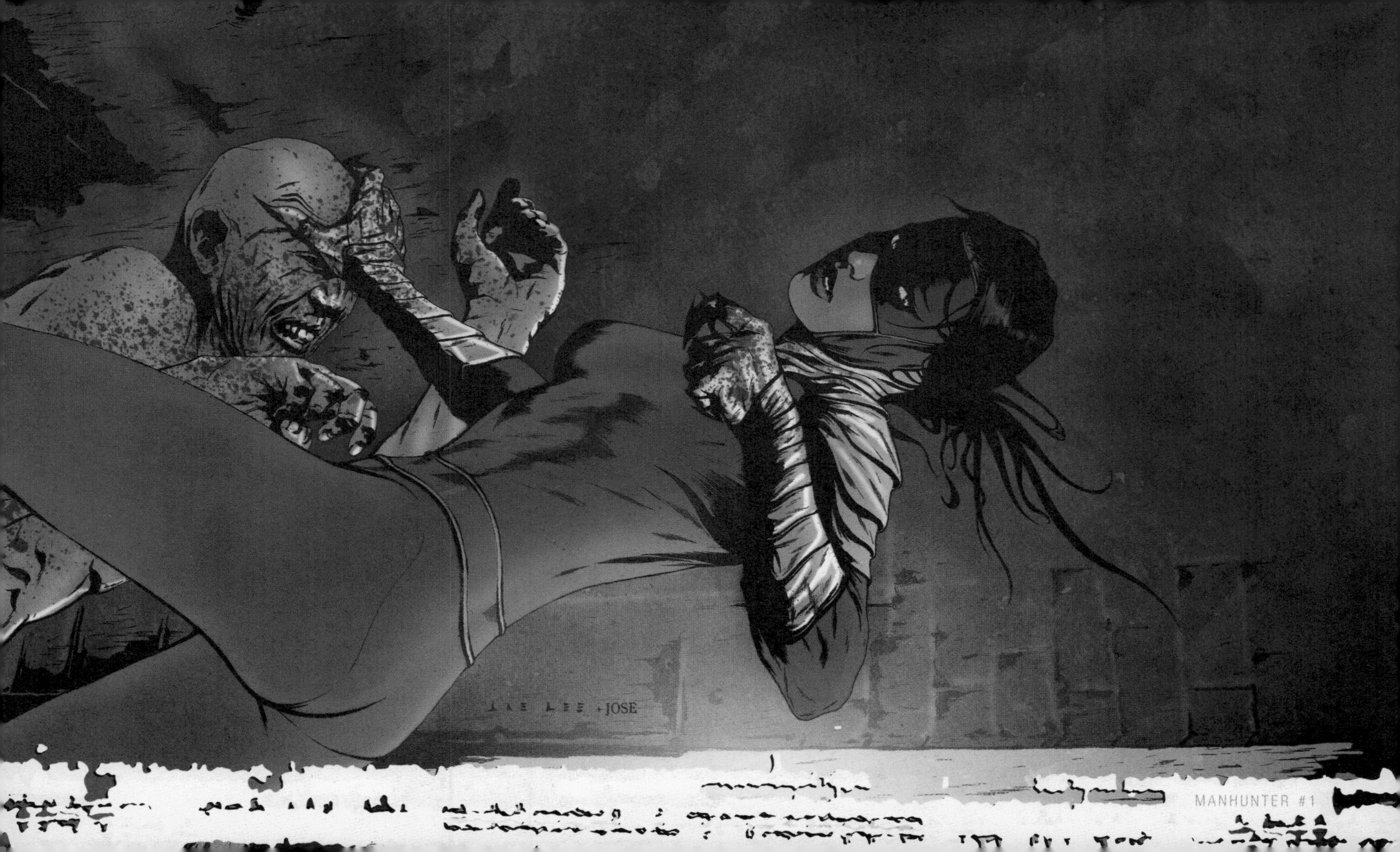
JAE LEE +JOSE
MANHUNTER #1

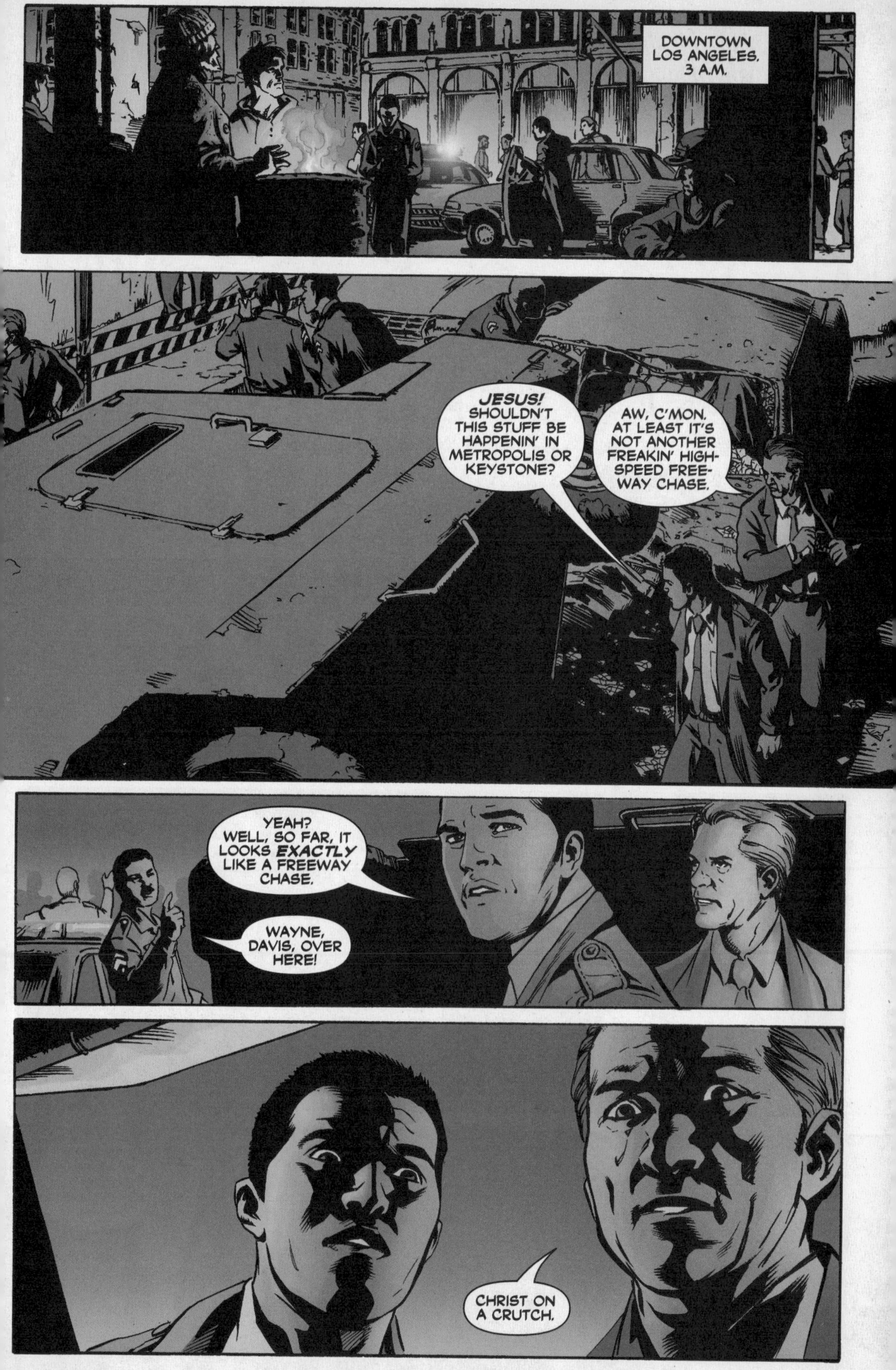
DOWNTOWN LOS ANGELES, 3 A.M.
JESUS! SHOULDN'T THIS STUFF BE HAPPENIN' IN METROPOLIS OR KEYSTONE?
AW, C'MON. AT LEAST IT'S NOT ANOTHER FREAKIN' HIGH-SPEED FREEWAY CHASE.
YEAH? WELL, SO FAR, IT LOOKS EXACTLY LIKE A FREEWAY CHASE.
WAYNE, DAVIS, OVER HERE!
CHRIST ON A CRUTCH.

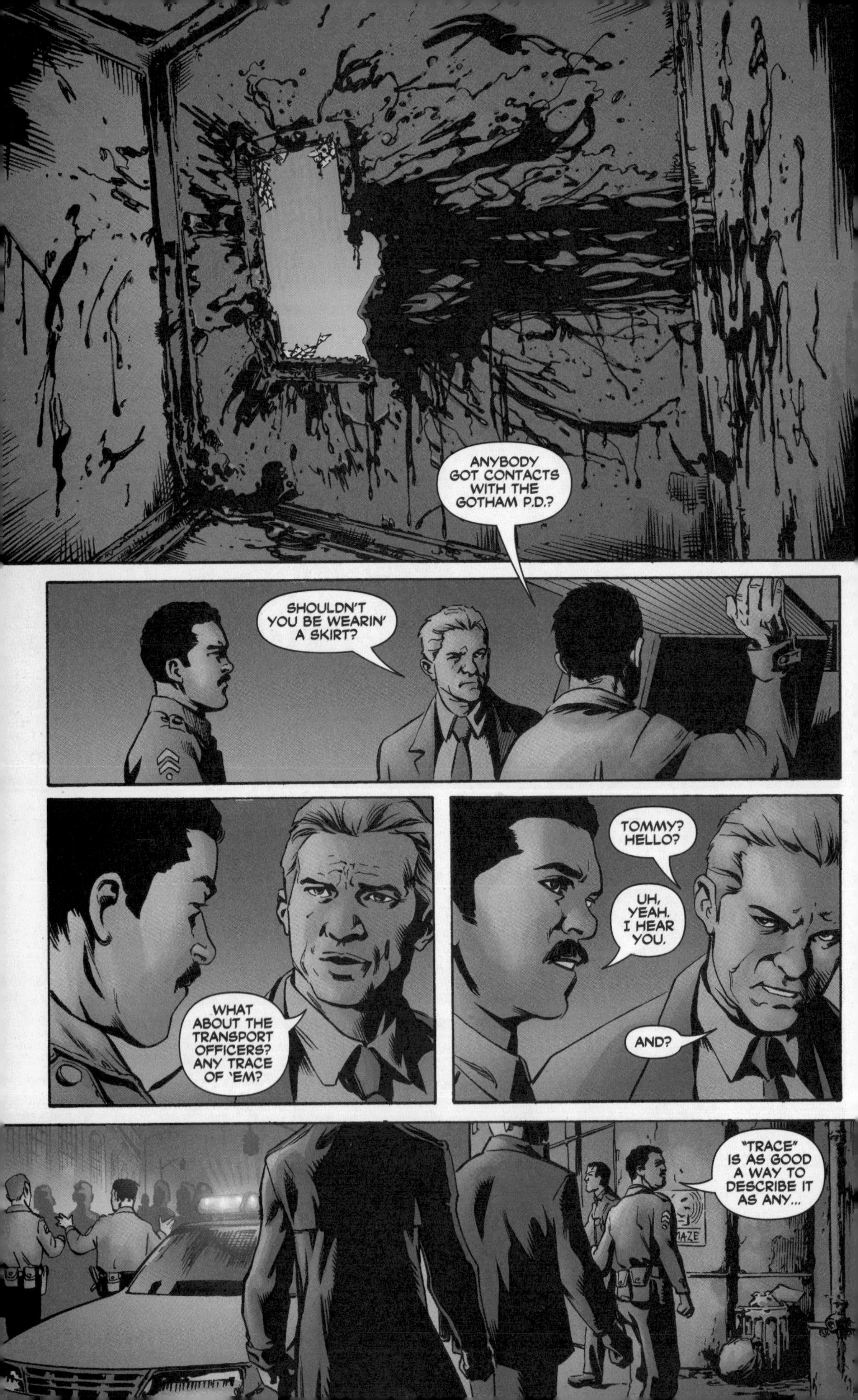
ANYBODY GOT CONTACTS WITH THE GOTHAM P.D.?
SHOULDN'T YOU BE WEARIN' A SKIRT?
WHAT ABOUT THE TRANSPORT OFFICERS? ANY TRACE OF 'EM?
TOMMY? HELLO?
UH, YEAH, I HEAR YOU.
AND?
"TRACE" IS AS GOOD A WAY TO DESCRIBE IT AS ANY...
MAZE

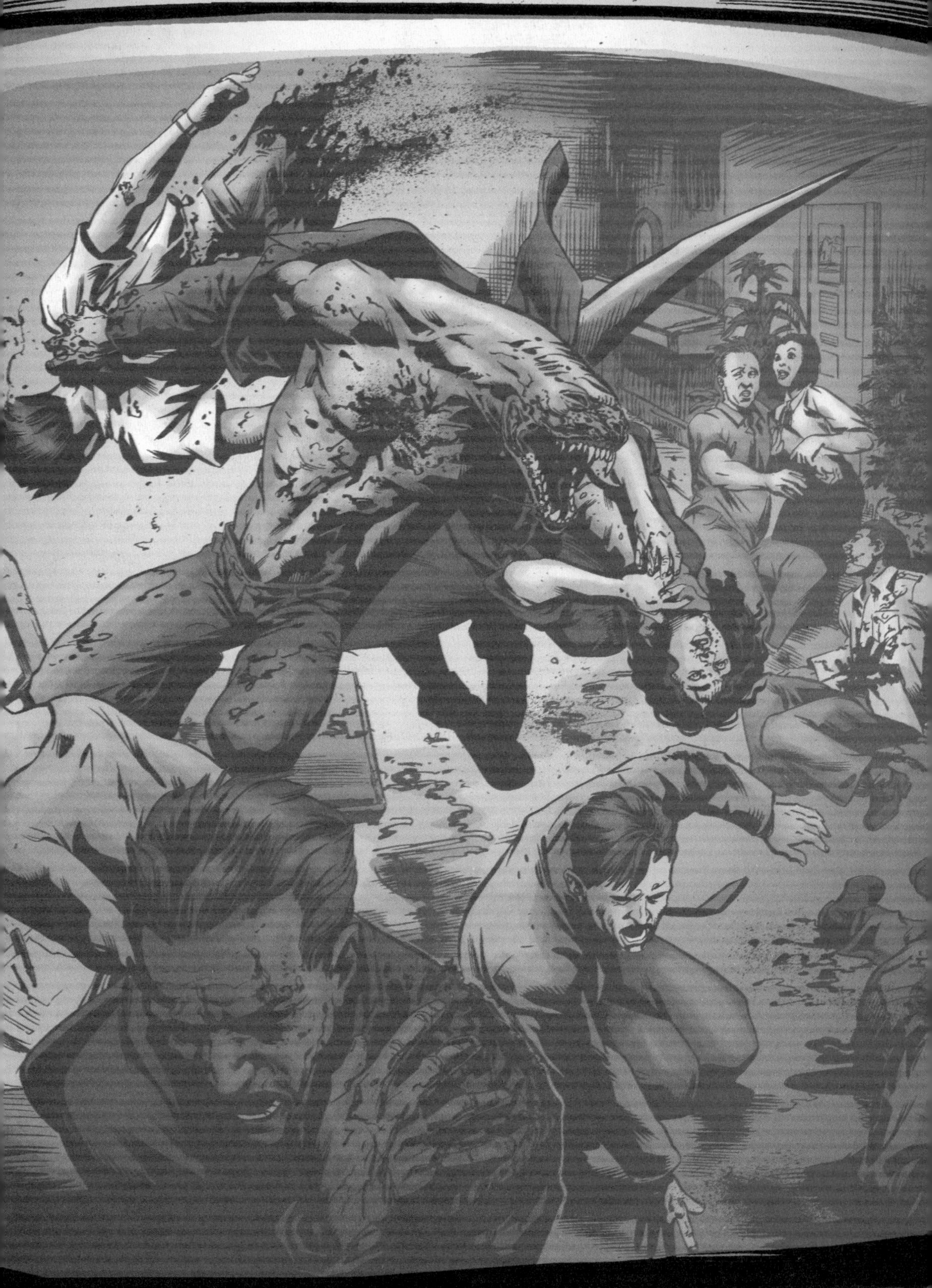

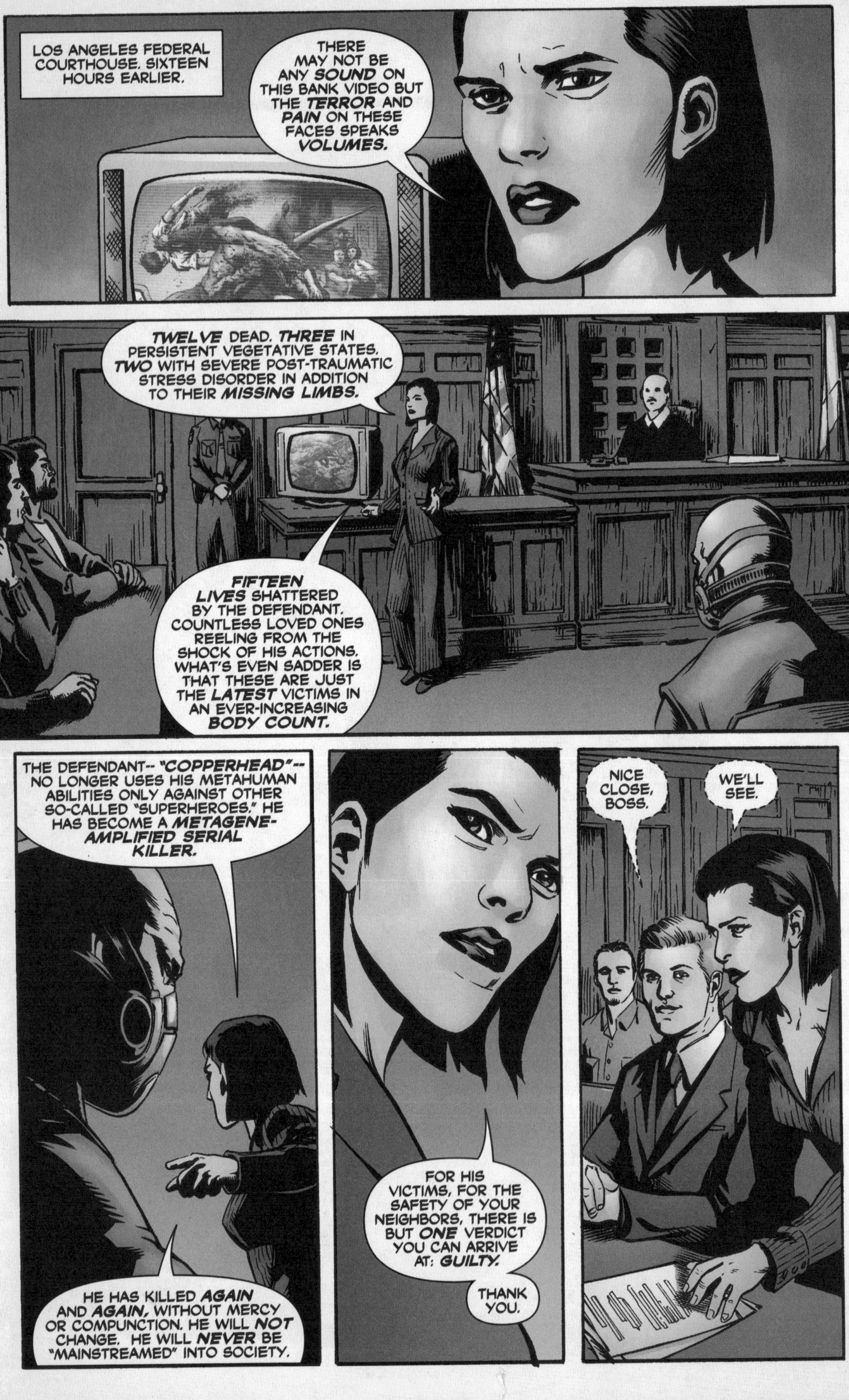
LOS ANGELES FEDERAL COURTHOUSE. SIXTEEN HOURS EARLIER.
THERE MAY NOT BE ANY SOUND ON THIS BANK VIDEO BUT THE TERROR AND PAIN ON THESE FACES SPEAKS VOLUMES.
TWELVE DEAD. THREE IN PERSISTENT VEGETATIVE STATES. TWO WITH SEVERE POST-TRAUMATIC STRESS DISORDER IN ADDITION TO THEIR MISSING LIMBS.
FIFTEEN LIVES SHATTERED BY THE DEFENDANT. COUNTLESS LOVED ONES REELING FROM THE SHOCK OF HIS ACTIONS. WHAT'S EVEN SADDER IS THAT THESE ARE JUST THE LATEST VICTIMS IN AN EVER-INCREASING BODY COUNT.
THE DEFENDANT-- "COPPERHEAD"-- NO LONGER USES HIS METAHUMAN ABILITIES ONLY AGAINST OTHER SO-CALLED "SUPERHEROES." HE HAS BECOME A METAGENE-AMPLIFIED SERIAL KILLER.
HE HAS KILLED AGAIN AND AGAIN, WITHOUT MERCY OR COMPUNCTION. HE WILL NOT CHANGE. HE WILL NEVER BE "MAINSTREAMED" INTO SOCIETY.
FOR HIS VICTIMS, FOR THE SAFETY OF YOUR NEIGHBORS, THERE IS BUT ONE VERDICT YOU CAN ARRIVE AT: GUILTY.
THANK YOU.
NICE CLOSE, BOSS.
WE'LL SEE.

THE *META-HUMAN* GENE.

THAT, LADIES AND GENTLEMEN OF THE JURY, IS WHAT THIS CASE HINGES UPON.

THERE IS NO ARGUING THAT COPPERHEAD HAS COMMITTED THESE HEINOUS ACTS. MS. SPENCER IS RIGHT. WHAT YOU SAW ON THE TAPE *SHOULD* SICKEN YOU. IT SICKENS *ME.*

BUT IT SHOULD ALSO MAKE YOU ASK *THIS* QUESTION: WHAT *SANE* HUMAN BEING COULD BRING SUCH DESTRUCTION UPON HIS FELLOW MAN?

THE ANSWER: *NONE.* MY CLIENT IS THE VICTIM OF *EVOLUTION* GONE AWRY.

THE PROSECUTION WOULD LIKE YOU TO BELIEVE THAT COPPERHEAD *ENJOYS* HIS CURRENT STATE. BUT *LOOK* AT HIM. BOUND AND SEDATED, OR AN UNCONTROL-LABLE CANNIBAL KILLER-- WHO WOULD *CHOOSE* SUCH A LIFE?

TO KILL HIM WOULD BE TOO EASY. YES, THE IMMEDIATE CATHARSIS OF HIS EXECUTION MIGHT EASE THE VICTIMS' PAIN MOMENTARILY.

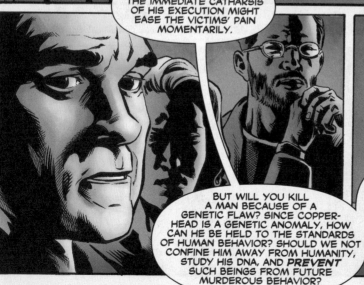

BUT WILL YOU KILL A MAN BECAUSE OF A GENETIC FLAW? SINCE COPPER-HEAD IS A GENETIC ANOMALY, HOW CAN HE BE HELD TO THE STANDARDS OF HUMAN BEHAVIOR? SHOULD WE NOT CONFINE HIM AWAY FROM HUMANITY, STUDY HIS DNA, AND *PREVENT* SUCH BEINGS FROM FUTURE MURDEROUS BEHAVIOR?

NOT GUILTY, LADIES AND GENTLEMEN. NO MORE SO THAN YOU ARE OF CHOOSING YOUR EYE COLOR.

THANK YOU.

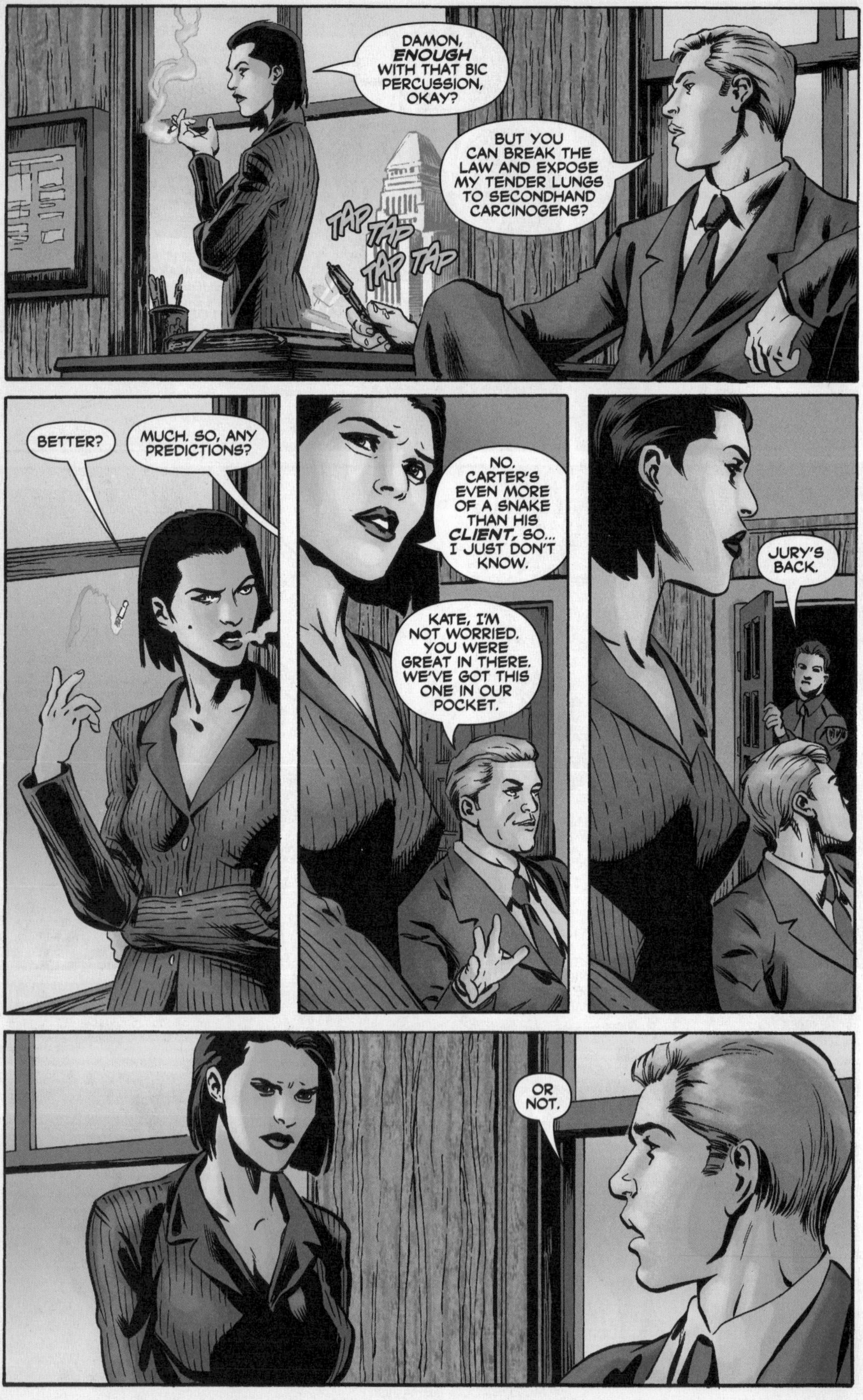
DAMON, **ENOUGH** WITH THAT BIC PERCUSSION, OKAY?
BUT YOU CAN BREAK THE LAW AND EXPOSE MY TENDER LUNGS TO SECONDHAND CARCINOGENS?
TAP TAP TAP TAP
BETTER?
MUCH. SO, ANY PREDICTIONS?
NO. CARTER'S EVEN MORE OF A SNAKE THAN HIS **CLIENT,** SO... I JUST DON'T KNOW.
KATE, I'M NOT WORRIED. YOU WERE GREAT IN THERE. WE'VE GOT THIS ONE IN OUR POCKET.
JURY'S BACK.
OR NOT.

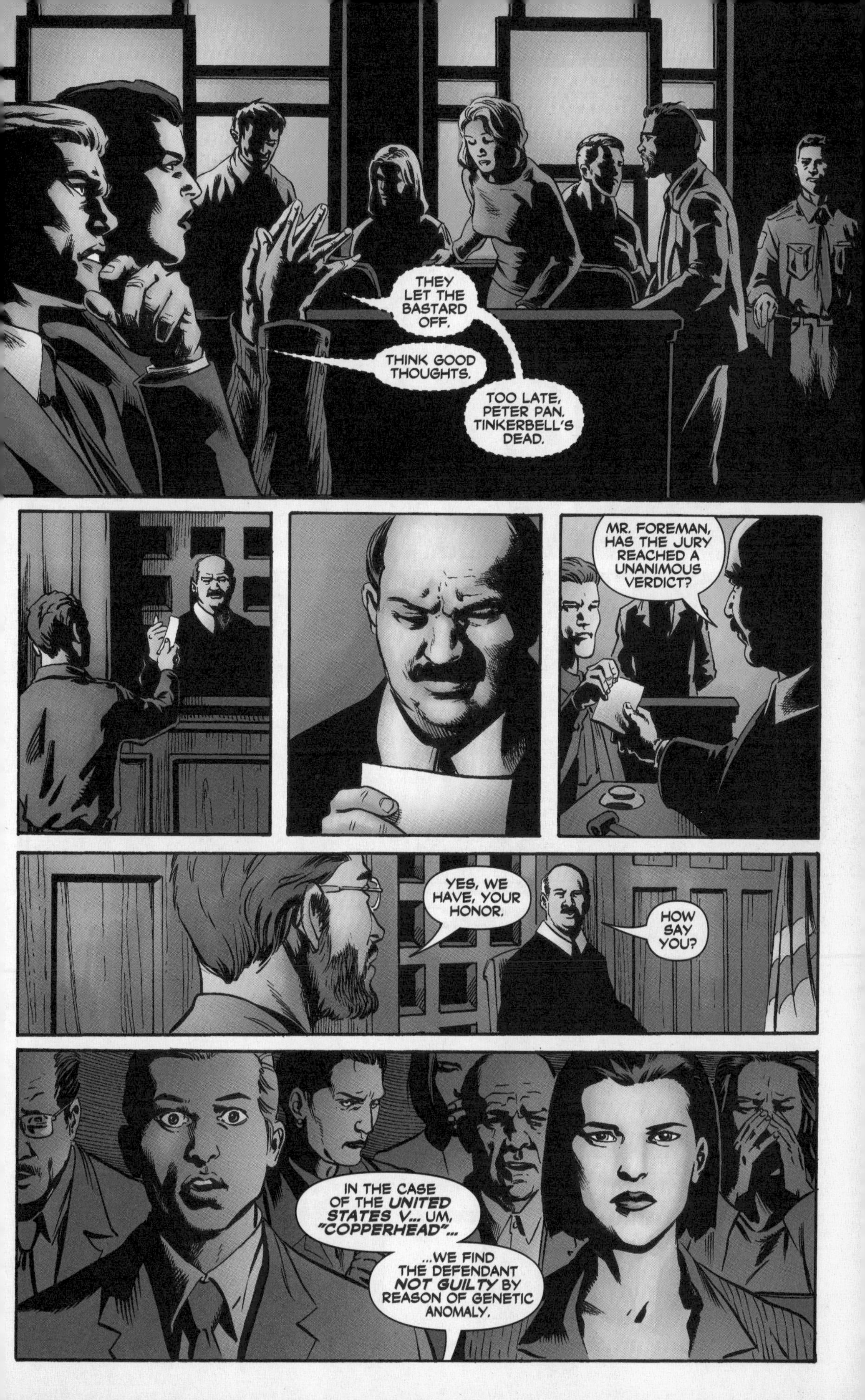
THEY LET THE BASTARD OFF.
THINK GOOD THOUGHTS.
TOO LATE, PETER PAN. TINKERBELL'S DEAD.
MR. FOREMAN, HAS THE JURY REACHED A UNANIMOUS VERDICT?
YES, WE HAVE, YOUR HONOR.
HOW SAY YOU?
IN THE CASE OF THE *UNITED STATES V...* UM, *"COPPERHEAD"*...
...WE FIND THE DEFENDANT *NOT GUILTY* BY REASON OF GENETIC ANOMALY.

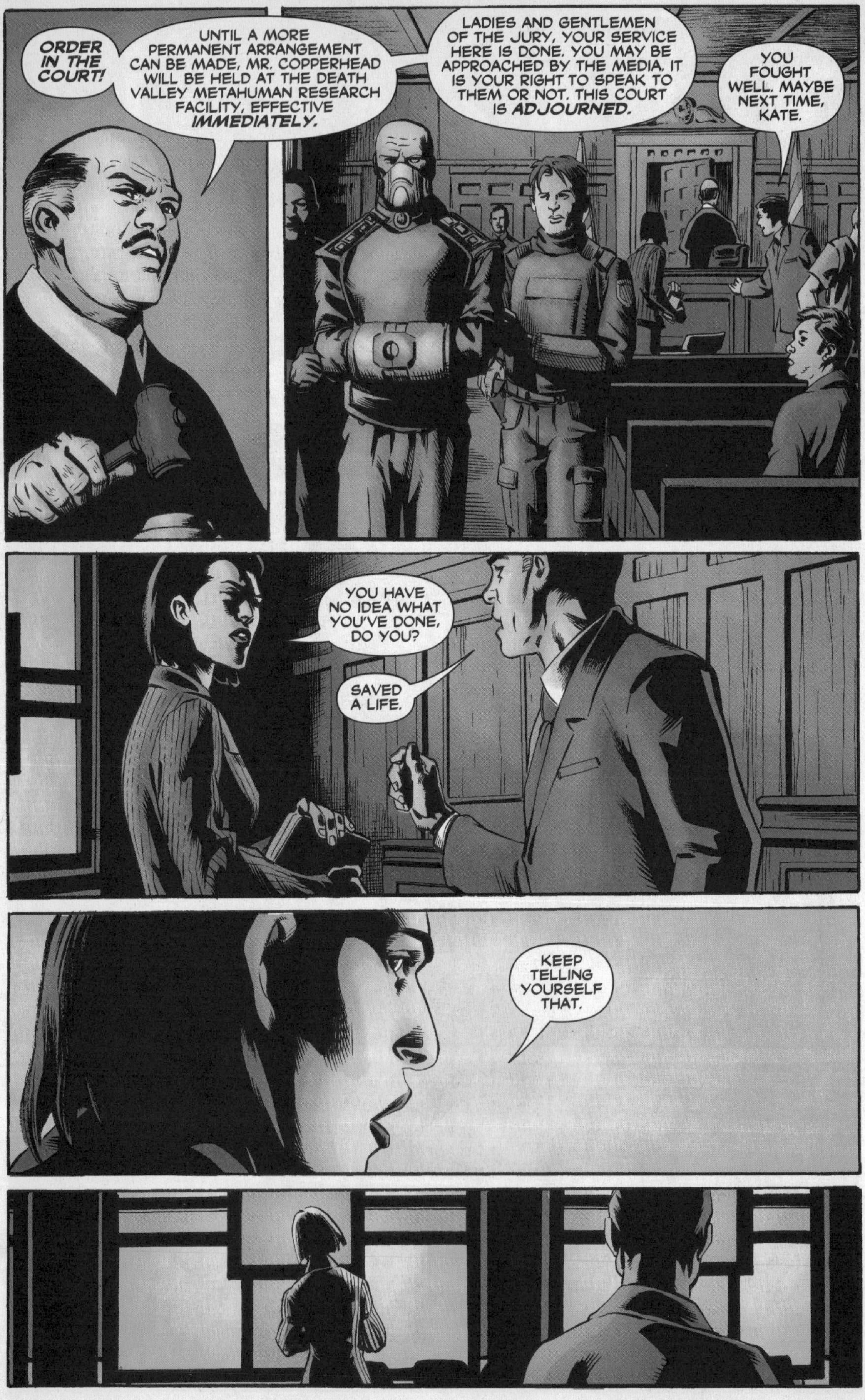
ORDER IN THE COURT!
UNTIL A MORE PERMANENT ARRANGEMENT CAN BE MADE, MR. COPPERHEAD WILL BE HELD AT THE DEATH VALLEY METAHUMAN RESEARCH FACILITY, EFFECTIVE IMMEDIATELY.
LADIES AND GENTLEMEN OF THE JURY, YOUR SERVICE HERE IS DONE. YOU MAY BE APPROACHED BY THE MEDIA. IT IS YOUR RIGHT TO SPEAK TO THEM OR NOT. THIS COURT IS ADJOURNED.
YOU FOUGHT WELL. MAYBE NEXT TIME, KATE.
YOU HAVE NO IDEA WHAT YOU'VE DONE, DO YOU?
SAVED A LIFE.
KEEP TELLING YOURSELF THAT.

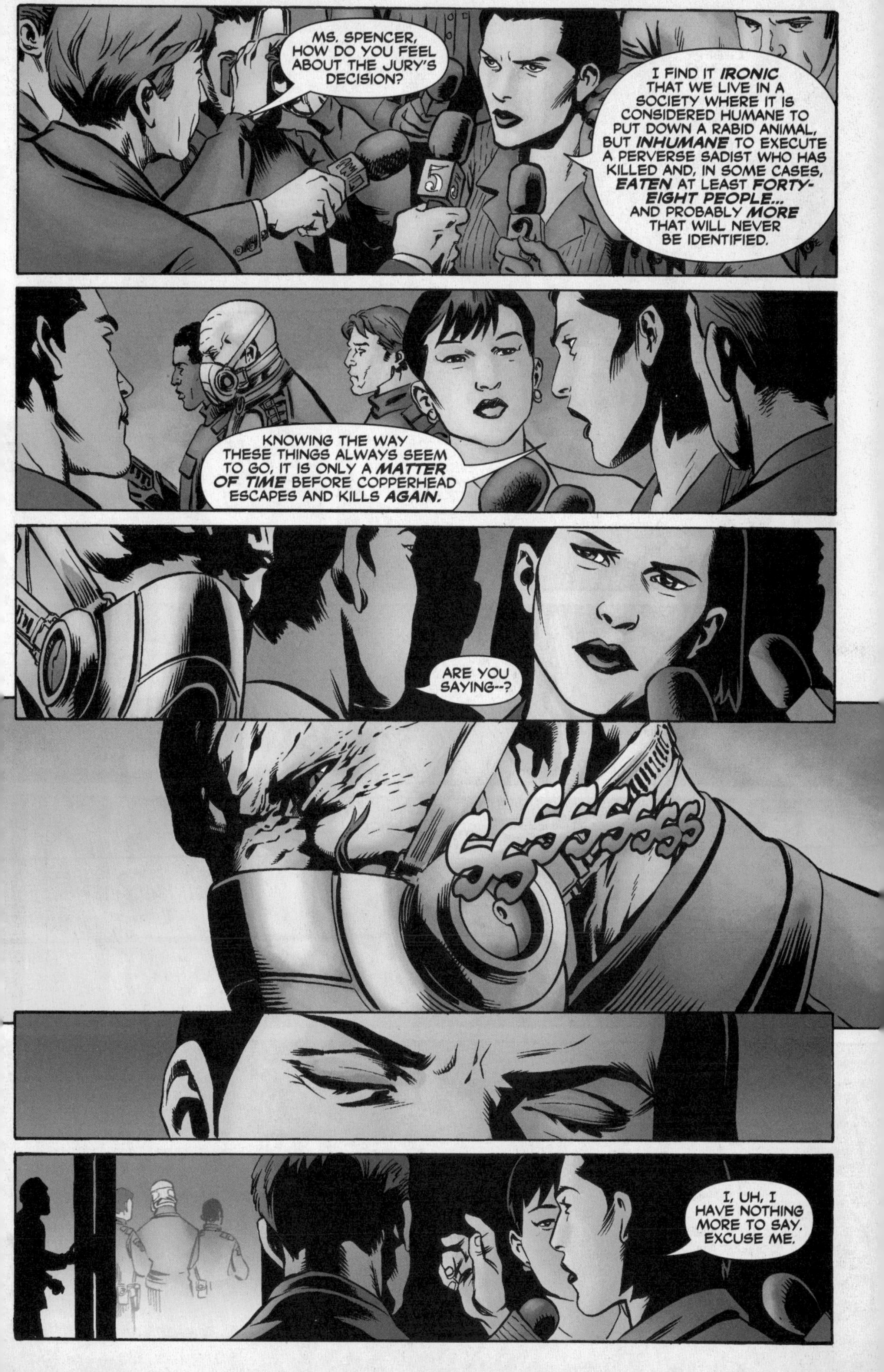
MS. SPENCER, HOW DO YOU FEEL ABOUT THE JURY'S DECISION?
I FIND IT IRONIC THAT WE LIVE IN A SOCIETY WHERE IT IS CONSIDERED HUMANE TO PUT DOWN A RABID ANIMAL, BUT INHUMANE TO EXECUTE A PERVERSE SADIST WHO HAS KILLED AND, IN SOME CASES, EATEN AT LEAST FORTY-EIGHT PEOPLE... AND PROBABLY MORE THAT WILL NEVER BE IDENTIFIED.
KNOWING THE WAY THESE THINGS ALWAYS SEEM TO GO, IT IS ONLY A MATTER OF TIME BEFORE COPPERHEAD ESCAPES AND KILLS AGAIN.
ARE YOU SAYING--?
SSSSSSSS
I, UH, I HAVE NOTHING MORE TO SAY. EXCUSE ME.

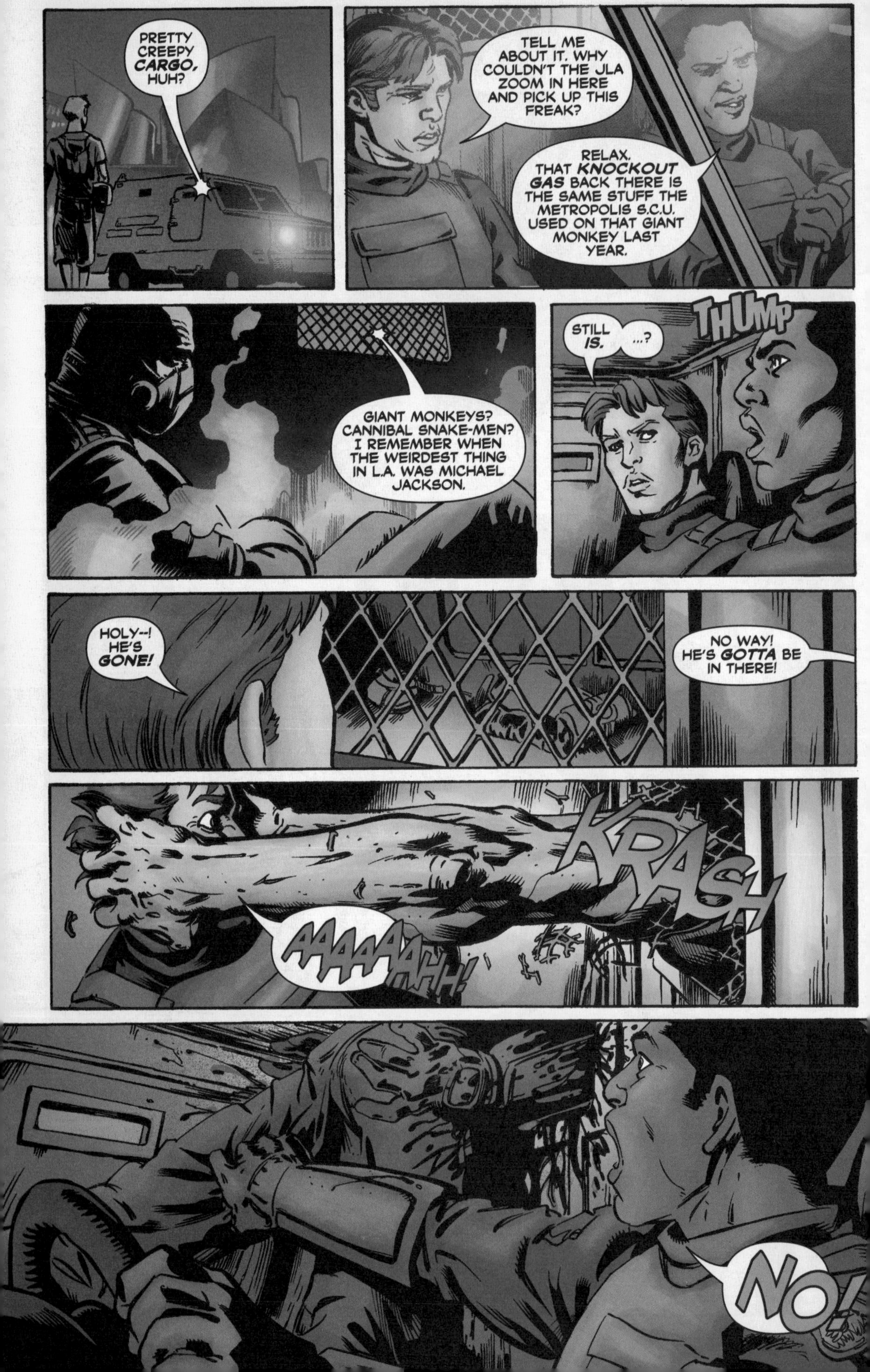
PRETTY CREEPY CARGO, HUH?
TELL ME ABOUT IT. WHY COULDN'T THE JLA ZOOM IN HERE AND PICK UP THIS FREAK?
RELAX. THAT KNOCKOUT GAS BACK THERE IS THE SAME STUFF THE METROPOLIS S.C.U. USED ON THAT GIANT MONKEY LAST YEAR.
GIANT MONKEYS? CANNIBAL SNAKE-MEN? I REMEMBER WHEN THE WEIRDEST THING IN L.A. WAS MICHAEL JACKSON.
STILL IS.
...?
THUMP
HOLY--! HE'S GONE!
NO WAY! HE'S GOTTA BE IN THERE!
KRASH
AAAAAAHH!
NO!

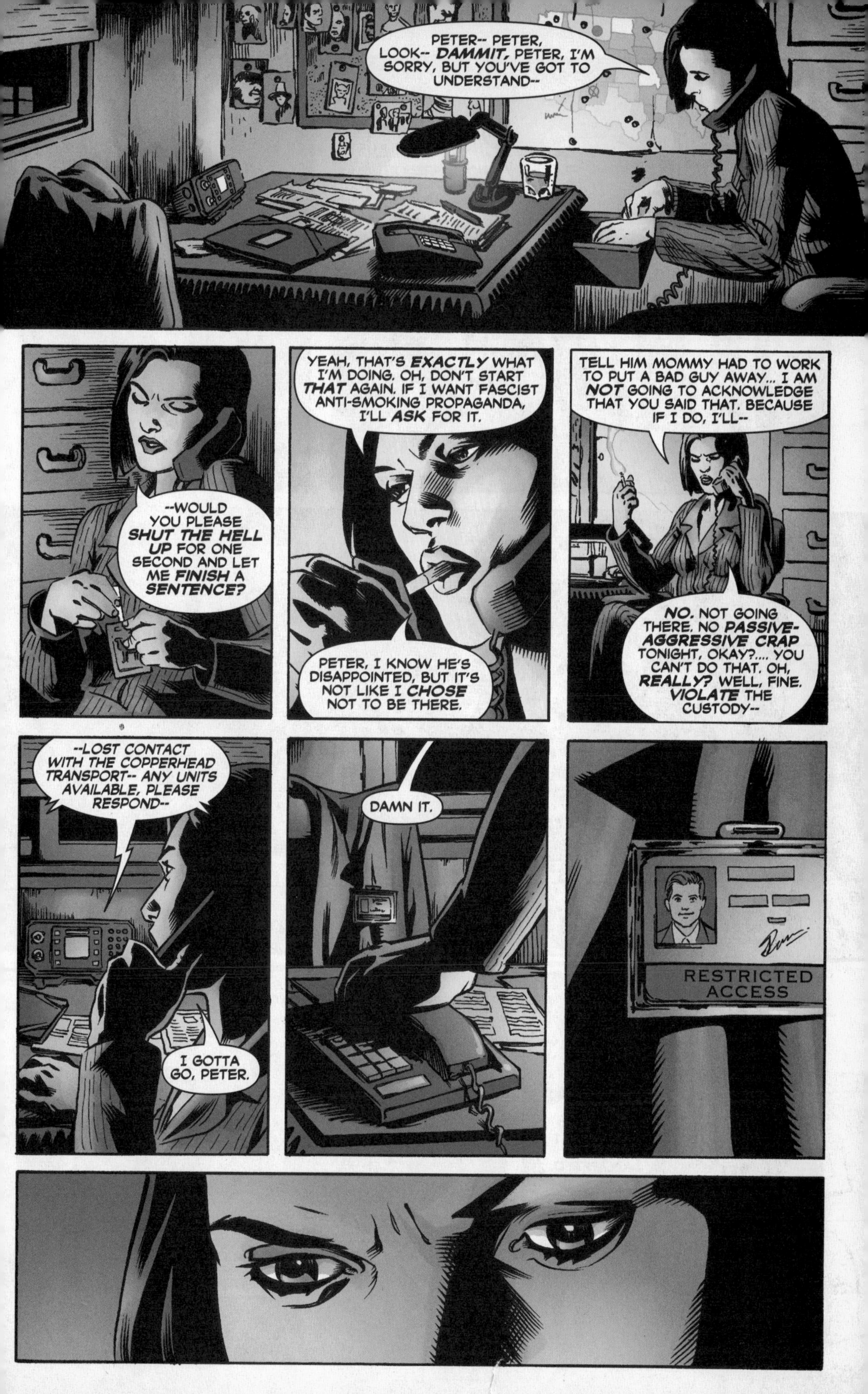
PETER-- PETER, LOOK-- DAMMIT, PETER, I'M SORRY, BUT YOU'VE GOT TO UNDERSTAND--
--WOULD YOU PLEASE SHUT THE HELL UP FOR ONE SECOND AND LET ME FINISH A SENTENCE?
YEAH, THAT'S EXACTLY WHAT I'M DOING. OH, DON'T START THAT AGAIN. IF I WANT FASCIST ANTI-SMOKING PROPAGANDA, I'LL ASK FOR IT.
PETER, I KNOW HE'S DISAPPOINTED, BUT IT'S NOT LIKE I CHOSE NOT TO BE THERE.
TELL HIM MOMMY HAD TO WORK TO PUT A BAD GUY AWAY... I AM NOT GOING TO ACKNOWLEDGE THAT YOU SAID THAT. BECAUSE IF I DO, I'LL--
NO. NOT GOING THERE. NO PASSIVE-AGGRESSIVE CRAP TONIGHT, OKAY?.... YOU CAN'T DO THAT. OH, REALLY? WELL, FINE. VIOLATE THE CUSTODY--
--LOST CONTACT WITH THE COPPERHEAD TRANSPORT-- ANY UNITS AVAILABLE, PLEASE RESPOND--
I GOTTA GO, PETER.
DAMN IT.
RESTRICTED ACCESS

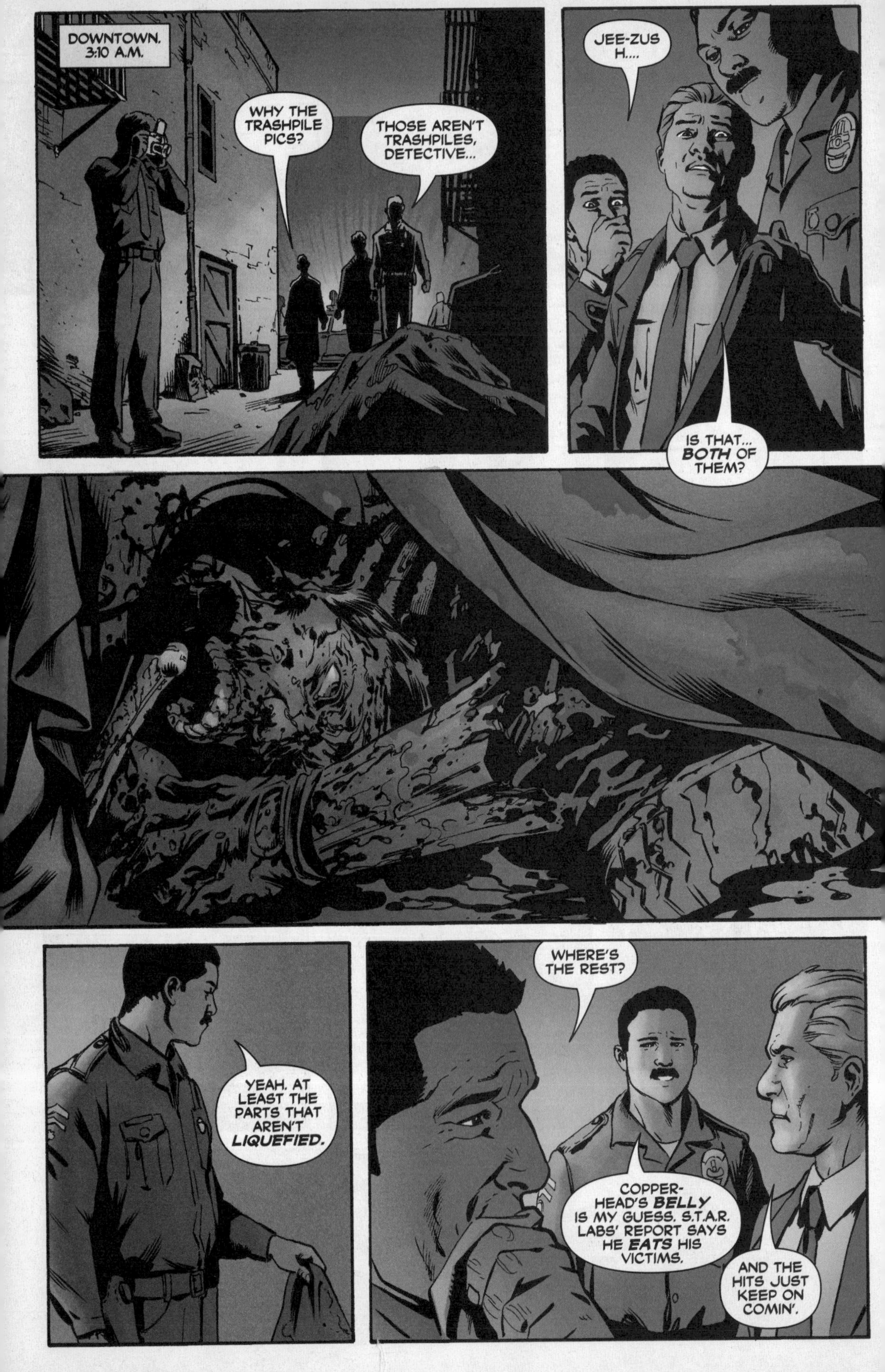
DOWNTOWN. 3:10 A.M.
WHY THE TRASHPILE PICS?
THOSE AREN'T TRASHPILES, DETECTIVE...
JEE-ZUS H....
IS THAT... BOTH OF THEM?
YEAH. AT LEAST THE PARTS THAT AREN'T LIQUEFIED.
WHERE'S THE REST?
COPPER-HEAD'S BELLY IS MY GUESS. S.T.A.R. LABS' REPORT SAYS HE EATS HIS VICTIMS.
AND THE HITS JUST KEEP ON COMIN'.

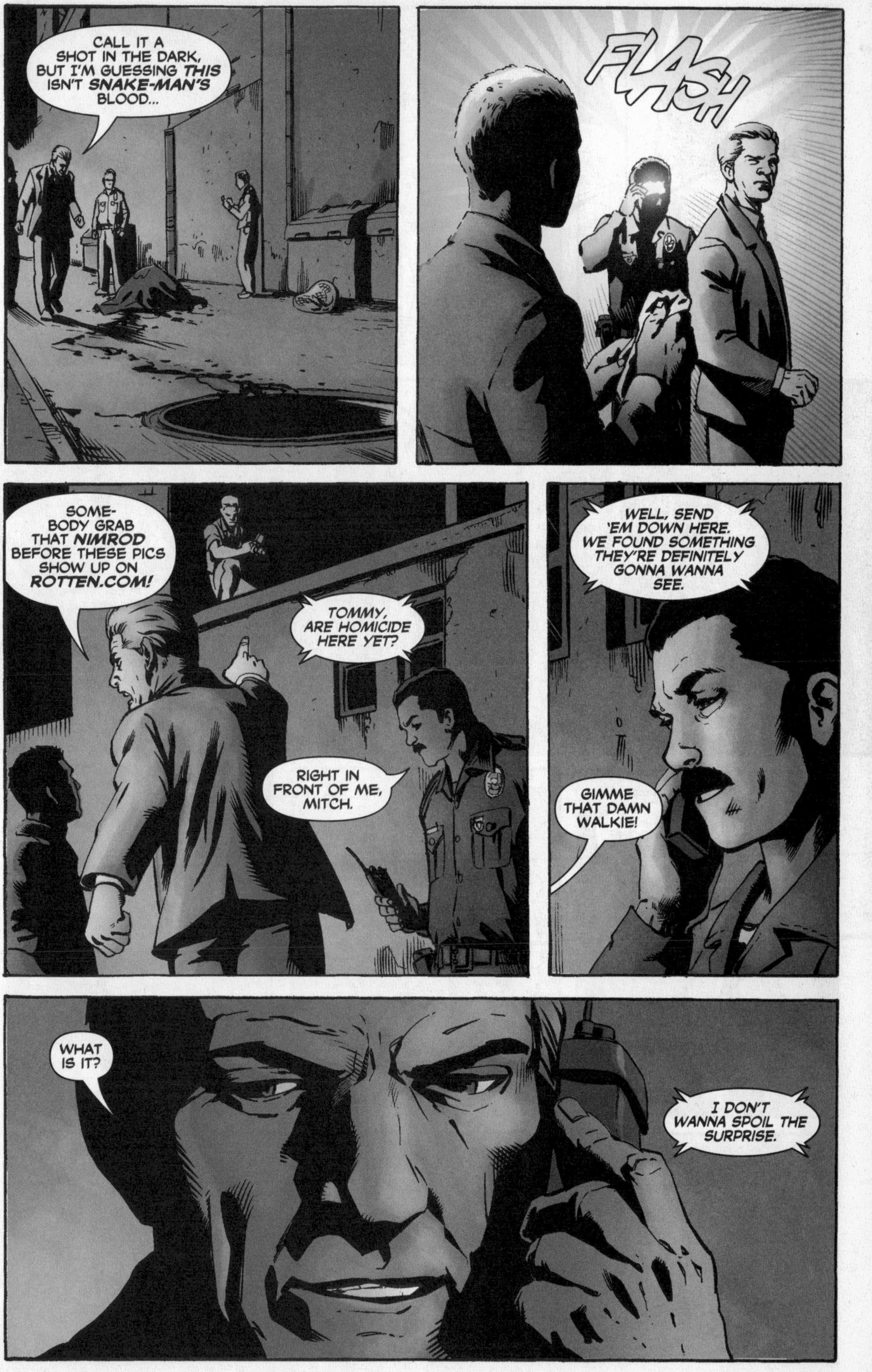
CALL IT A SHOT IN THE DARK, BUT I'M GUESSING THIS ISN'T SNAKE-MAN'S BLOOD...
FLASH
SOME-BODY GRAB THAT NIMROD BEFORE THESE PICS SHOW UP ON ROTTEN.COM!
TOMMY, ARE HOMICIDE HERE YET?
RIGHT IN FRONT OF ME, MITCH.
GIMME THAT DAMN WALKIE!
WELL, SEND 'EM DOWN HERE. WE FOUND SOMETHING THEY'RE DEFINITELY GONNA WANNA SEE.
WHAT IS IT?
I DON'T WANNA SPOIL THE SURPRISE.

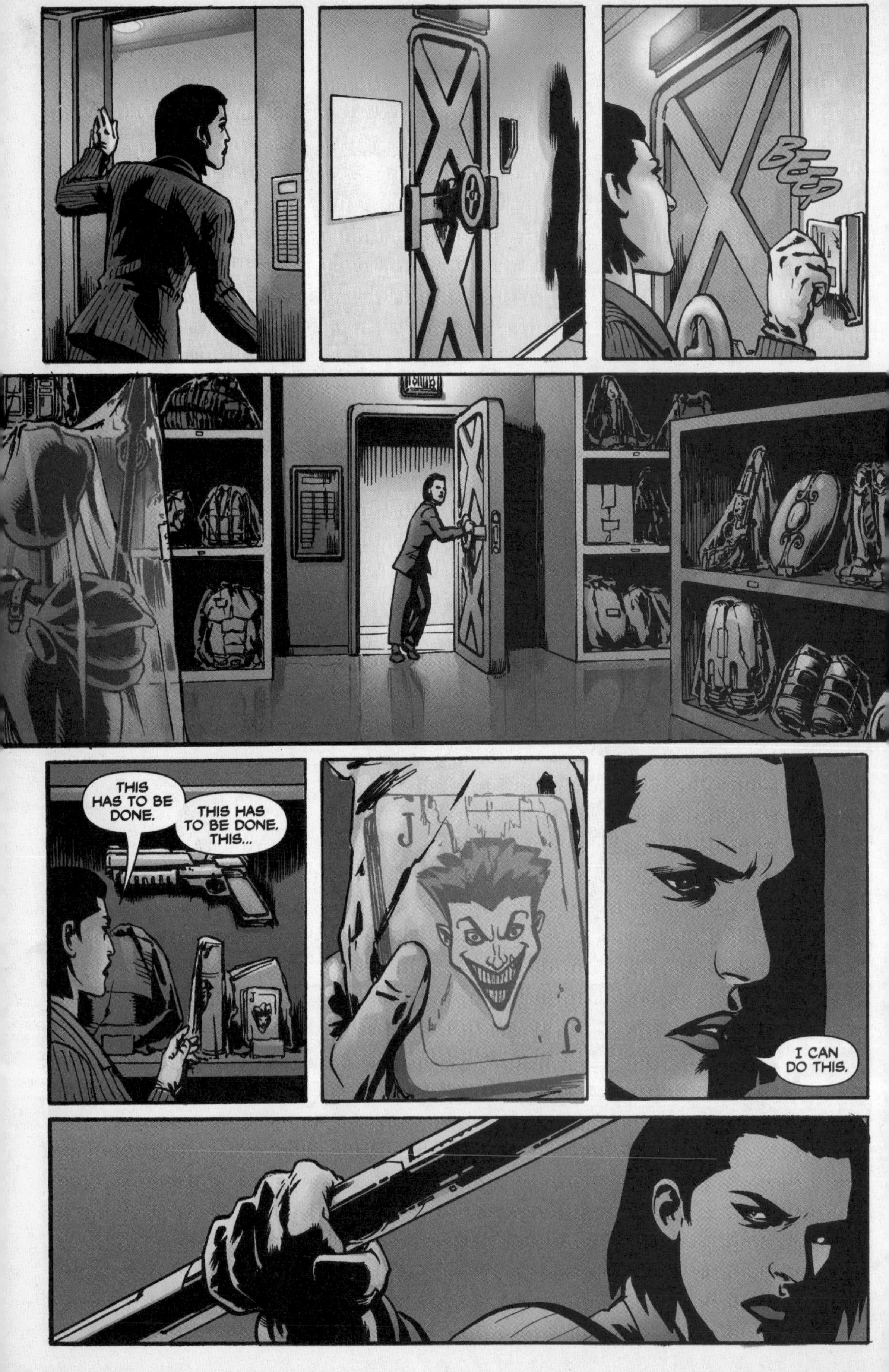
BEEP
THIS HAS TO BE DONE.
THIS HAS TO BE DONE. THIS...
I CAN DO THIS.

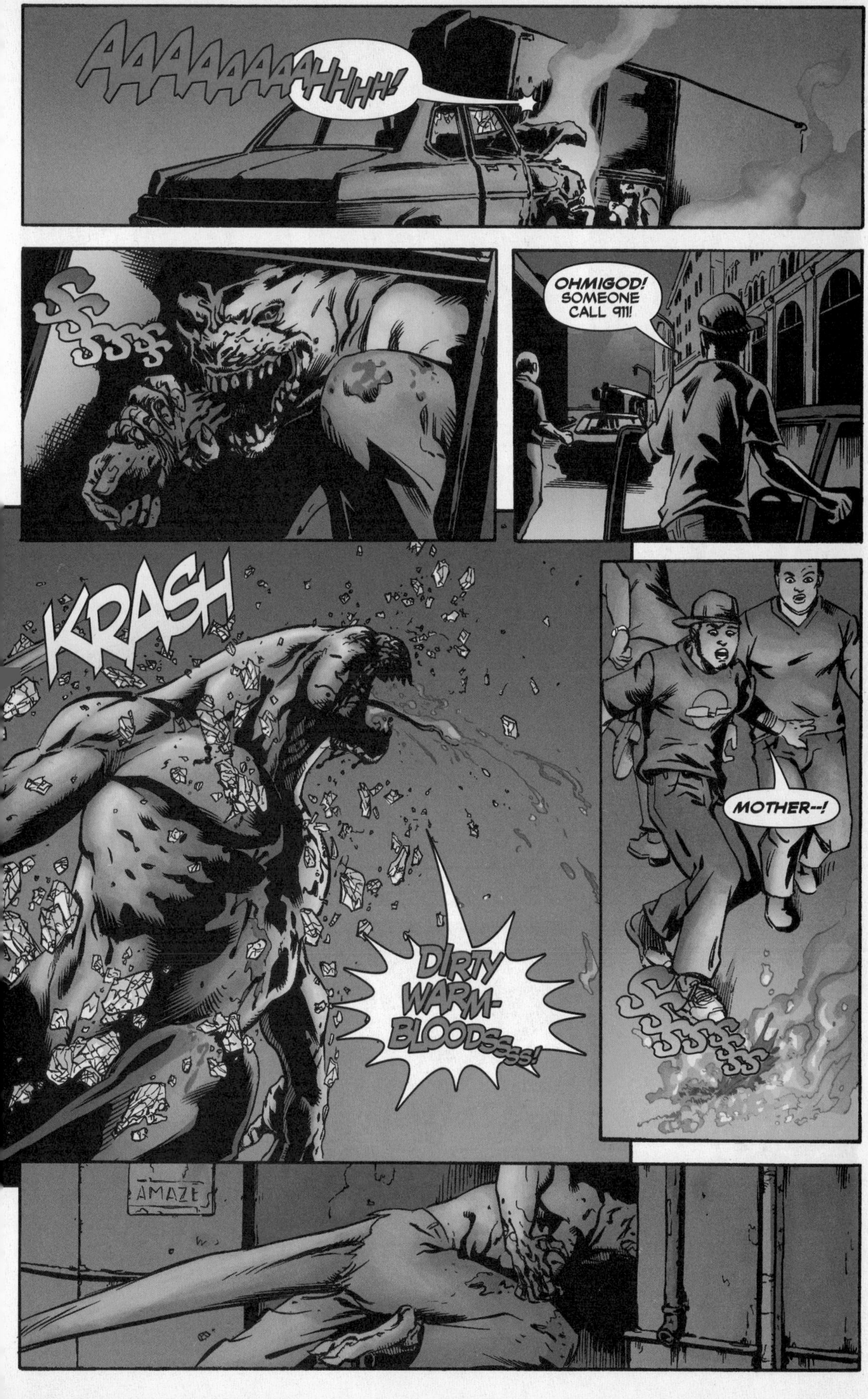
AAAAAAAAHHHH!
SSSSS
OHMIGOD! SOMEONE CALL 911!
KRASH
DIRTY WARM-BLOODSsss!
MOTHER--!
SSSSSS
AMAZE

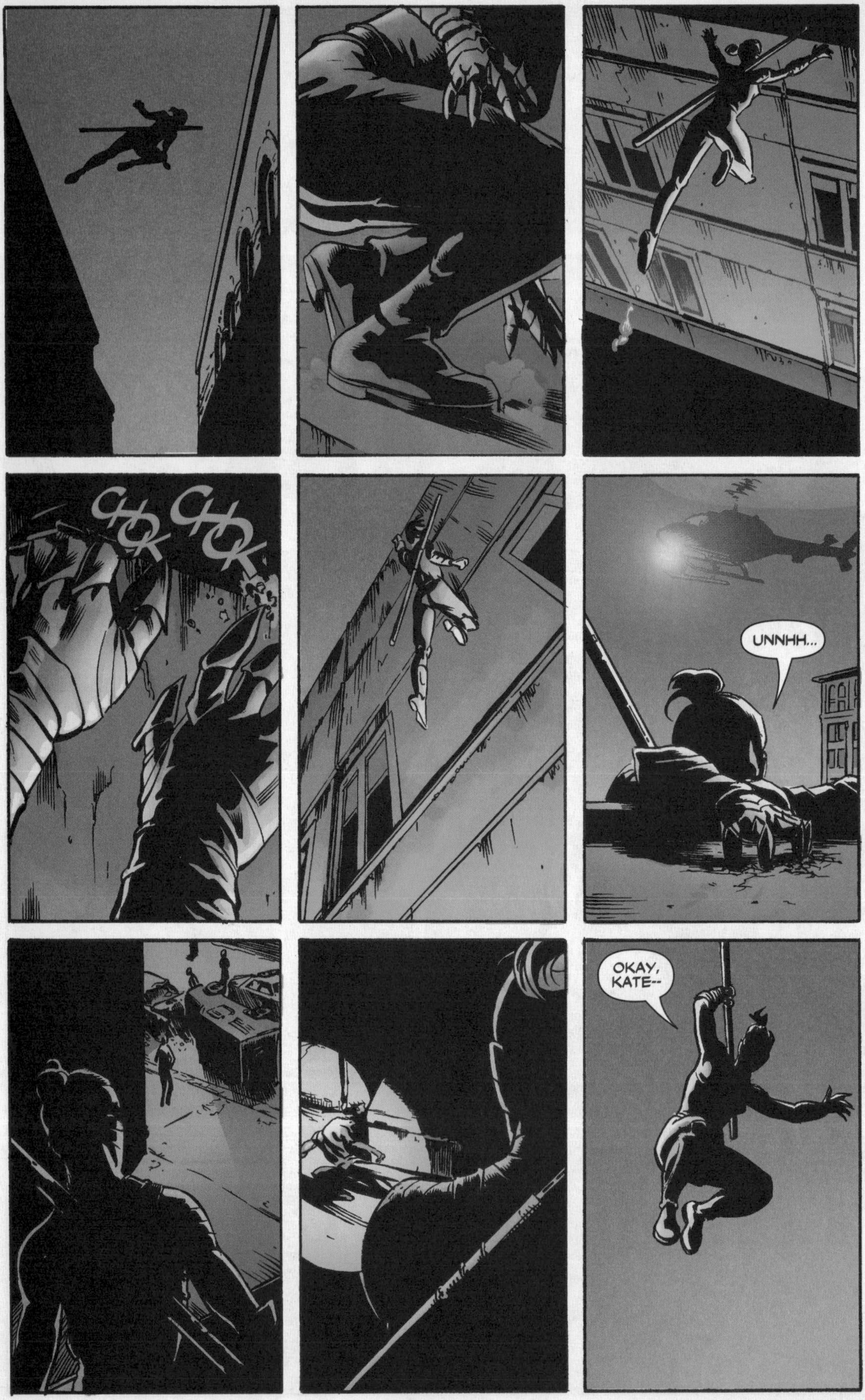
CHOK CHOK
UNNHH...
OKAY, KATE--

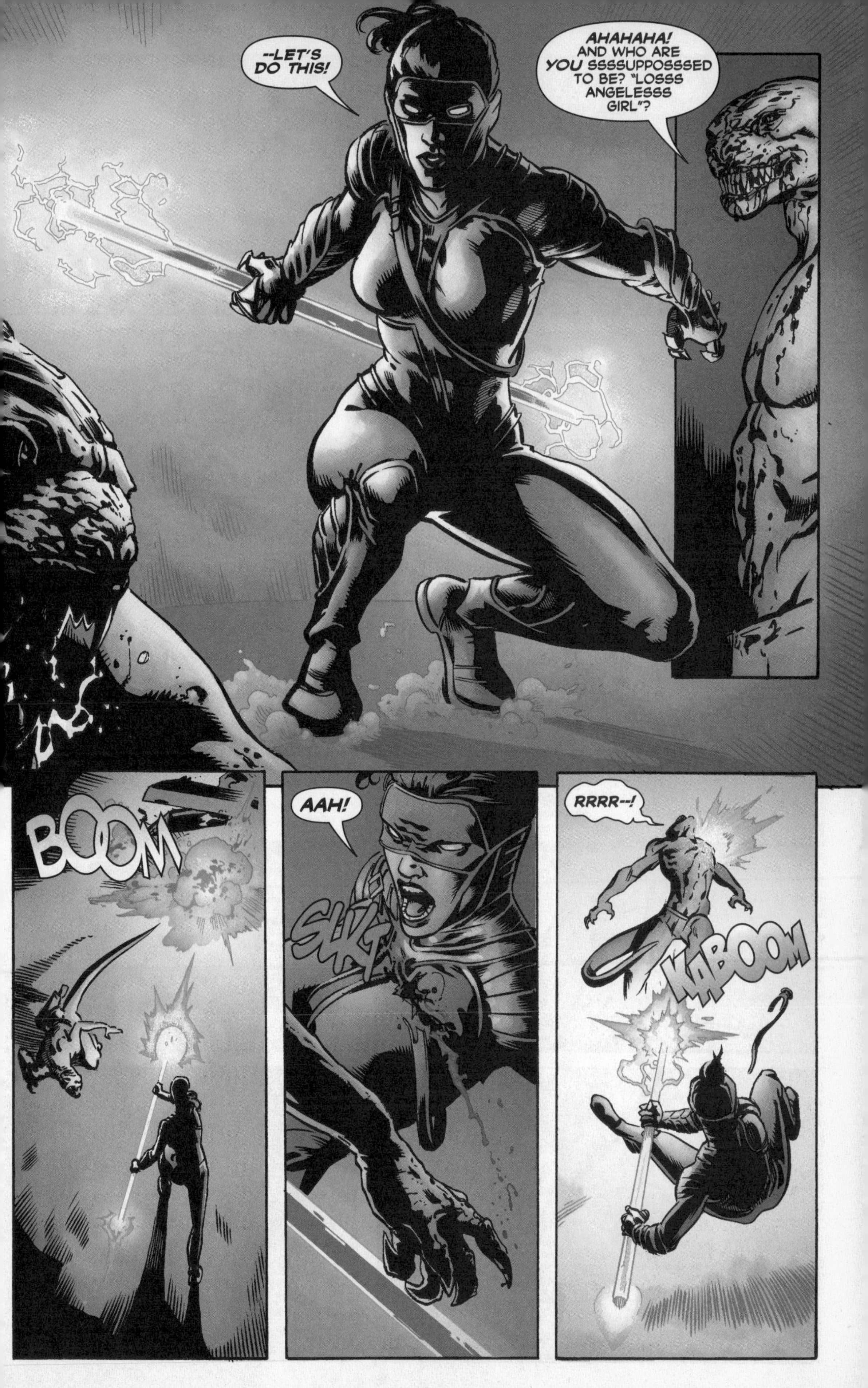

--LET'S DO THIS!
AHAHAHA! AND WHO ARE YOU SSSSUPPOSSSSED TO BE? "LOSSS ANGELESSS GIRL"?
BOOM
AAH!
SLK
RRRR--!
KABOOM

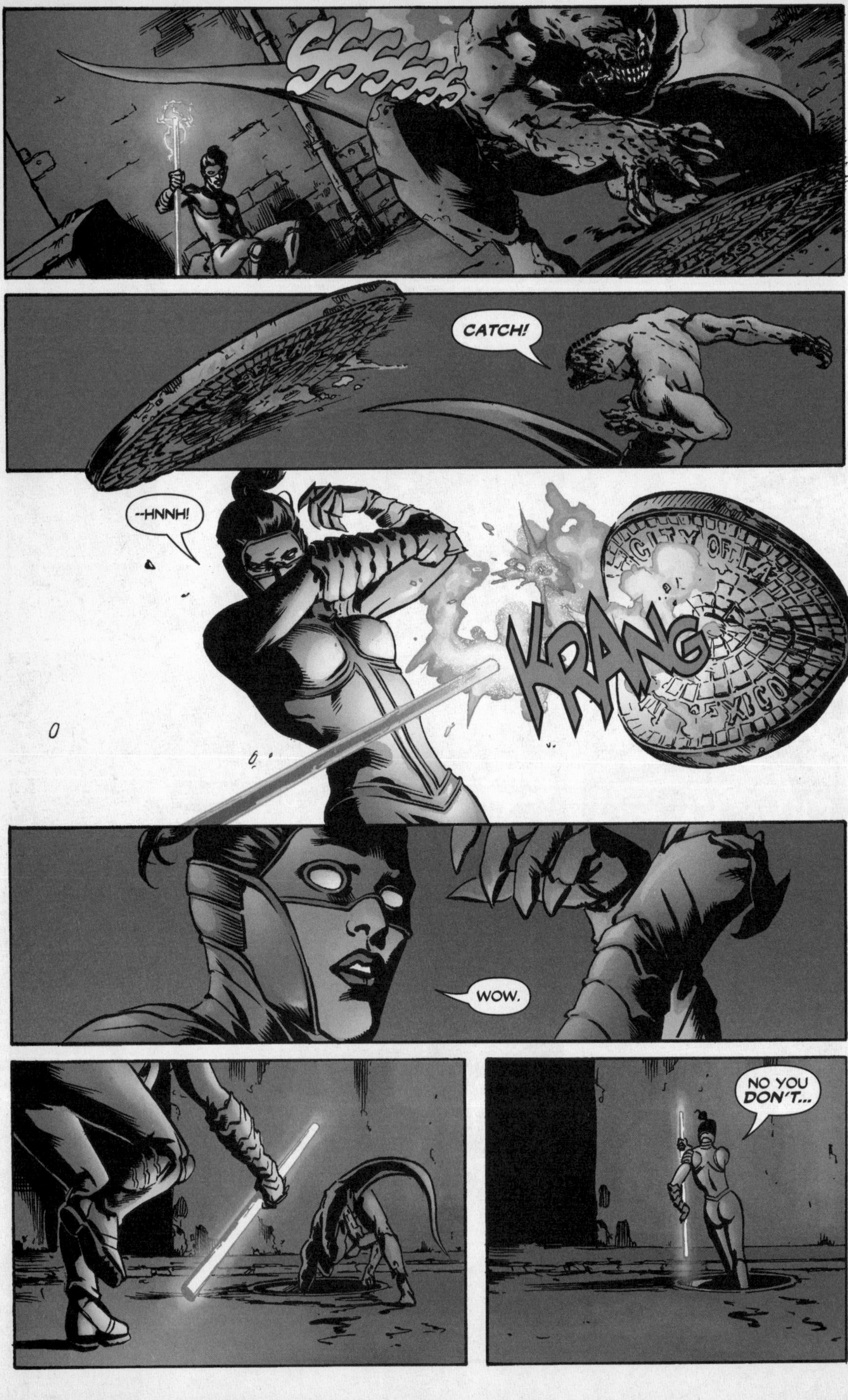
SSSSSS
CATCH!
--HNNH!
CITY OF L.A.
MEXICO
KRANG
WOW.
NO YOU DON'T...

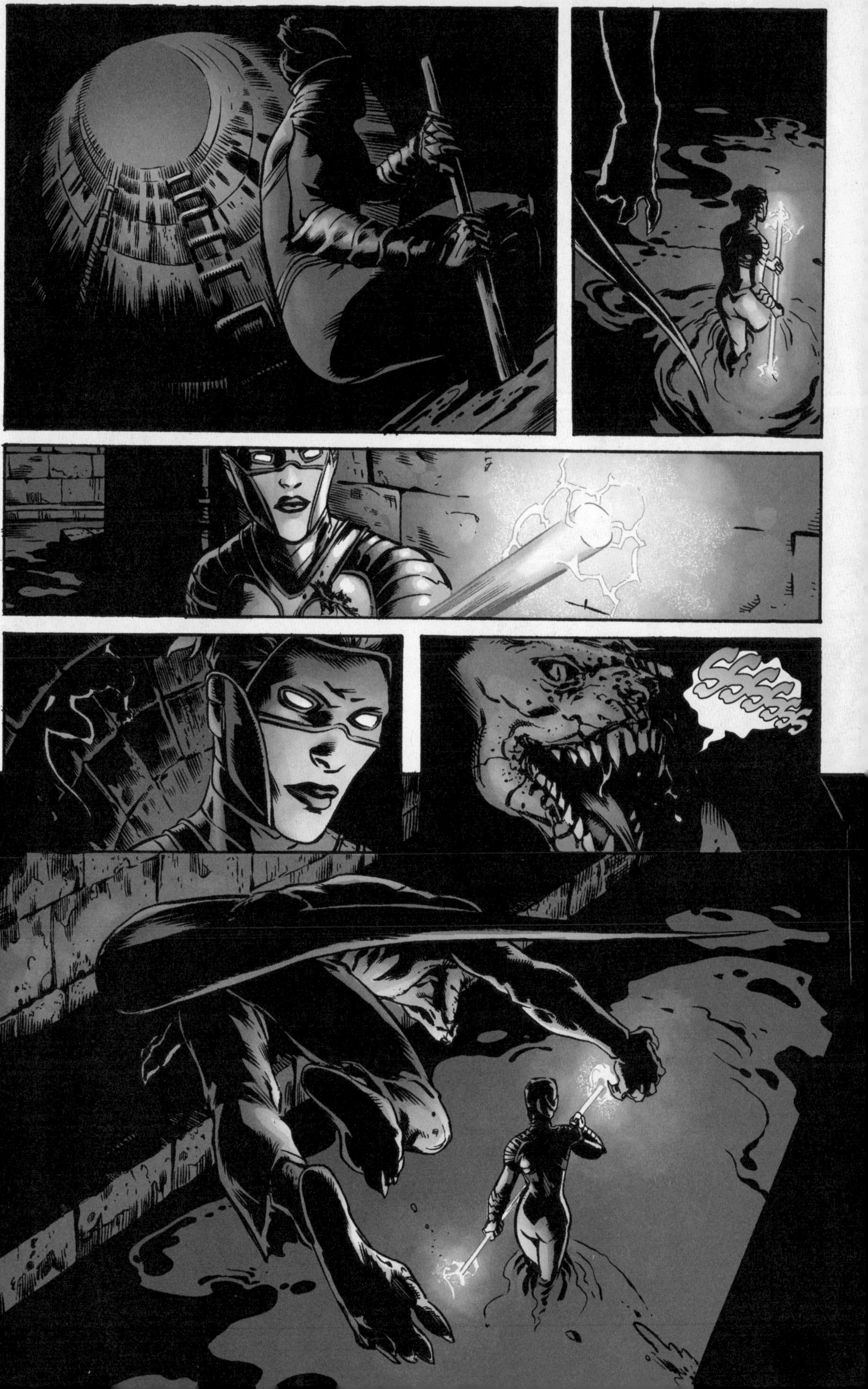
SSSSSS

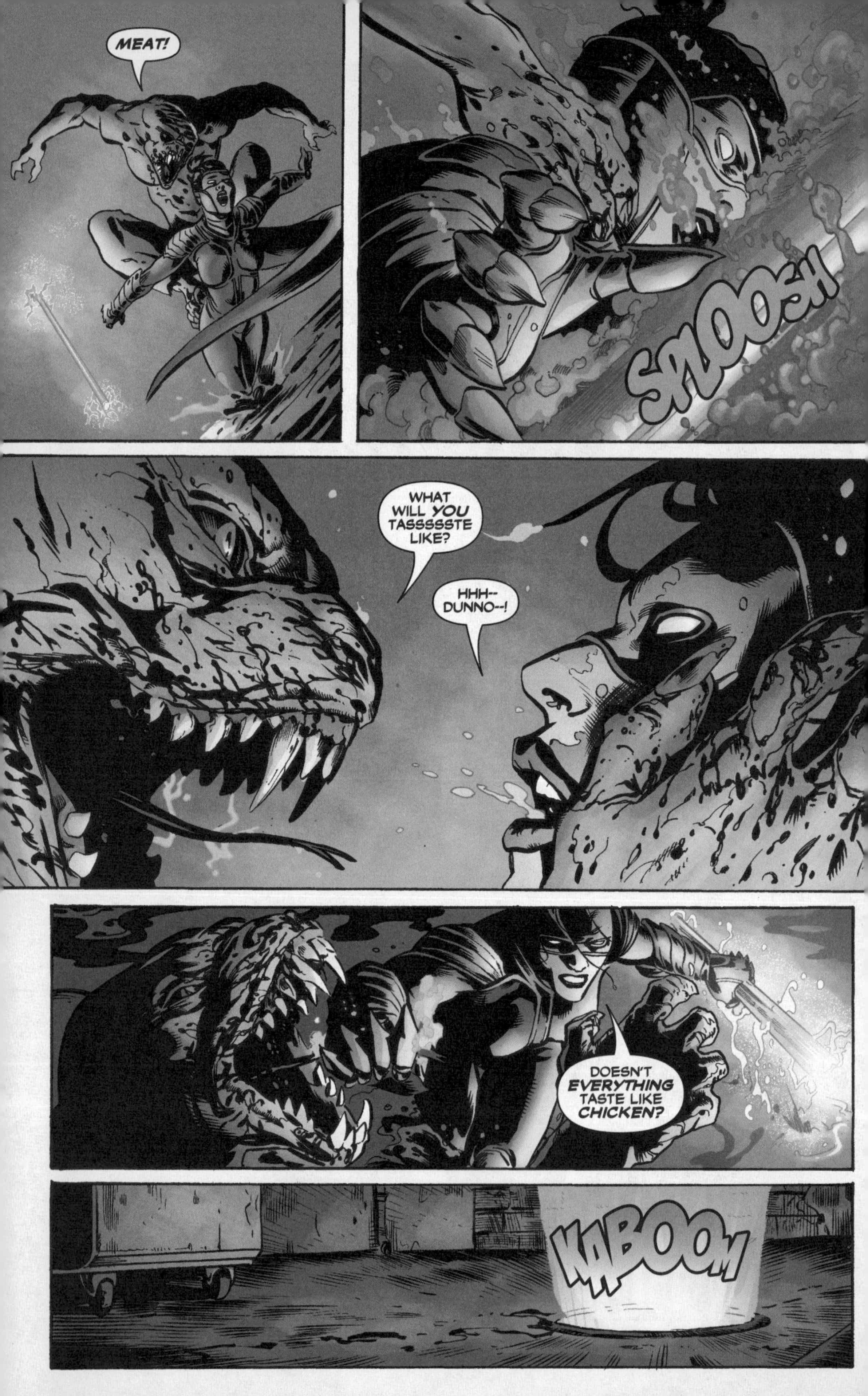
MEAT!
SPLOOSH
WHAT WILL YOU TASSSSSTE LIKE?
HHH-- DUNNO--!
DOESN'T EVERYTHING TASTE LIKE CHICKEN?
KABOOM

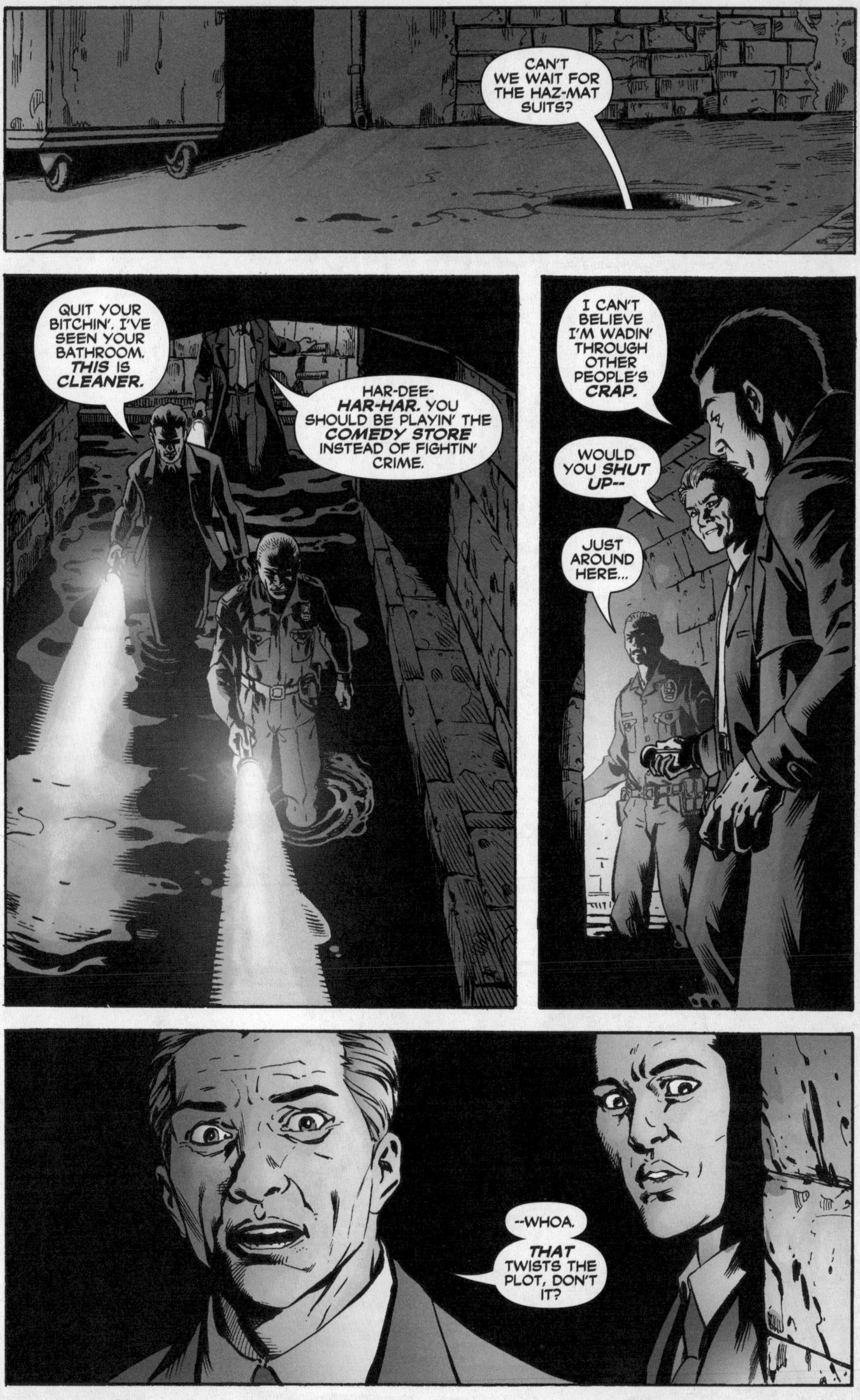
CAN'T WE WAIT FOR THE HAZ-MAT SUITS?
QUIT YOUR BITCHIN'. I'VE SEEN YOUR BATHROOM. THIS IS CLEANER.
HAR-DEE-HAR-HAR. YOU SHOULD BE PLAYIN' THE COMEDY STORE INSTEAD OF FIGHTIN' CRIME.
I CAN'T BELIEVE I'M WADIN' THROUGH OTHER PEOPLE'S CRAP.
WOULD YOU SHUT UP--
JUST AROUND HERE...
--WHOA. THAT TWISTS THE PLOT, DON'T IT?

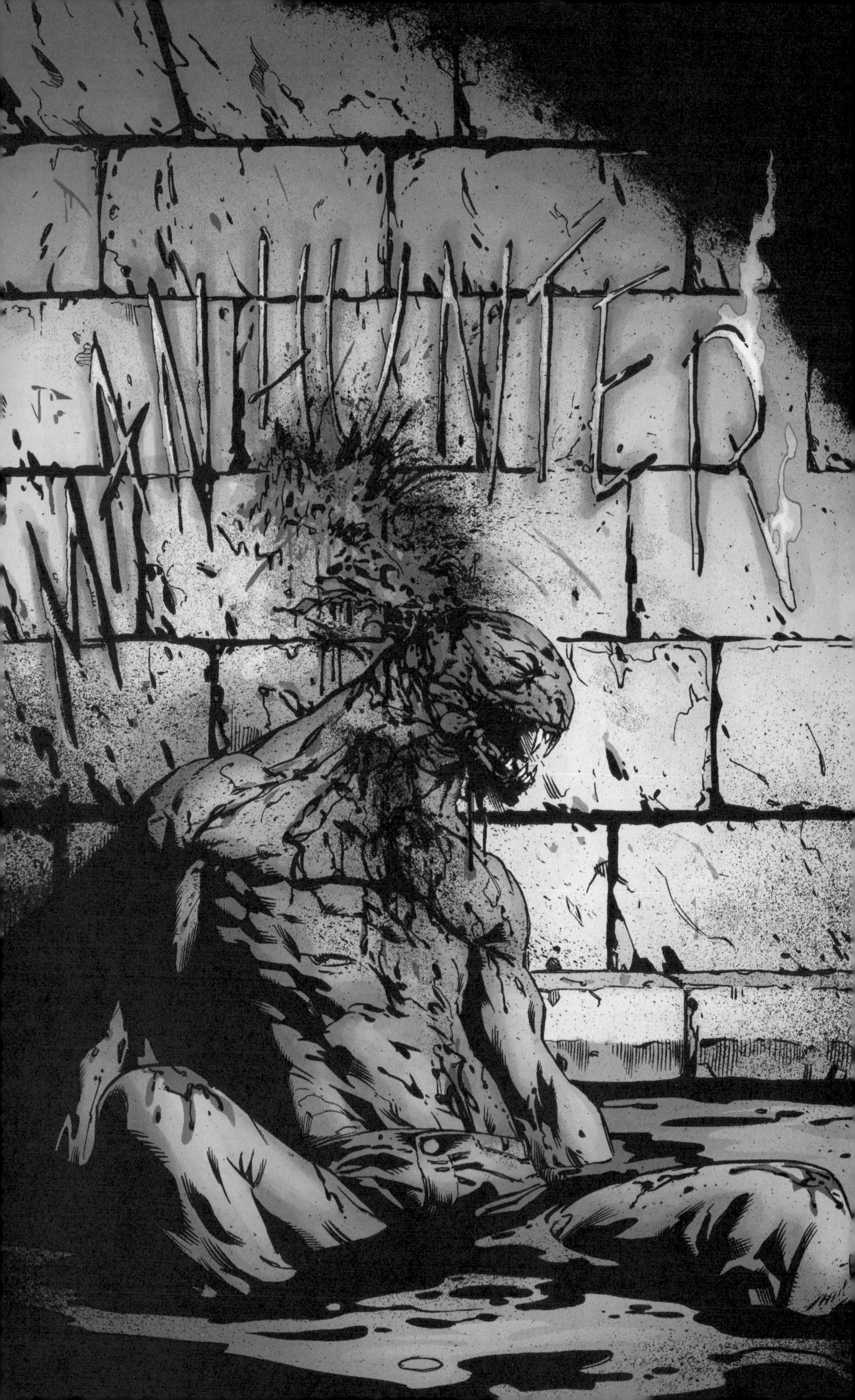
MANHUNTER

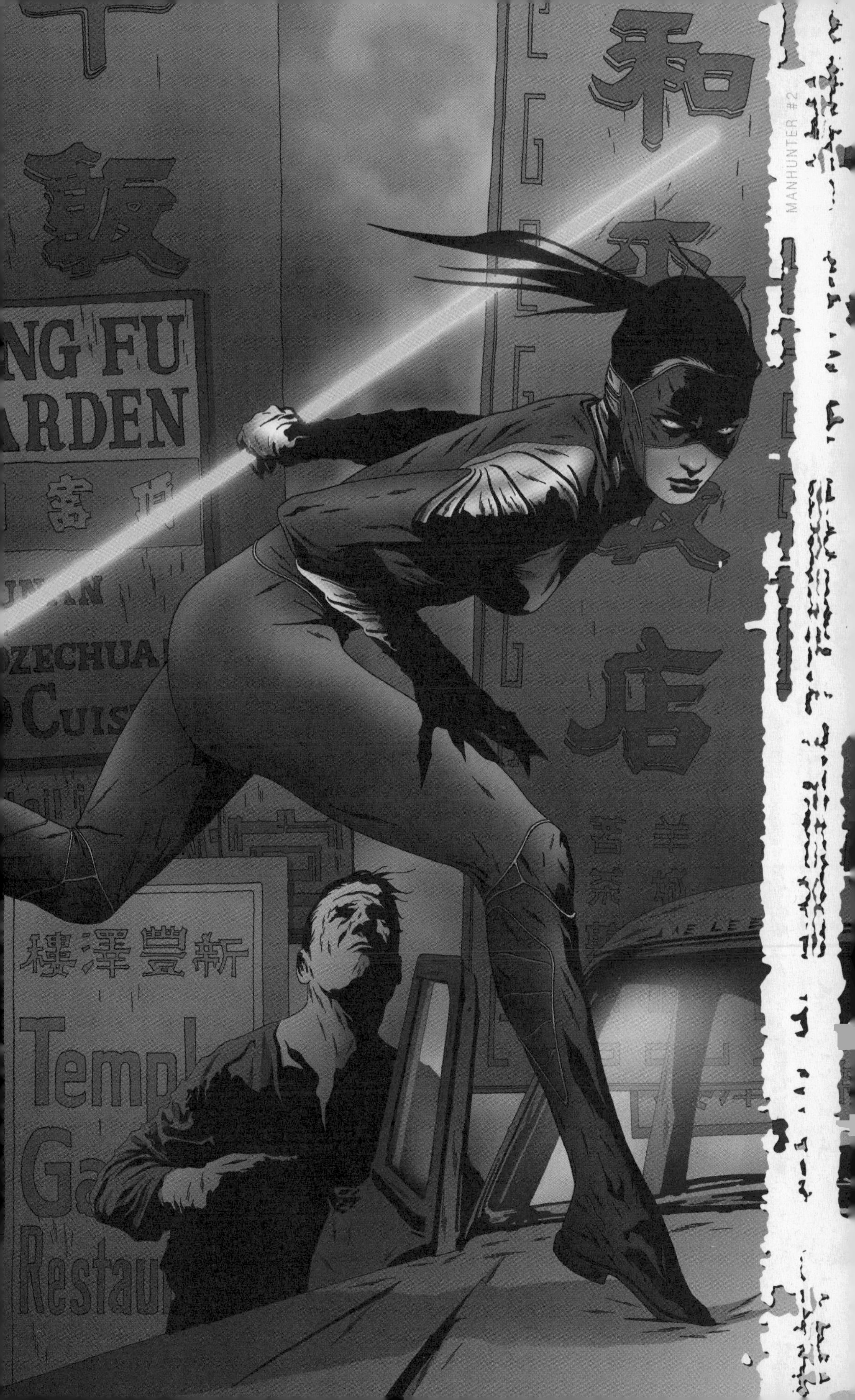
NG FU
ARDEN
ZECHUA
CUIS
樓澤豐新
Templ
Ga
Restau
MANHUNTER #2

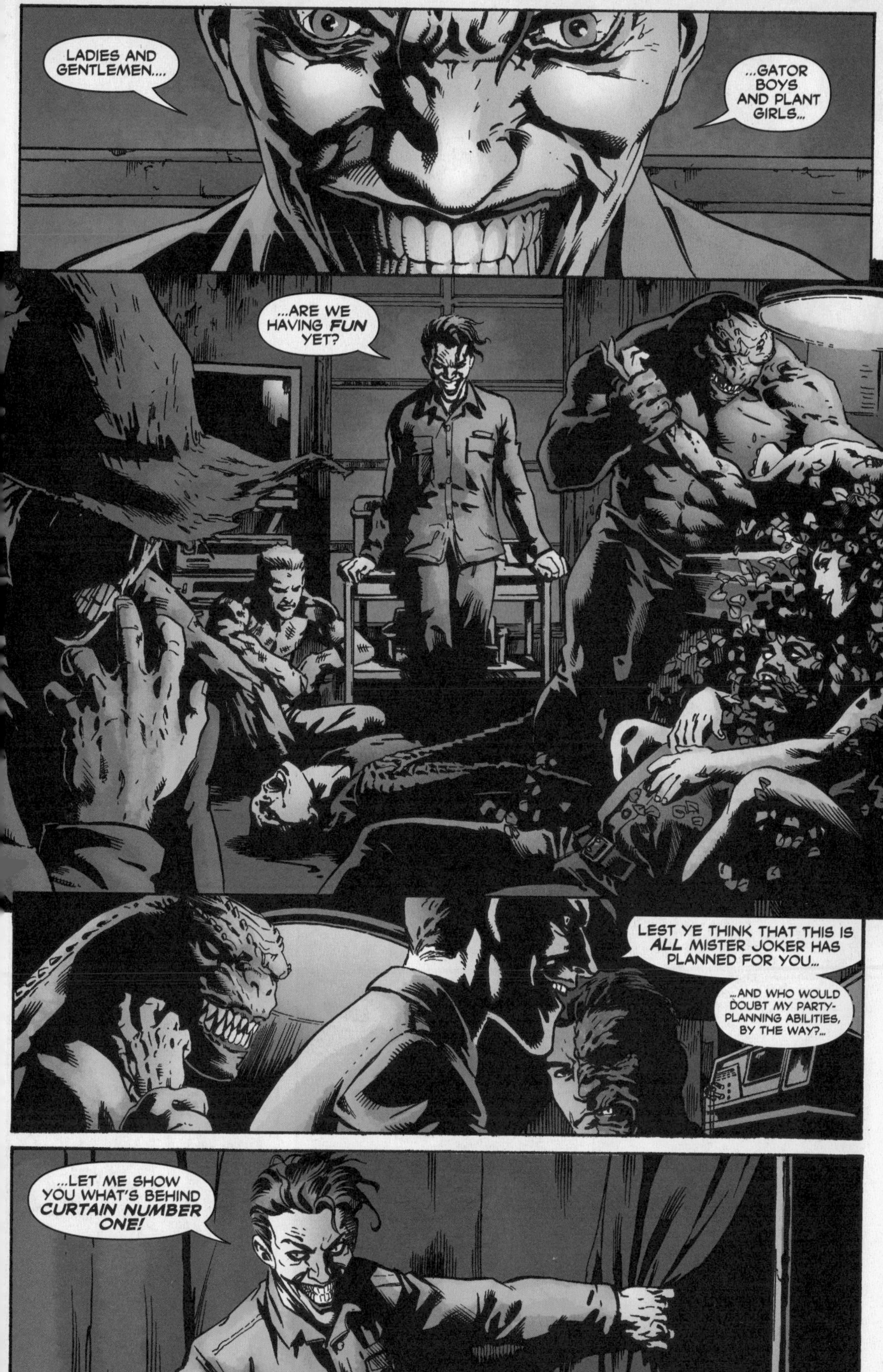
LADIES AND GENTLEMEN....
...GATOR BOYS AND PLANT GIRLS...
...ARE WE HAVING FUN YET?
LEST YE THINK THAT THIS IS ALL MISTER JOKER HAS PLANNED FOR YOU...
...AND WHO WOULD DOUBT MY PARTY-PLANNING ABILITIES, BY THE WAY?...
...LET ME SHOW YOU WHAT'S BEHIND CURTAIN NUMBER ONE!

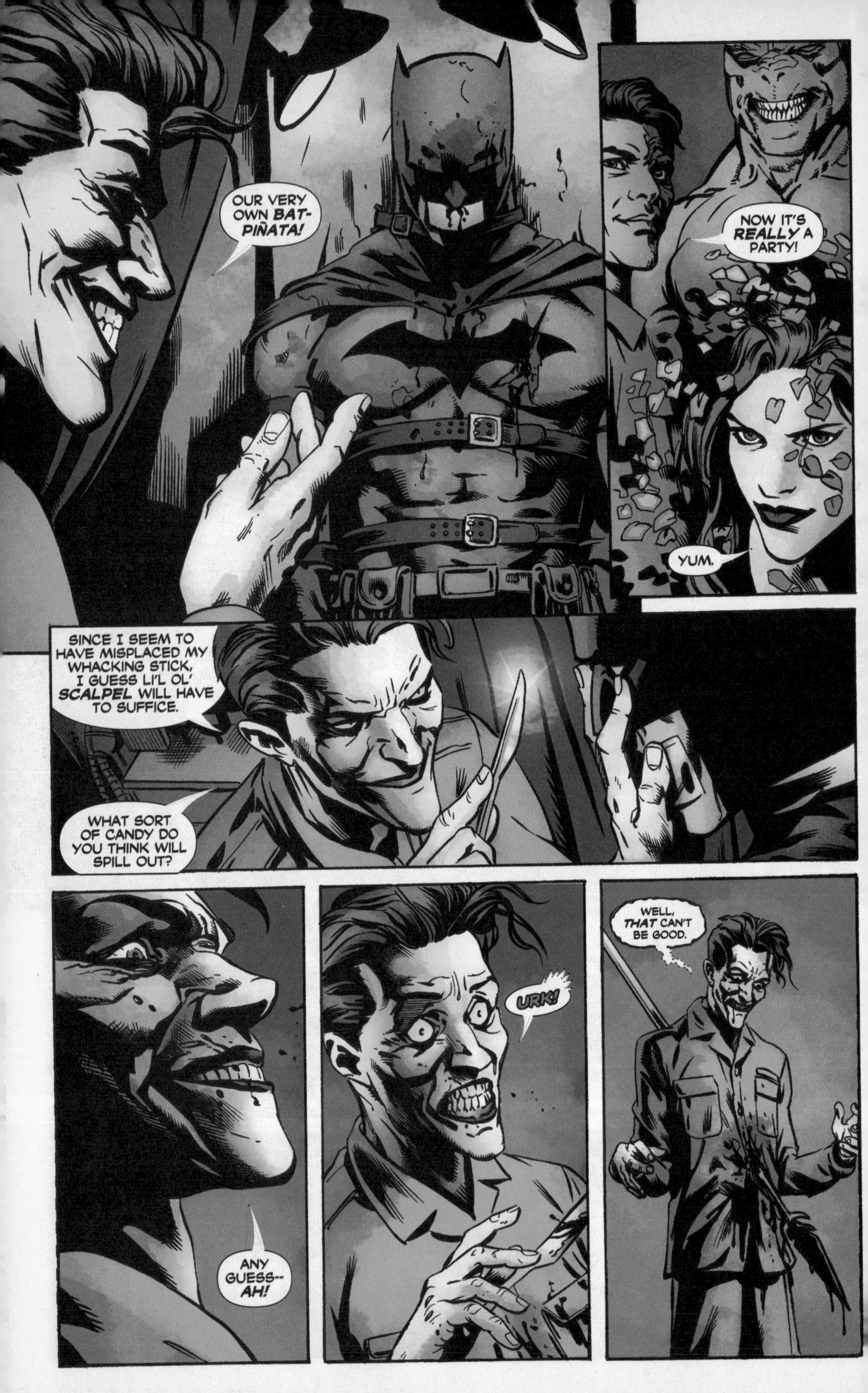
OUR VERY OWN BAT-PIÑATA!
NOW IT'S REALLY A PARTY!
YUM.
SINCE I SEEM TO HAVE MISPLACED MY WHACKING STICK, I GUESS LI'L OL' SCALPEL WILL HAVE TO SUFFICE.
WHAT SORT OF CANDY DO YOU THINK WILL SPILL OUT?
ANY GUESS-- AH!
URK!
WELL, THAT CAN'T BE GOOD.

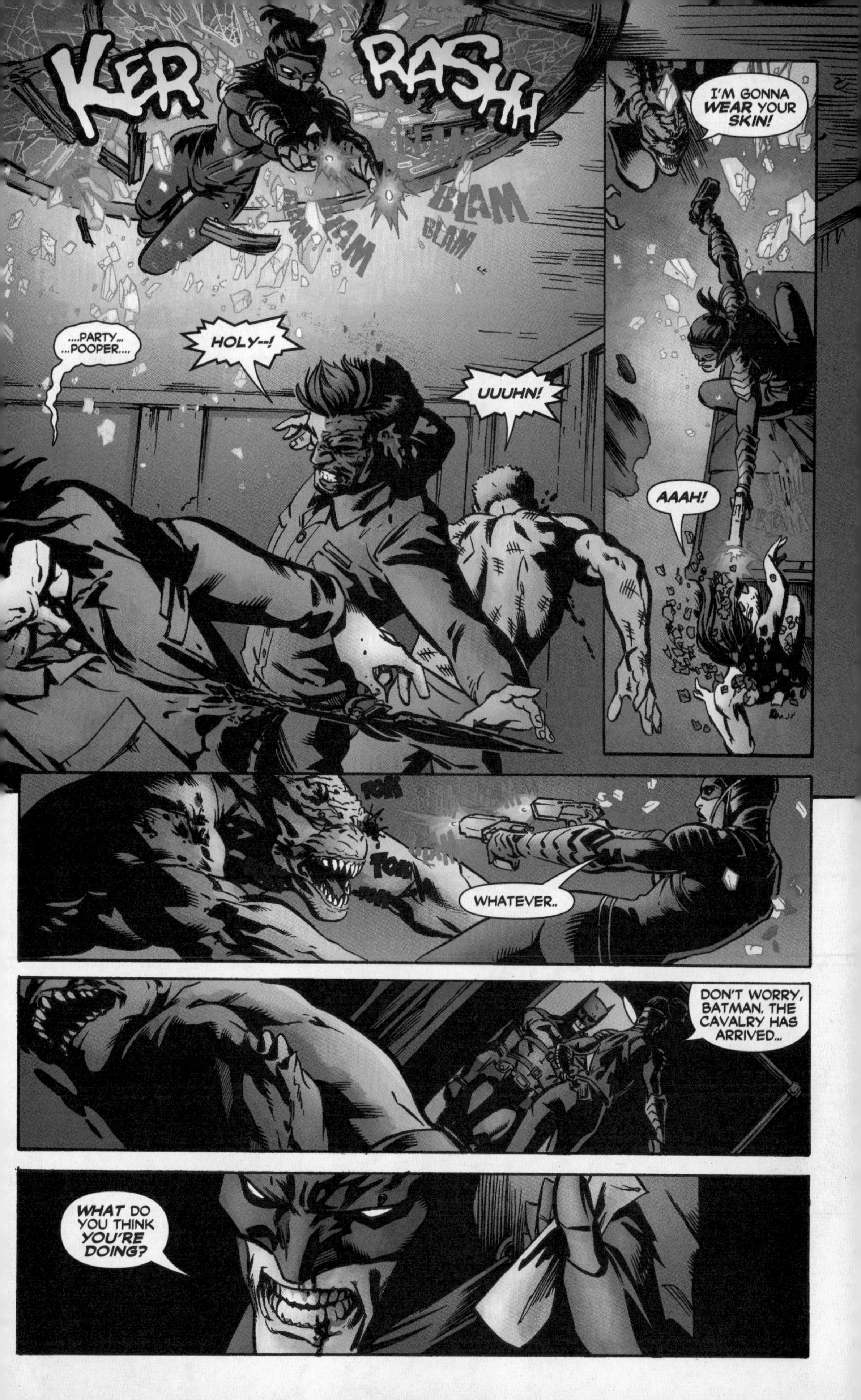
KER RASHH
BLAM
BLAM
...PARTY... ...POOPER....
HOLY--!
UUUHN!
I'M GONNA WEAR YOUR SKIN!
AAAH!
WHATEVER..
DON'T WORRY, BATMAN. THE CAVALRY HAS ARRIVED...
WHAT DO YOU THINK YOU'RE DOING?

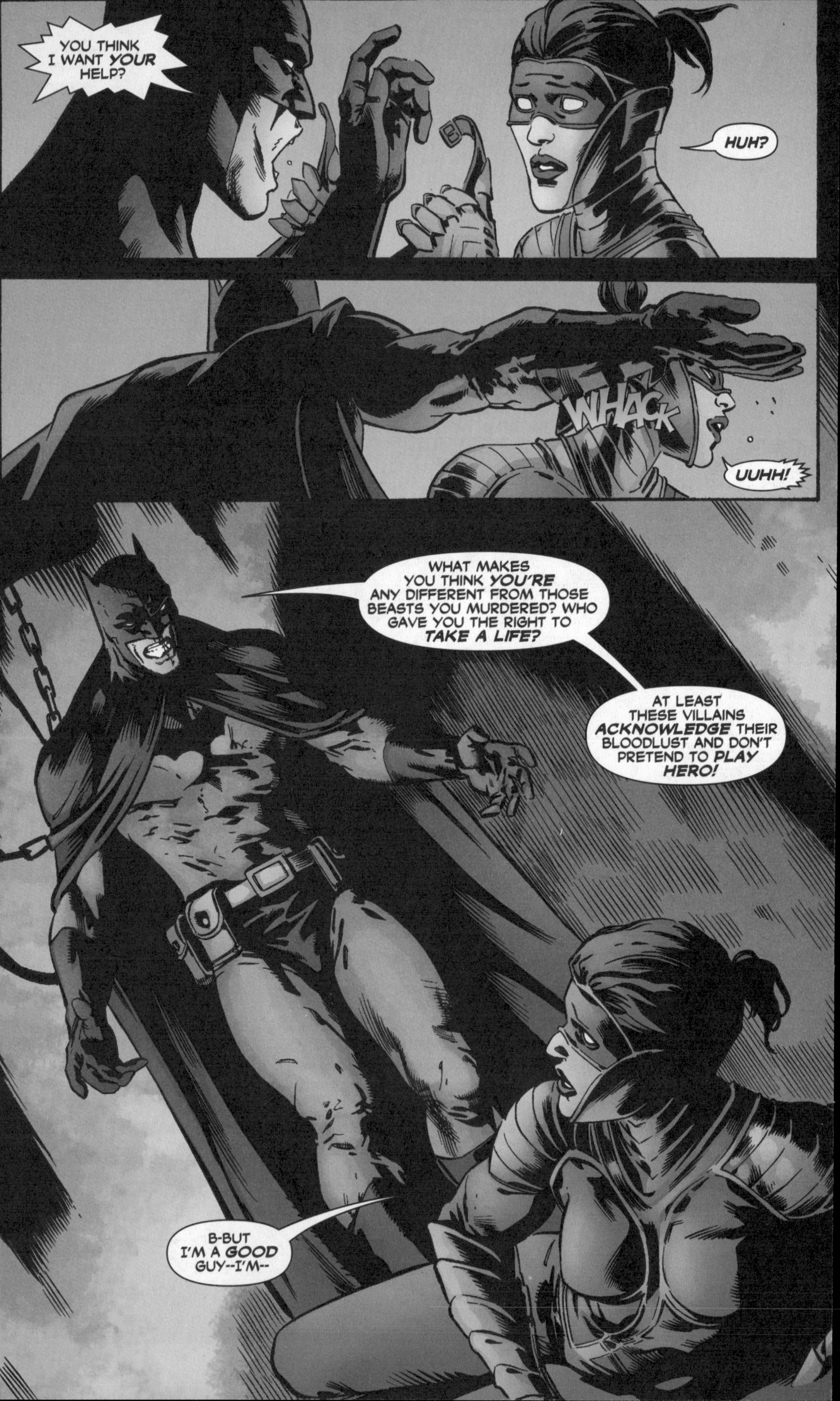
YOU THINK I WANT YOUR HELP?
HUH?
WHACK
UUHH!
WHAT MAKES YOU THINK YOU'RE ANY DIFFERENT FROM THOSE BEASTS YOU MURDERED? WHO GAVE YOU THE RIGHT TO TAKE A LIFE?
AT LEAST THESE VILLAINS ACKNOWLEDGE THEIR BLOODLUST AND DON'T PRETEND TO PLAY HERO!
B-BUT I'M A GOOD GUY--I'M--

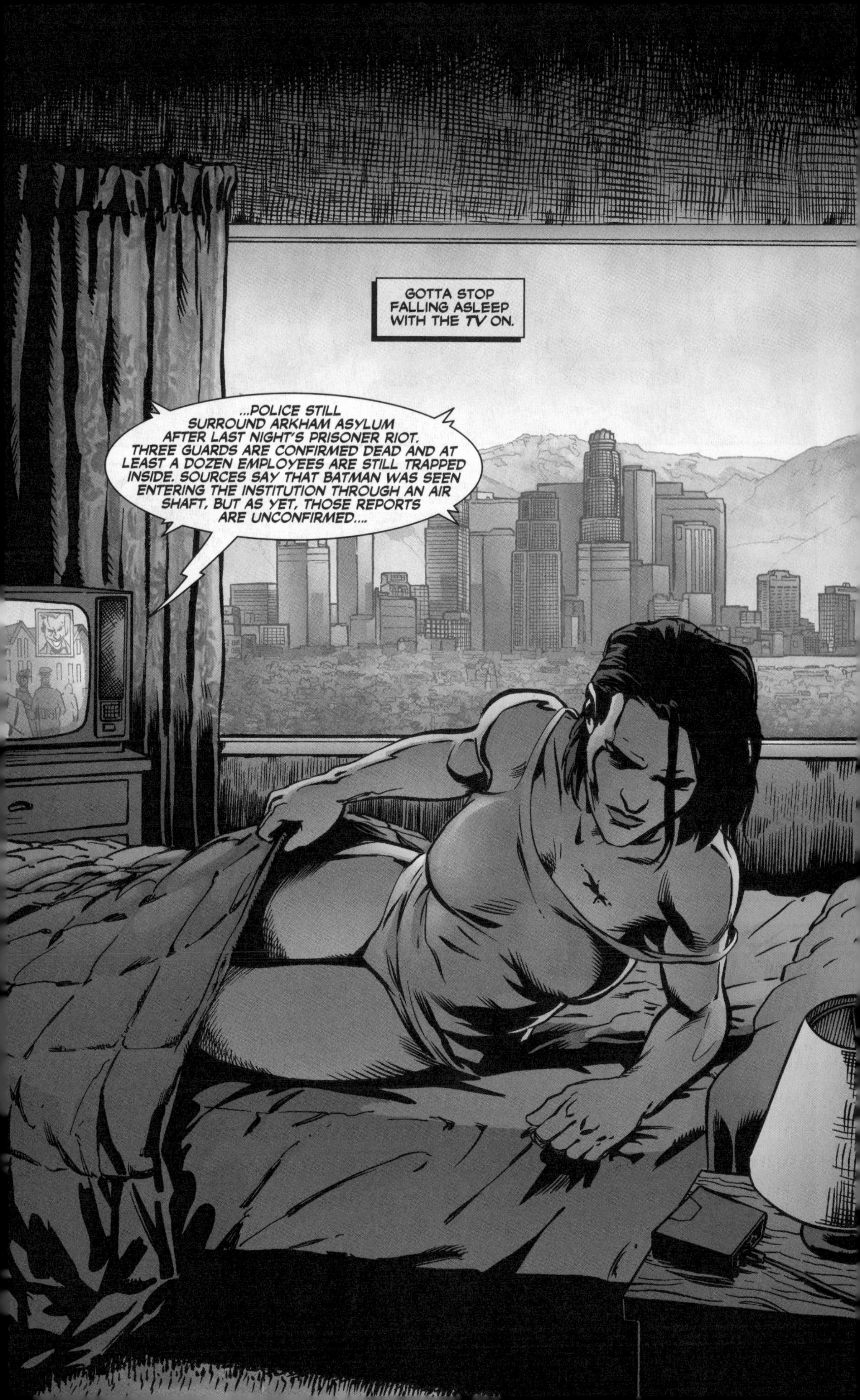
GOTTA STOP FALLING ASLEEP WITH THE TV ON.
...POLICE STILL SURROUND ARKHAM ASYLUM AFTER LAST NIGHT'S PRISONER RIOT. THREE GUARDS ARE CONFIRMED DEAD AND AT LEAST A DOZEN EMPLOYEES ARE STILL TRAPPED INSIDE. SOURCES SAY THAT BATMAN WAS SEEN ENTERING THE INSTITUTION THROUGH AN AIR SHAFT, BUT AS YET, THOSE REPORTS ARE UNCONFIRMED....

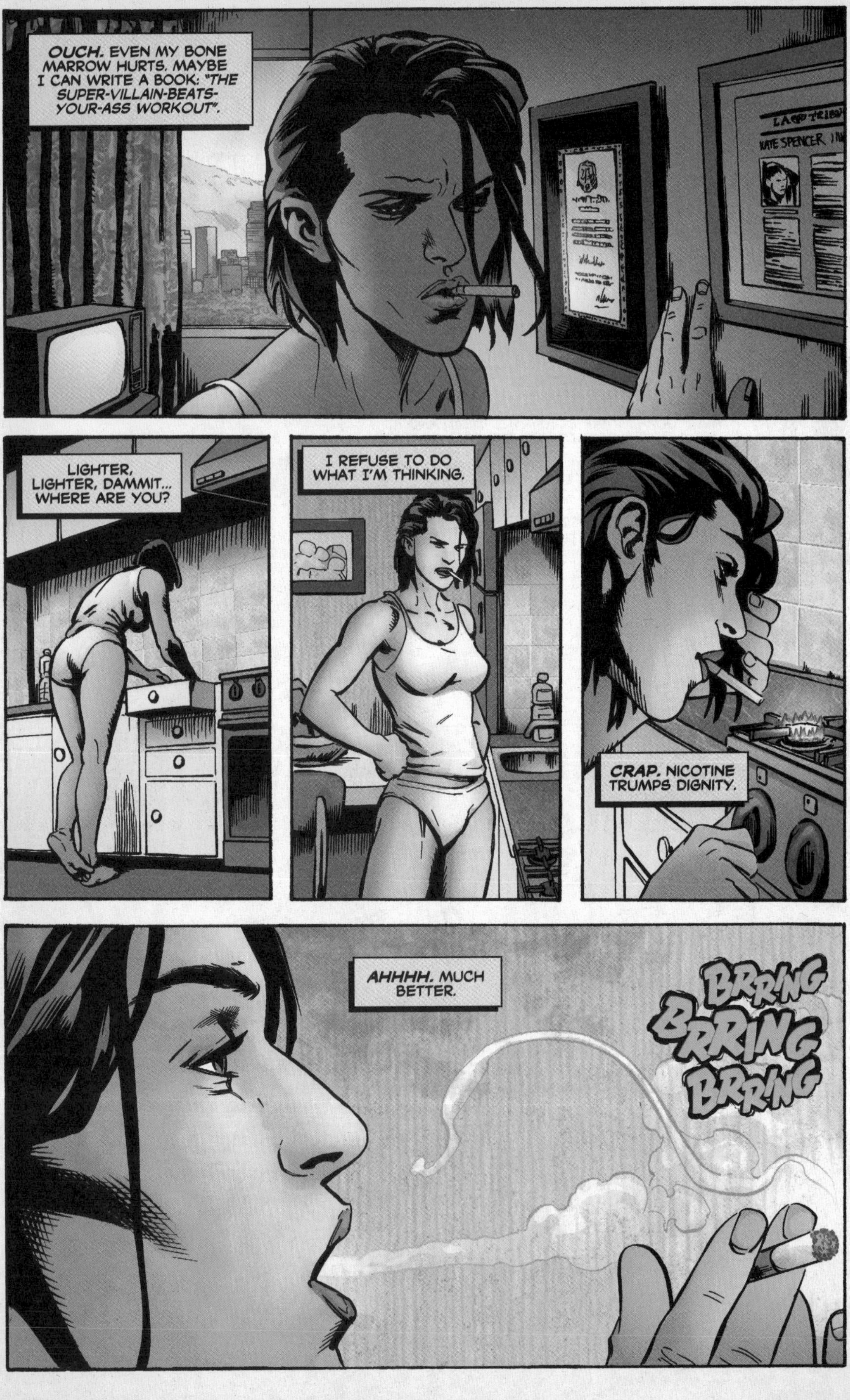
OUCH. EVEN MY BONE MARROW HURTS. MAYBE I CAN WRITE A BOOK: "THE SUPER-VILLAIN-BEATS-YOUR-ASS WORKOUT".
LIGHTER, LIGHTER, DAMMIT... WHERE ARE YOU?
I REFUSE TO DO WHAT I'M THINKING.
CRAP. NICOTINE TRUMPS DIGNITY.
AHHHH. MUCH BETTER.
BRRING BRRING BRRING

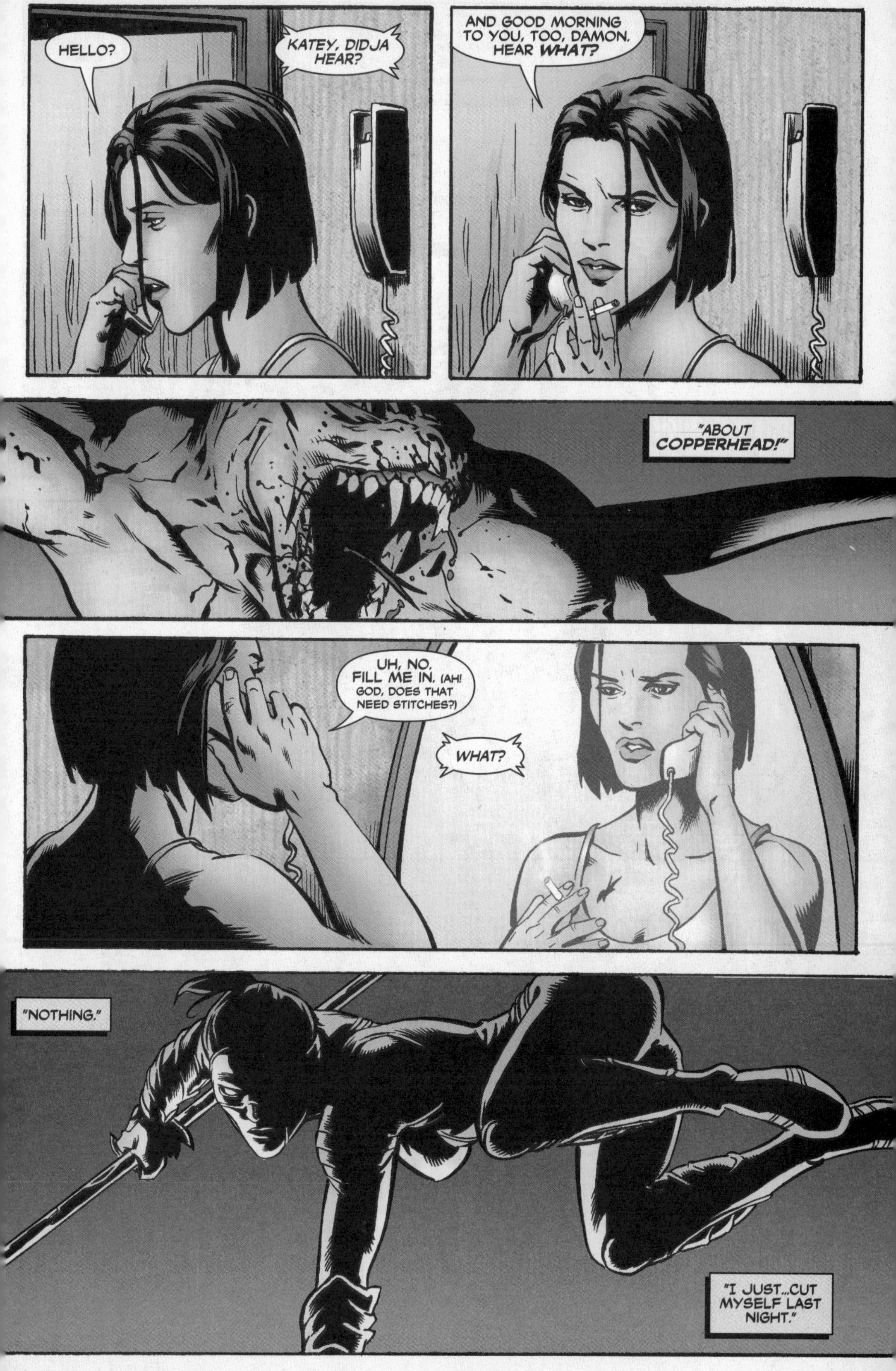
HELLO?
KATEY, DIDJA HEAR?
AND GOOD MORNING TO YOU, TOO, DAMON. HEAR WHAT?
"ABOUT COPPERHEAD!"
UH, NO. FILL ME IN. (AH! GOD, DOES THAT NEED STITCHES?)
WHAT?
"NOTHING."
"I JUST...CUT MYSELF LAST NIGHT."

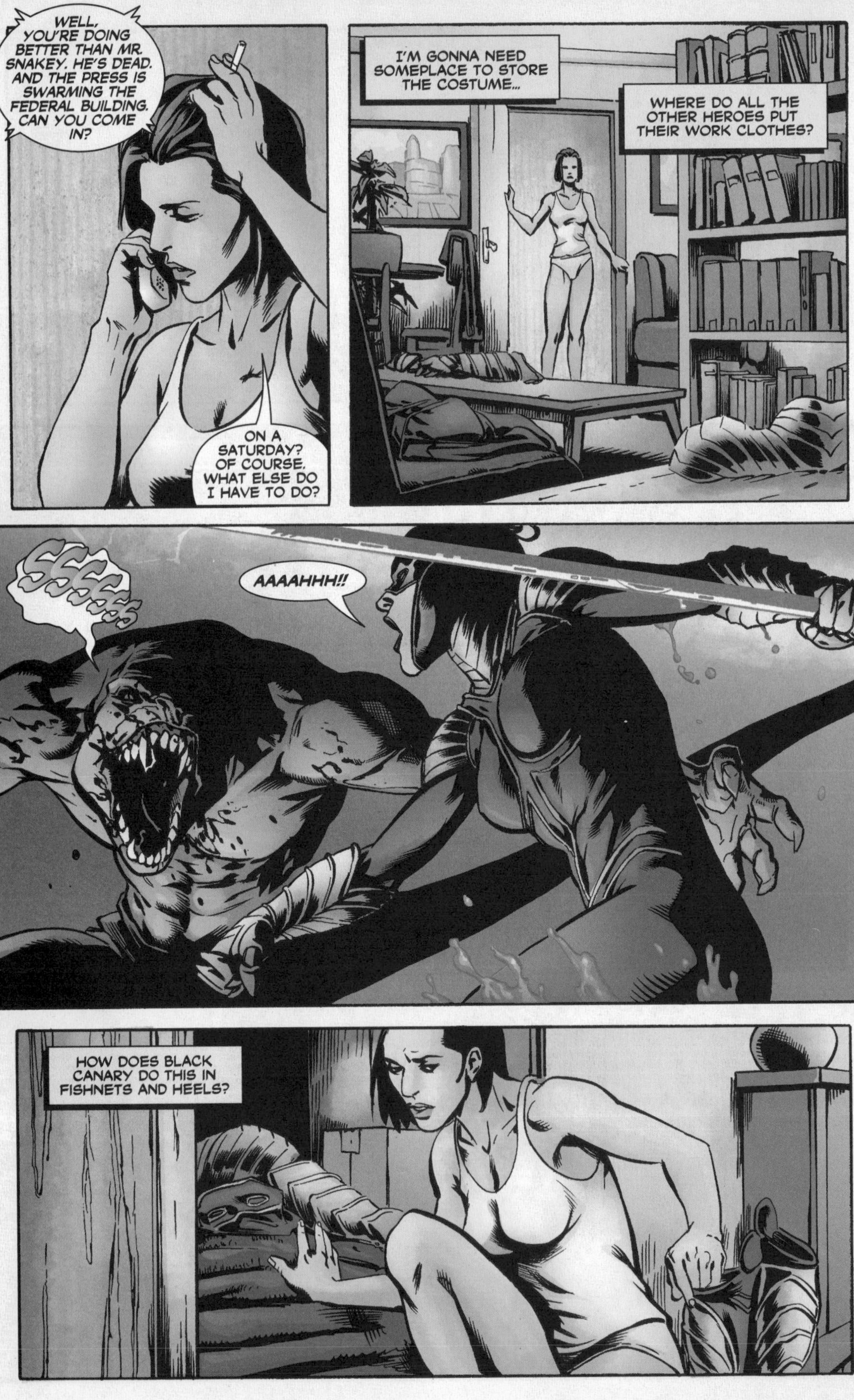
WELL, YOU'RE DOING BETTER THAN MR. SNAKEY. HE'S DEAD. AND THE PRESS IS SWARMING THE FEDERAL BUILDING. CAN YOU COME IN?
ON A SATURDAY? OF COURSE. WHAT ELSE DO I HAVE TO DO?
I'M GONNA NEED SOMEPLACE TO STORE THE COSTUME...
WHERE DO ALL THE OTHER HEROES PUT THEIR WORK CLOTHES?
SSSSSS
AAAAHHH!!
HOW DOES BLACK CANARY DO THIS IN FISHNETS AND HEELS?

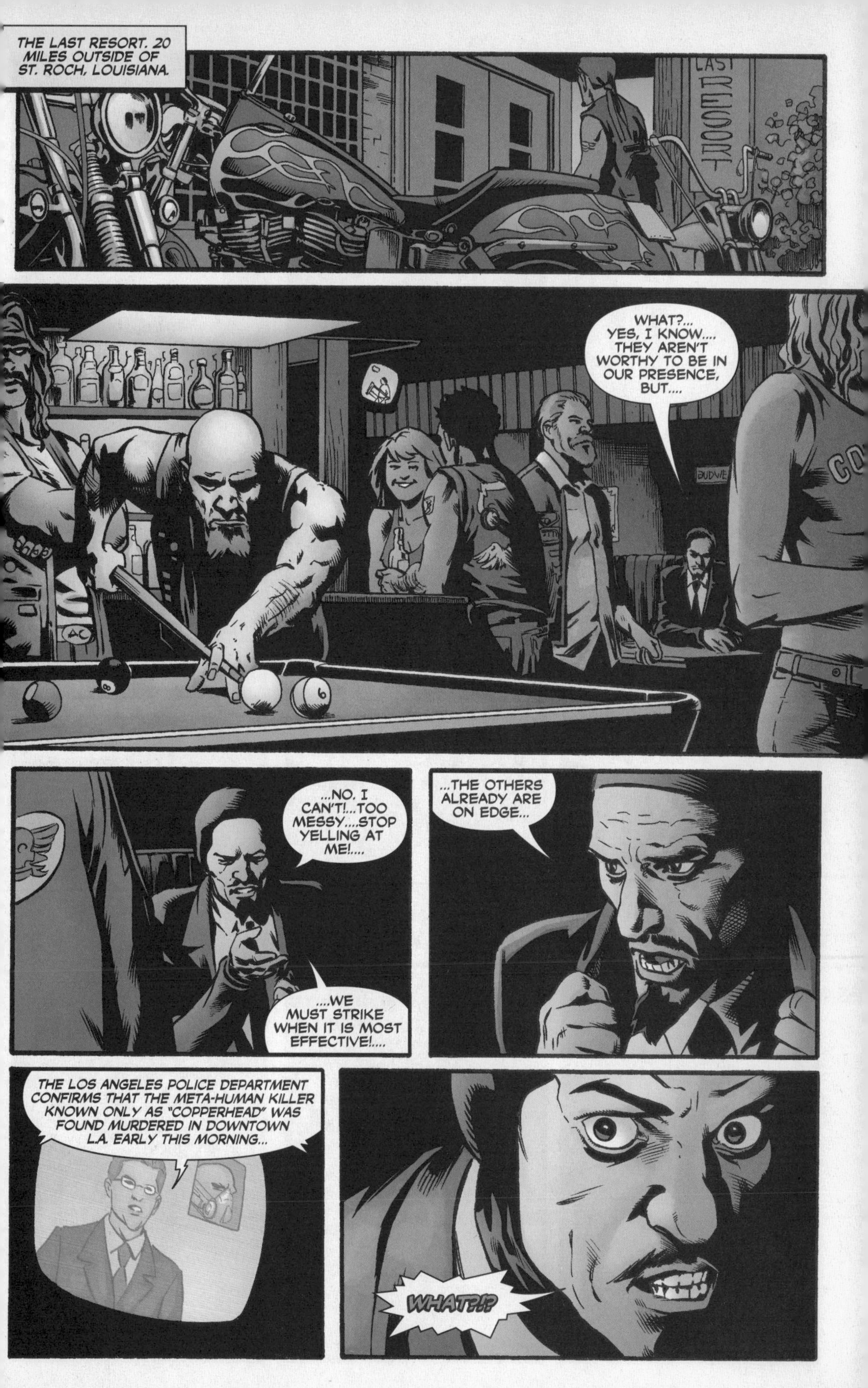
THE LAST RESORT. 20 MILES OUTSIDE OF ST. ROCH, LOUISIANA.
LAST RESORT
WHAT?... YES, I KNOW.... THEY AREN'T WORTHY TO BE IN OUR PRESENCE, BUT....
...NO, I CAN'T!...TOO MESSY....STOP YELLING AT ME!....
....WE MUST STRIKE WHEN IT IS MOST EFFECTIVE!....
...THE OTHERS ALREADY ARE ON EDGE...
THE LOS ANGELES POLICE DEPARTMENT CONFIRMS THAT THE META-HUMAN KILLER KNOWN ONLY AS "COPPERHEAD" WAS FOUND MURDERED IN DOWNTOWN L.A. EARLY THIS MORNING...
WHAT?!?

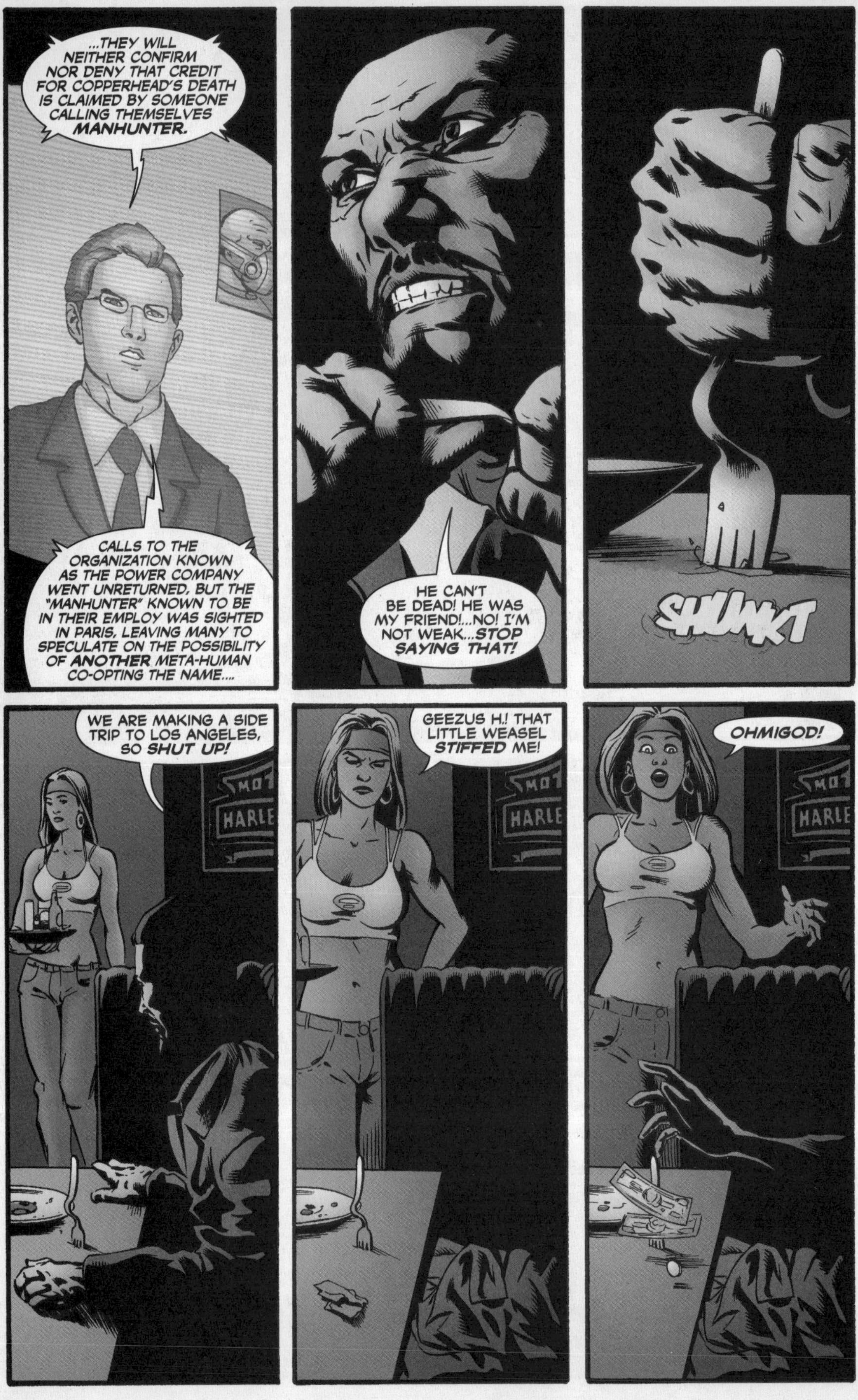
...THEY WILL NEITHER CONFIRM NOR DENY THAT CREDIT FOR COPPERHEAD'S DEATH IS CLAIMED BY SOMEONE CALLING THEMSELVES MANHUNTER.
CALLS TO THE ORGANIZATION KNOWN AS THE POWER COMPANY WENT UNRETURNED, BUT THE "MANHUNTER" KNOWN TO BE IN THEIR EMPLOY WAS SIGHTED IN PARIS, LEAVING MANY TO SPECULATE ON THE POSSIBILITY OF ANOTHER META-HUMAN CO-OPTING THE NAME....
HE CAN'T BE DEAD! HE WAS MY FRIEND!...NO! I'M NOT WEAK...STOP SAYING THAT!
SHUNKT
WE ARE MAKING A SIDE TRIP TO LOS ANGELES, SO SHUT UP!
GEEZUS H.! THAT LITTLE WEASEL STIFFED ME!
OHMIGOD!

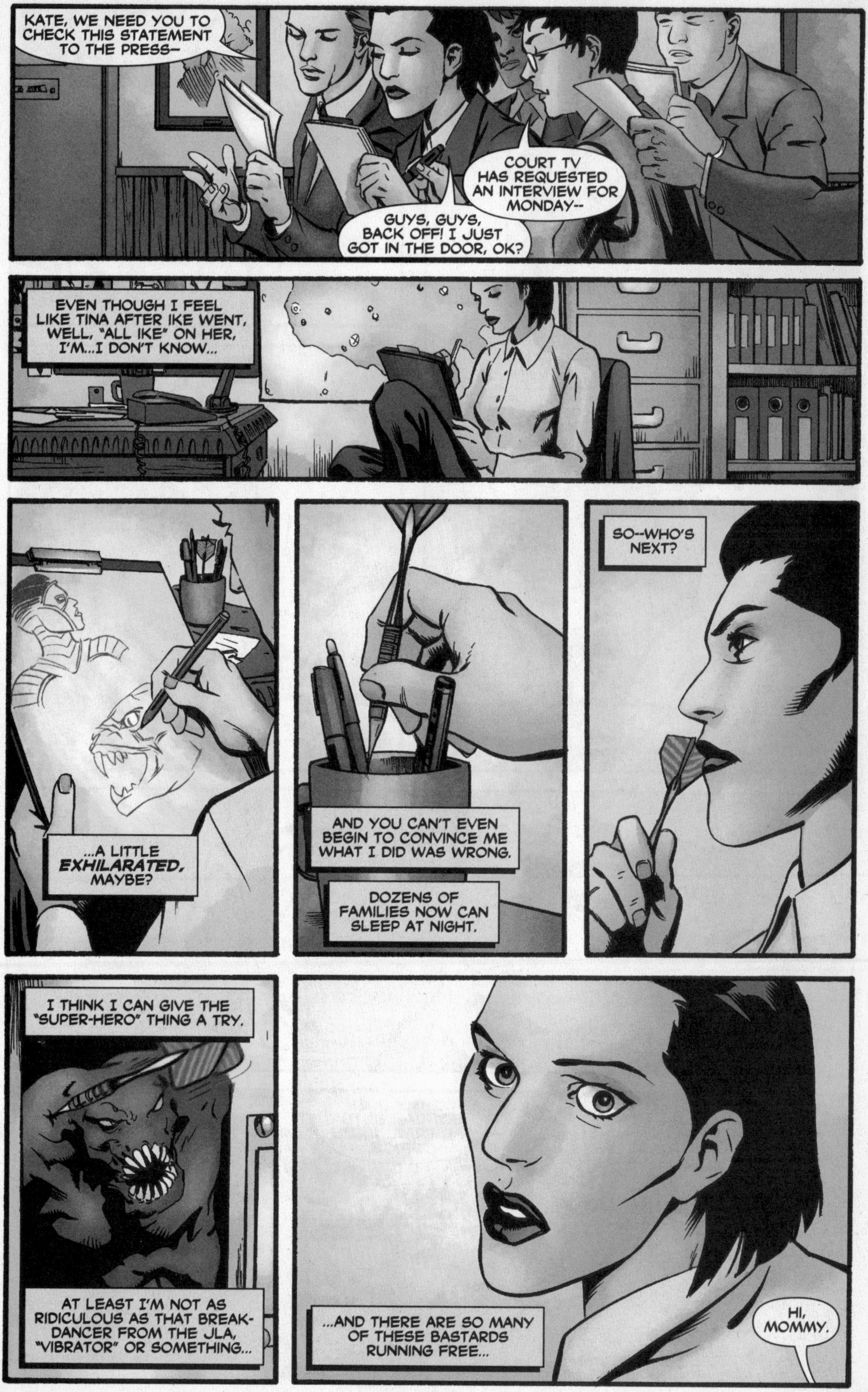
KATE, WE NEED YOU TO CHECK THIS STATEMENT TO THE PRESS--
COURT TV HAS REQUESTED AN INTERVIEW FOR MONDAY--
GUYS, GUYS, BACK OFF! I JUST GOT IN THE DOOR, OK?
EVEN THOUGH I FEEL LIKE TINA AFTER IKE WENT, WELL, "ALL IKE" ON HER, I'M...I DON'T KNOW...
...A LITTLE *EXHILARATED,* MAYBE?
AND YOU CAN'T EVEN BEGIN TO CONVINCE ME WHAT I DID WAS WRONG.
DOZENS OF FAMILIES NOW CAN SLEEP AT NIGHT.
SO--WHO'S NEXT?
I THINK I CAN GIVE THE "SUPER-HERO" THING A TRY.
AT LEAST I'M NOT AS RIDICULOUS AS THAT BREAK-DANCER FROM THE JLA, "VIBRATOR" OR SOMETHING...
...AND THERE ARE SO MANY OF THESE BASTARDS RUNNING FREE...
HI, MOMMY.

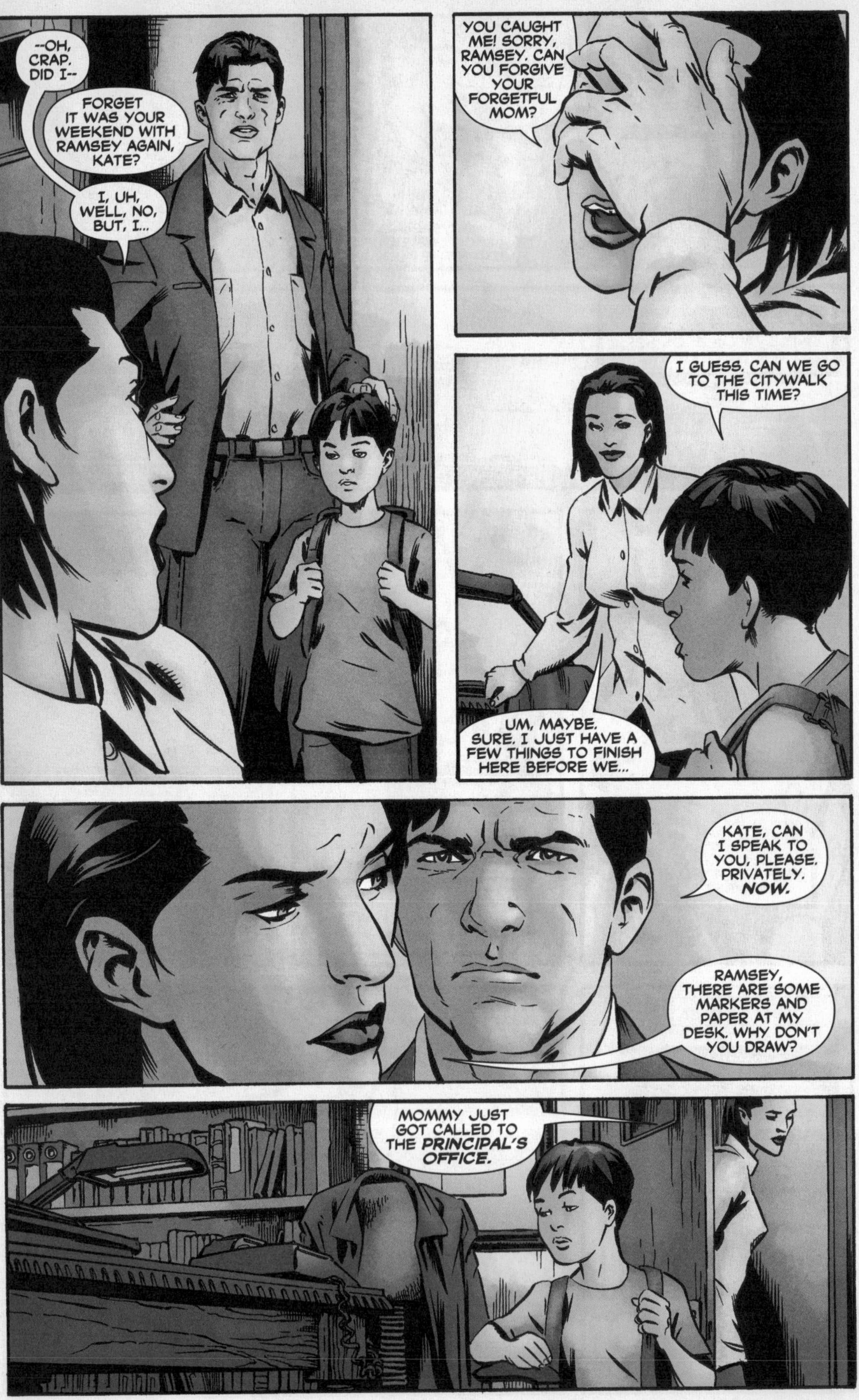
--OH, CRAP. DID I--
FORGET IT WAS YOUR WEEKEND WITH RAMSEY AGAIN, KATE?
I, UH, WELL, NO, BUT, I...
YOU CAUGHT ME! SORRY, RAMSEY. CAN YOU FORGIVE YOUR FORGETFUL MOM?
I GUESS. CAN WE GO TO THE CITYWALK THIS TIME?
UM, MAYBE. SURE. I JUST HAVE A FEW THINGS TO FINISH HERE BEFORE WE...
KATE, CAN I SPEAK TO YOU, PLEASE. PRIVATELY. *NOW.*
RAMSEY, THERE ARE SOME MARKERS AND PAPER AT MY DESK. WHY DON'T YOU DRAW?
MOMMY JUST GOT CALLED TO THE *PRINCIPAL'S OFFICE.*

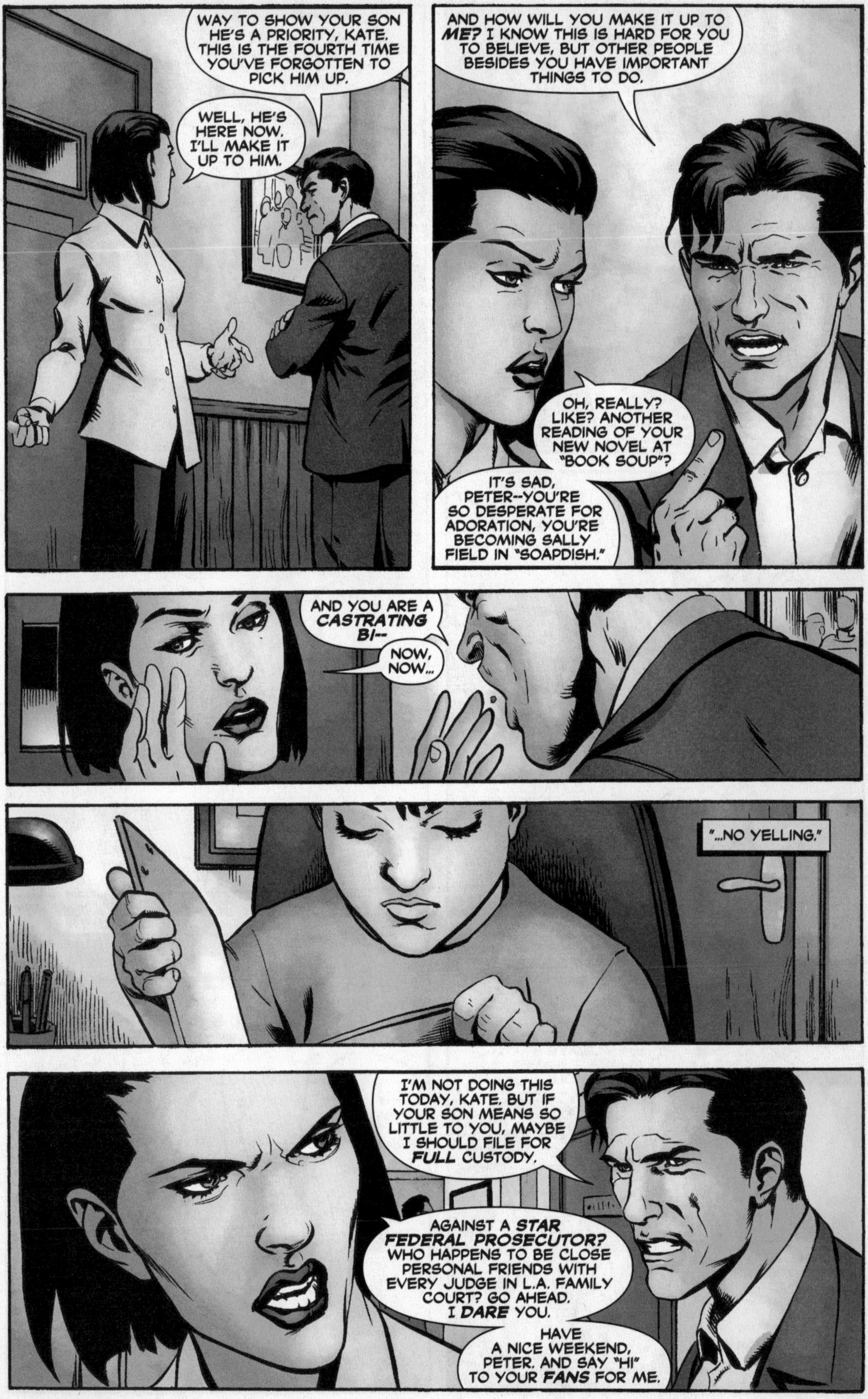
WAY TO SHOW YOUR SON HE'S A PRIORITY, KATE. THIS IS THE FOURTH TIME YOU'VE FORGOTTEN TO PICK HIM UP.
WELL, HE'S HERE NOW. I'LL MAKE IT UP TO HIM.
AND HOW WILL YOU MAKE IT UP TO ME? I KNOW THIS IS HARD FOR YOU TO BELIEVE, BUT OTHER PEOPLE BESIDES YOU HAVE IMPORTANT THINGS TO DO.
OH, REALLY? LIKE? ANOTHER READING OF YOUR NEW NOVEL AT "BOOK SOUP"?
IT'S SAD, PETER--YOU'RE SO DESPERATE FOR ADORATION, YOU'RE BECOMING SALLY FIELD IN "SOAPDISH."
AND YOU ARE A CASTRATING BI--
NOW, NOW...
"...NO YELLING."
I'M NOT DOING THIS TODAY, KATE. BUT IF YOUR SON MEANS SO LITTLE TO YOU, MAYBE I SHOULD FILE FOR FULL CUSTODY.
AGAINST A STAR FEDERAL PROSECUTOR? WHO HAPPENS TO BE CLOSE PERSONAL FRIENDS WITH EVERY JUDGE IN L.A. FAMILY COURT? GO AHEAD. I DARE YOU.
HAVE A NICE WEEKEND, PETER. AND SAY "HI" TO YOUR FANS FOR ME.

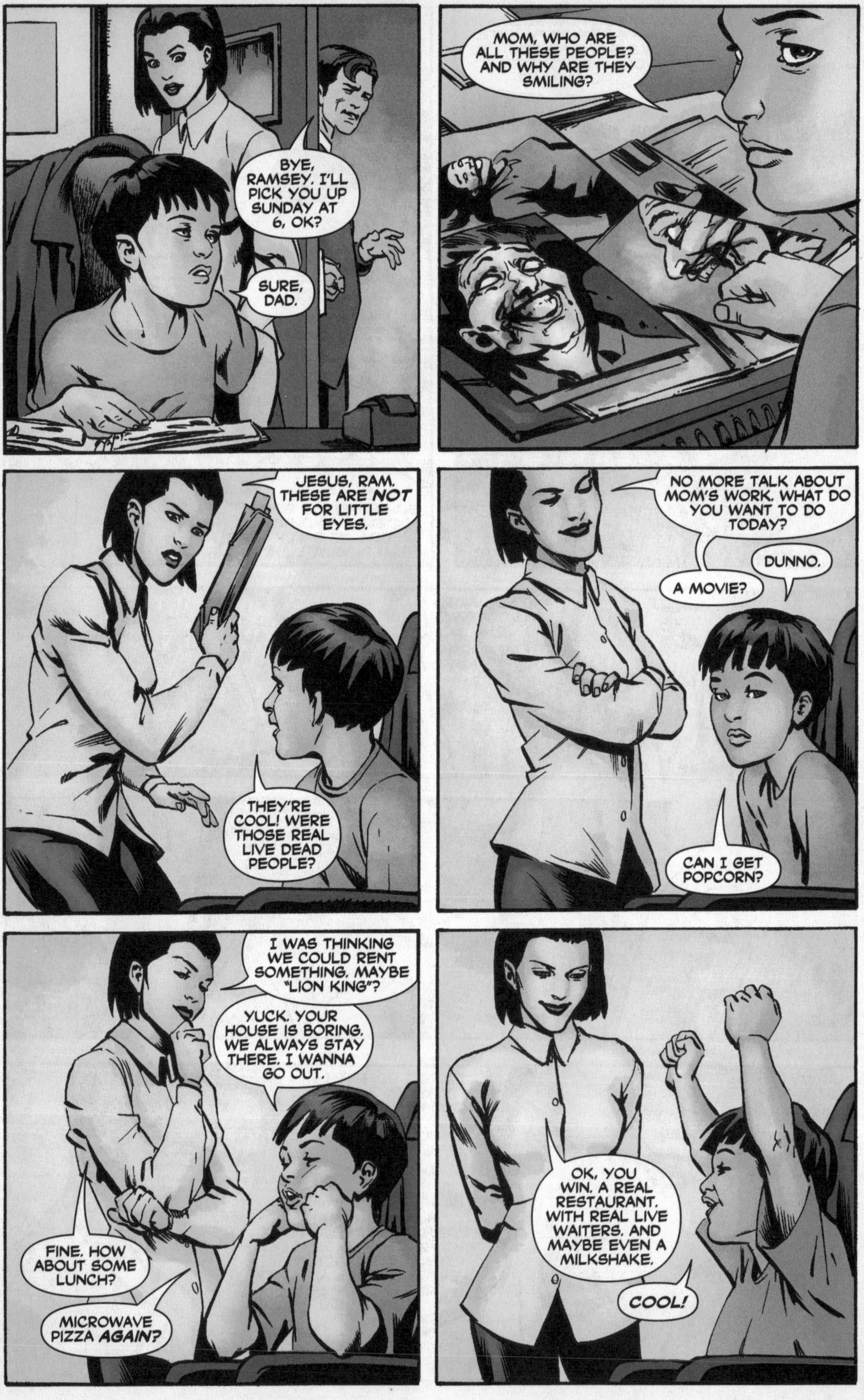
BYE, RAMSEY. I'LL PICK YOU UP SUNDAY AT 6, OK?
SURE, DAD.
MOM, WHO ARE ALL THESE PEOPLE? AND WHY ARE THEY SMILING?
JESUS, RAM. THESE ARE *NOT* FOR LITTLE EYES.
THEY'RE COOL! WERE THOSE REAL LIVE DEAD PEOPLE?
NO MORE TALK ABOUT MOM'S WORK. WHAT DO YOU WANT TO DO TODAY?
A MOVIE?
DUNNO.
CAN I GET POPCORN?
I WAS THINKING WE COULD RENT SOMETHING. MAYBE "LION KING"?
YUCK. YOUR HOUSE IS BORING. WE ALWAYS STAY THERE. I WANNA GO OUT.
FINE. HOW ABOUT SOME LUNCH?
MICROWAVE PIZZA *AGAIN?*
OK, YOU WIN. A REAL RESTAURANT. WITH REAL LIVE WAITERS. AND MAYBE EVEN A MILKSHAKE.
COOL!

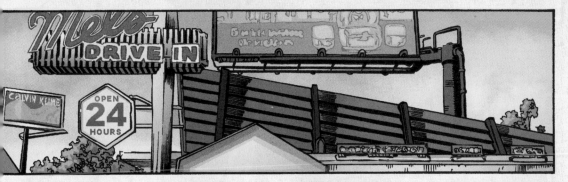

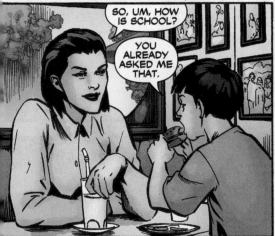

MEL'S
DRIVE IN
CALVIN KLINE
OPEN
24
HOURS
SO, UM, HOW IS SCHOOL?
YOU ALREADY ASKED ME THAT.
OH. YEAH. I KNOW. WELL, HOW'S "GANDALF"? HOUSEBROKEN YET?
UH-HUH.
OK, RAMSEY, GIMME A LITTLE HELP HERE? WHAT DO YOU WANT TO TALK ABOUT?
I GOTTA GO TO THE BATHROOM.
WAY TO GO, DONNA REED.
HELEN
EXCUSE ME, MA'AM. THERE'S, LIKE, NO SMOKING IN THE RESTAURANT. FOR LIKE THE PAST *FIVE YEARS.*

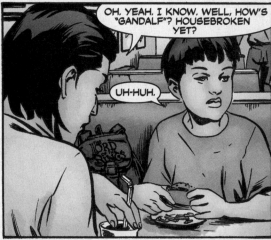

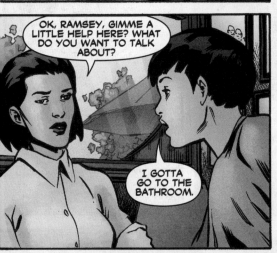

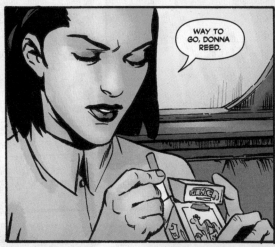

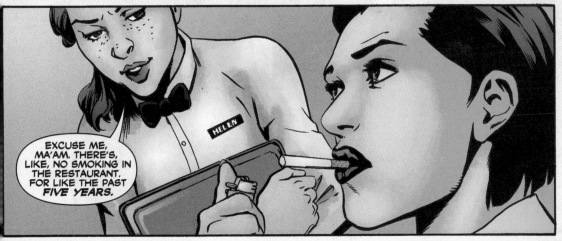

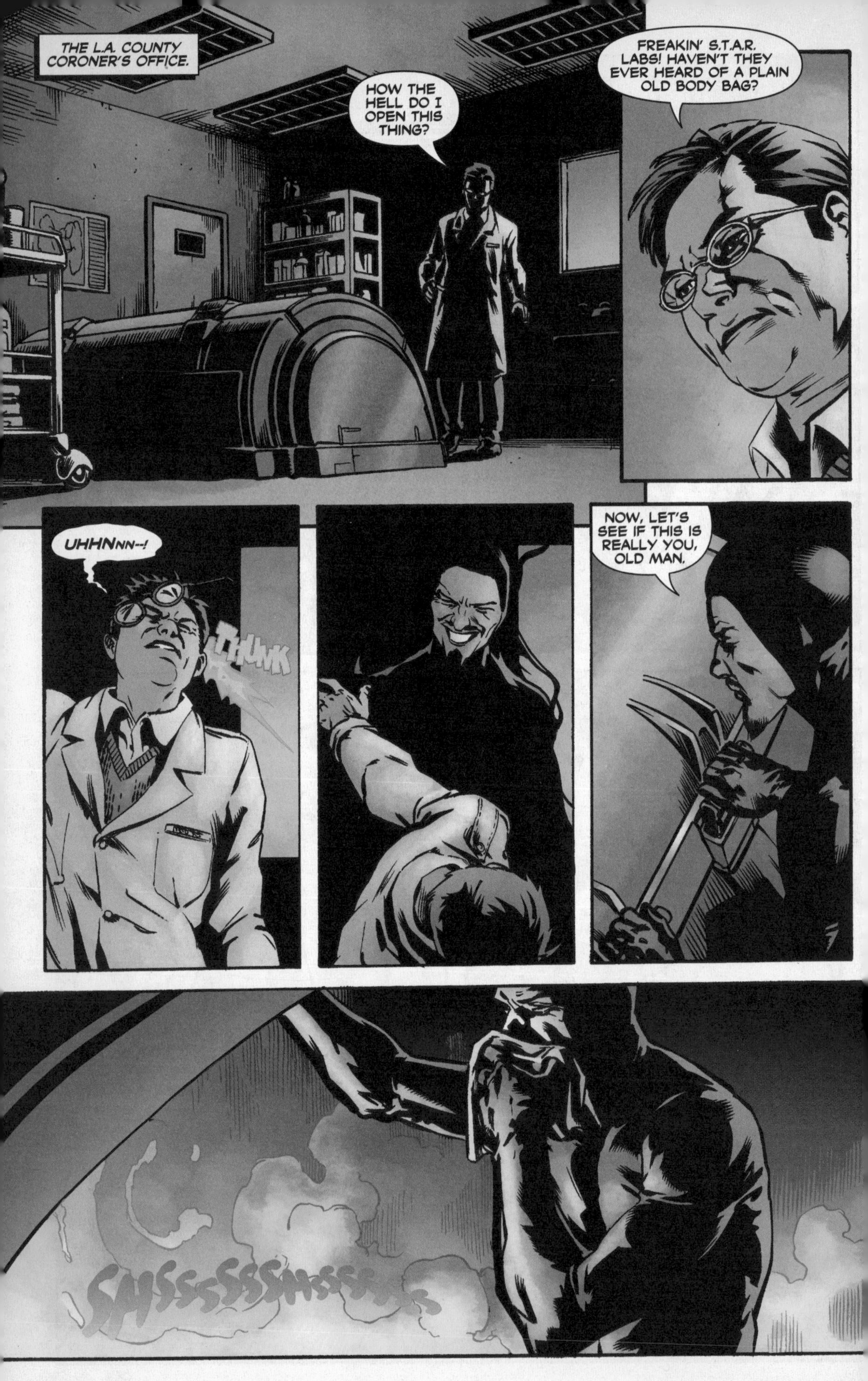
THE L.A. COUNTY CORONER'S OFFICE.
HOW THE HELL DO I OPEN THIS THING?
FREAKIN' S.T.A.R. LABS! HAVEN'T THEY EVER HEARD OF A PLAIN OLD BODY BAG?
UHHNNN--!
THUNK
NOW, LET'S SEE IF THIS IS REALLY YOU, OLD MAN.
SHSSSSSSHSSSSS

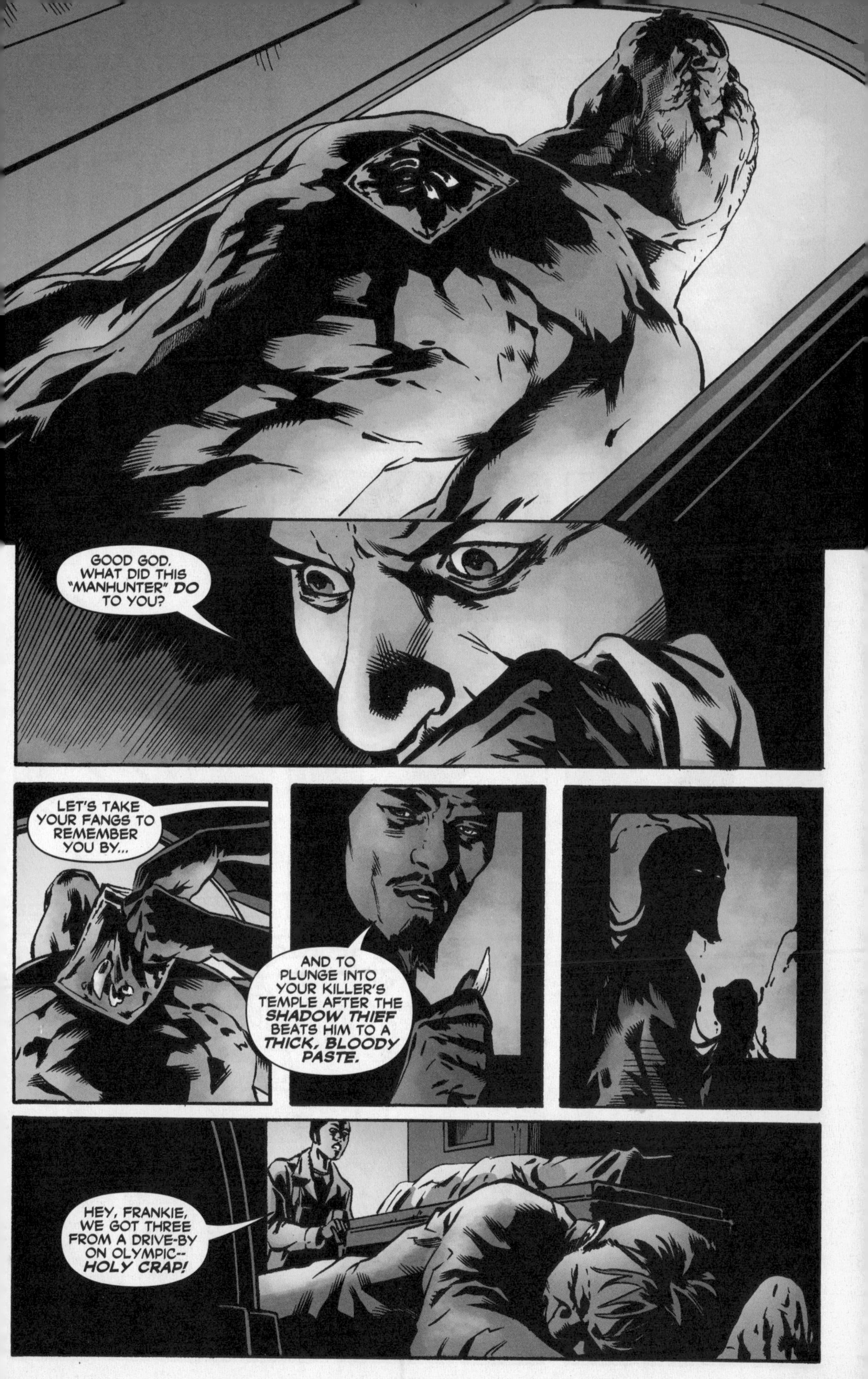
GOOD GOD, WHAT DID THIS "MANHUNTER" DO TO YOU?
LET'S TAKE YOUR FANGS TO REMEMBER YOU BY...
AND TO PLUNGE INTO YOUR KILLER'S TEMPLE AFTER THE SHADOW THIEF BEATS HIM TO A THICK, BLOODY PASTE.
HEY, FRANKIE, WE GOT THREE FROM A DRIVE-BY ON OLYMPIC-- HOLY CRAP!

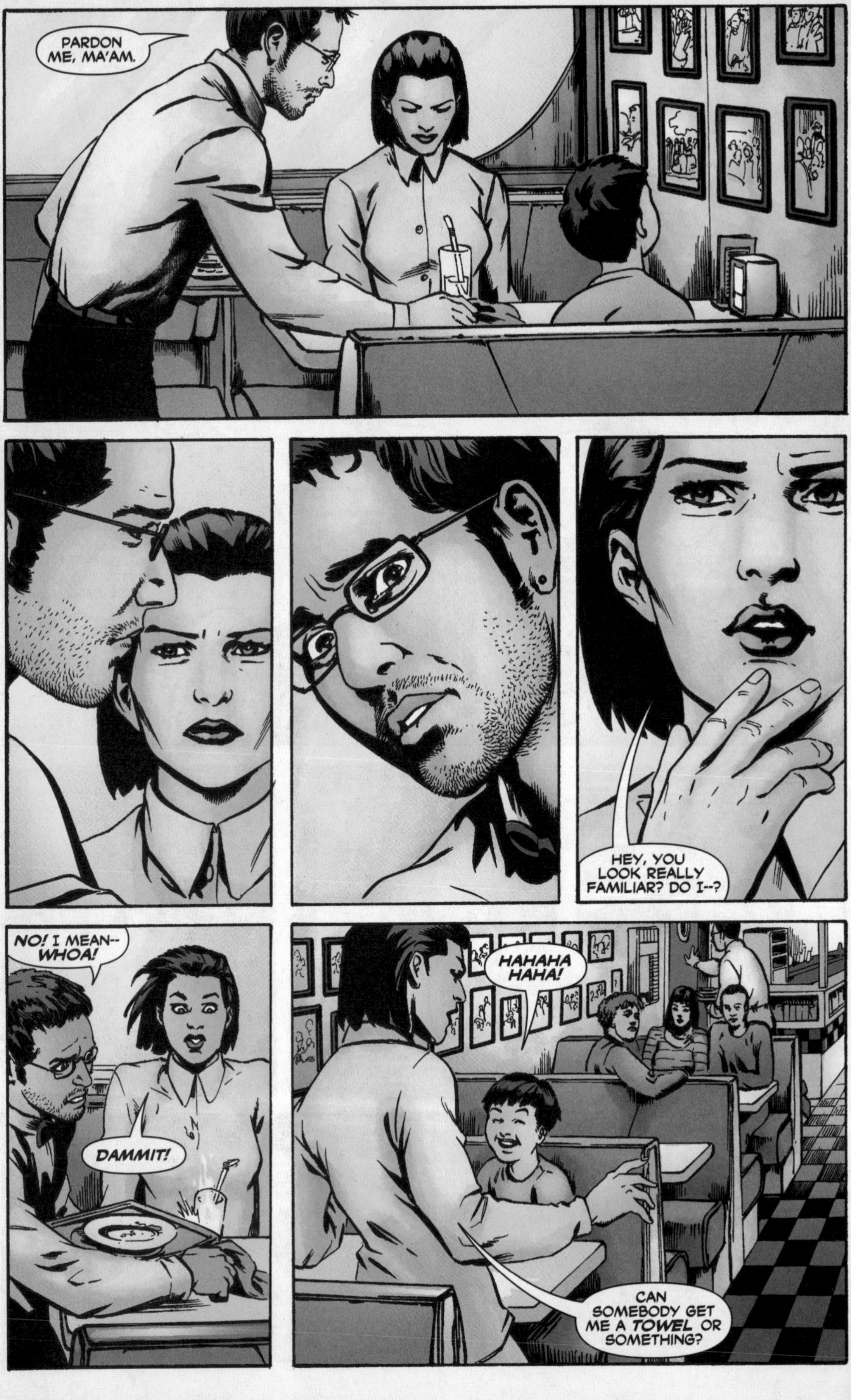
PARDON ME, MA'AM.
HEY, YOU LOOK REALLY FAMILIAR? DO I--?
NO! I MEAN-- WHOA!
DAMMIT!
HAHAHA HAHA!
CAN SOMEBODY GET ME A TOWEL OR SOMETHING?

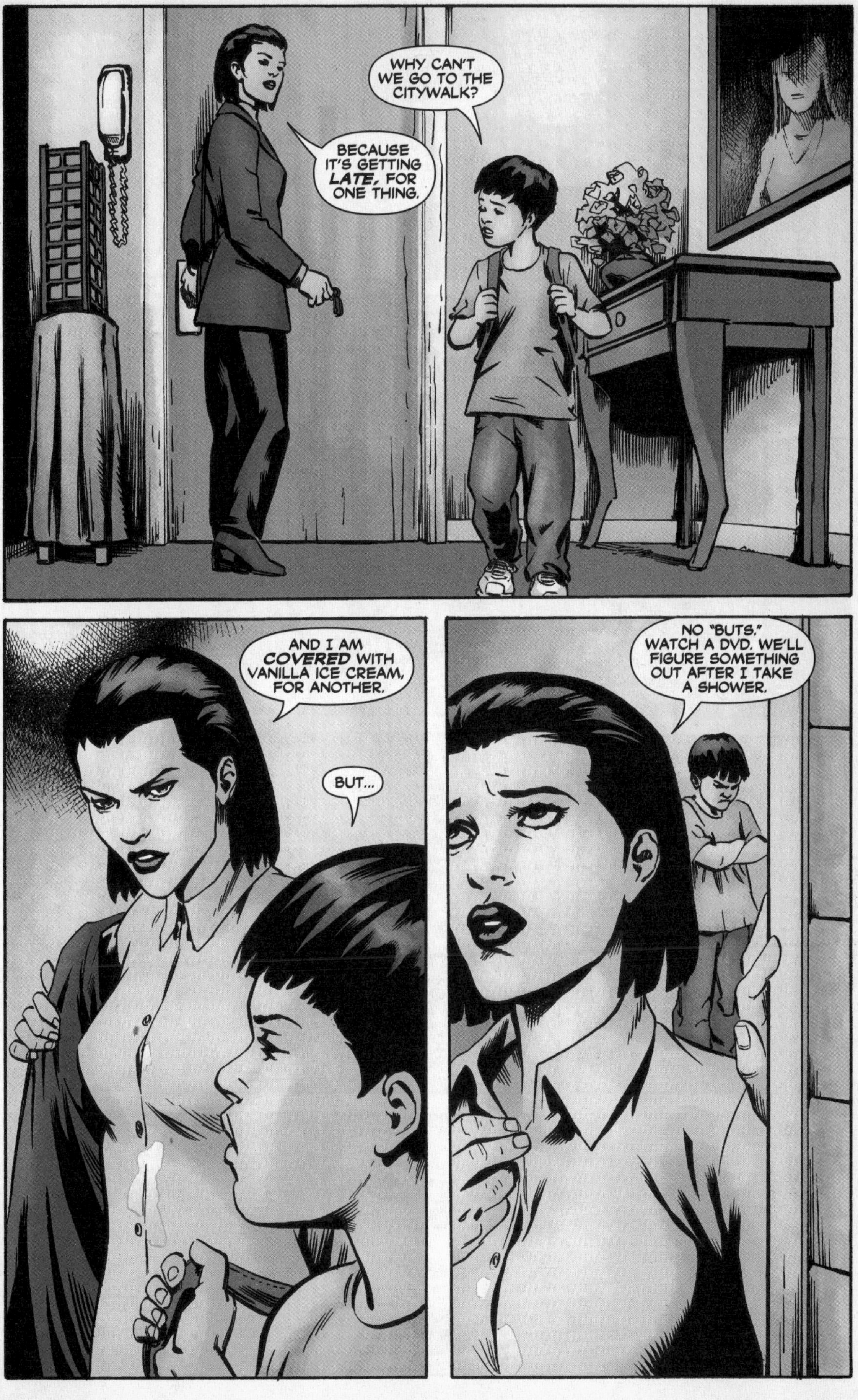
WHY CAN'T WE GO TO THE CITYWALK?
BECAUSE IT'S GETTING LATE, FOR ONE THING.
AND I AM COVERED WITH VANILLA ICE CREAM, FOR ANOTHER.
BUT...
NO "BUTS." WATCH A DVD. WE'LL FIGURE SOMETHING OUT AFTER I TAKE A SHOWER.

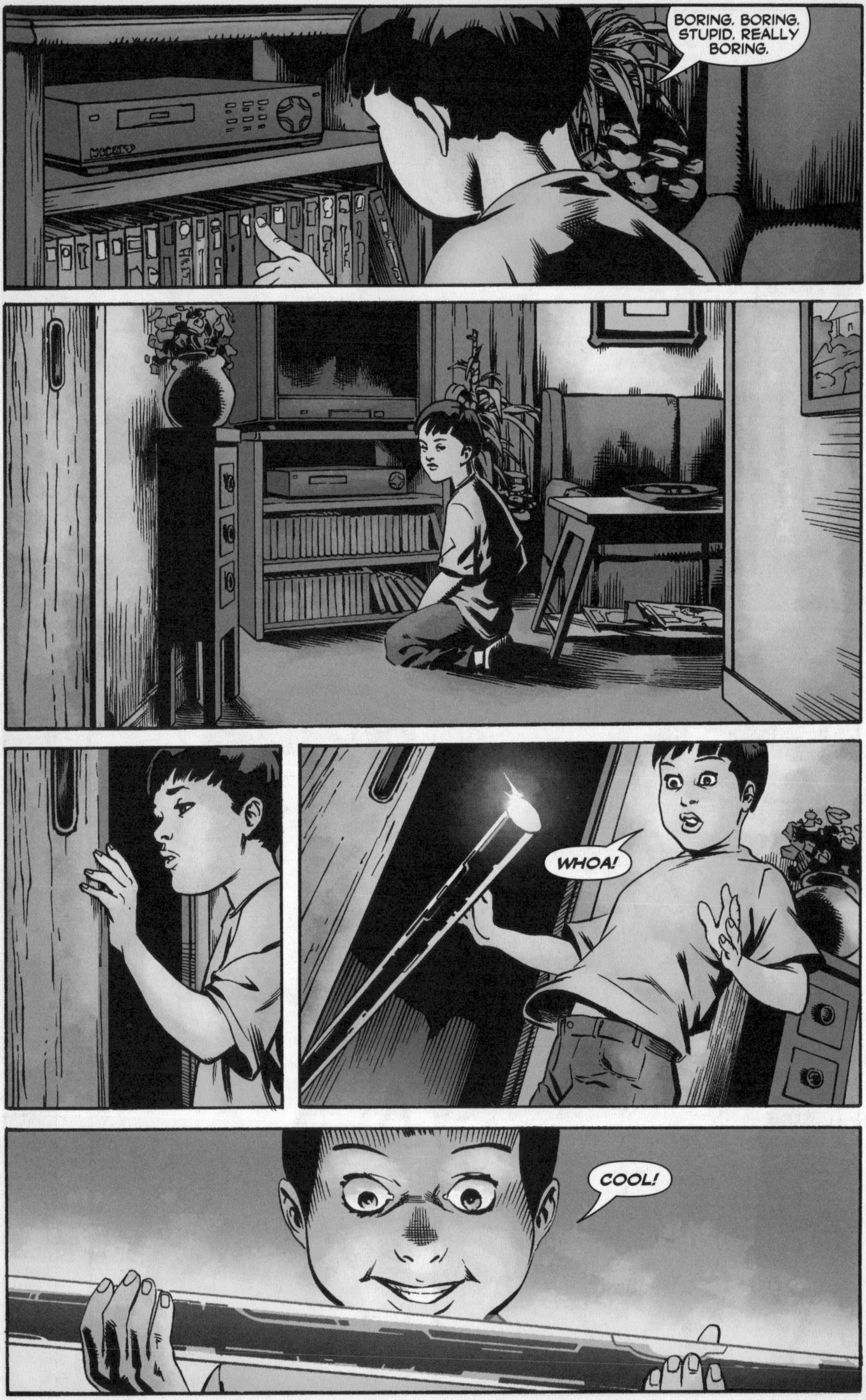

BORING. BORING. STUPID. REALLY BORING.
WHOA!
COOL!

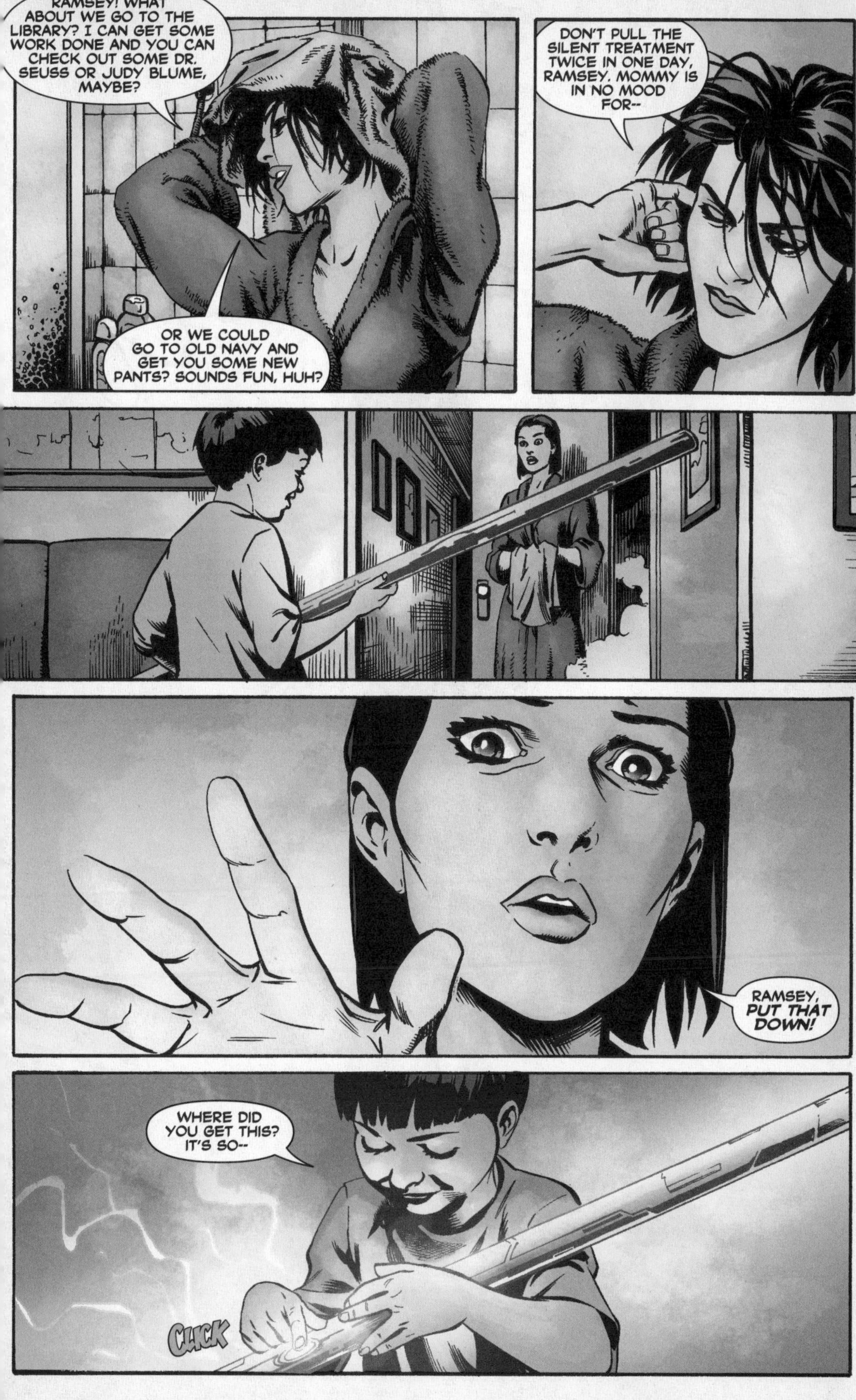
RAMSEY! WHAT ABOUT WE GO TO THE LIBRARY? I CAN GET SOME WORK DONE AND YOU CAN CHECK OUT SOME DR. SEUSS OR JUDY BLUME, MAYBE?
OR WE COULD GO TO OLD NAVY AND GET YOU SOME NEW PANTS? SOUNDS FUN, HUH?
DON'T PULL THE SILENT TREATMENT TWICE IN ONE DAY, RAMSEY. MOMMY IS IN NO MOOD FOR--
RAMSEY, PUT THAT DOWN!
WHERE DID YOU GET THIS? IT'S SO--
CLICK

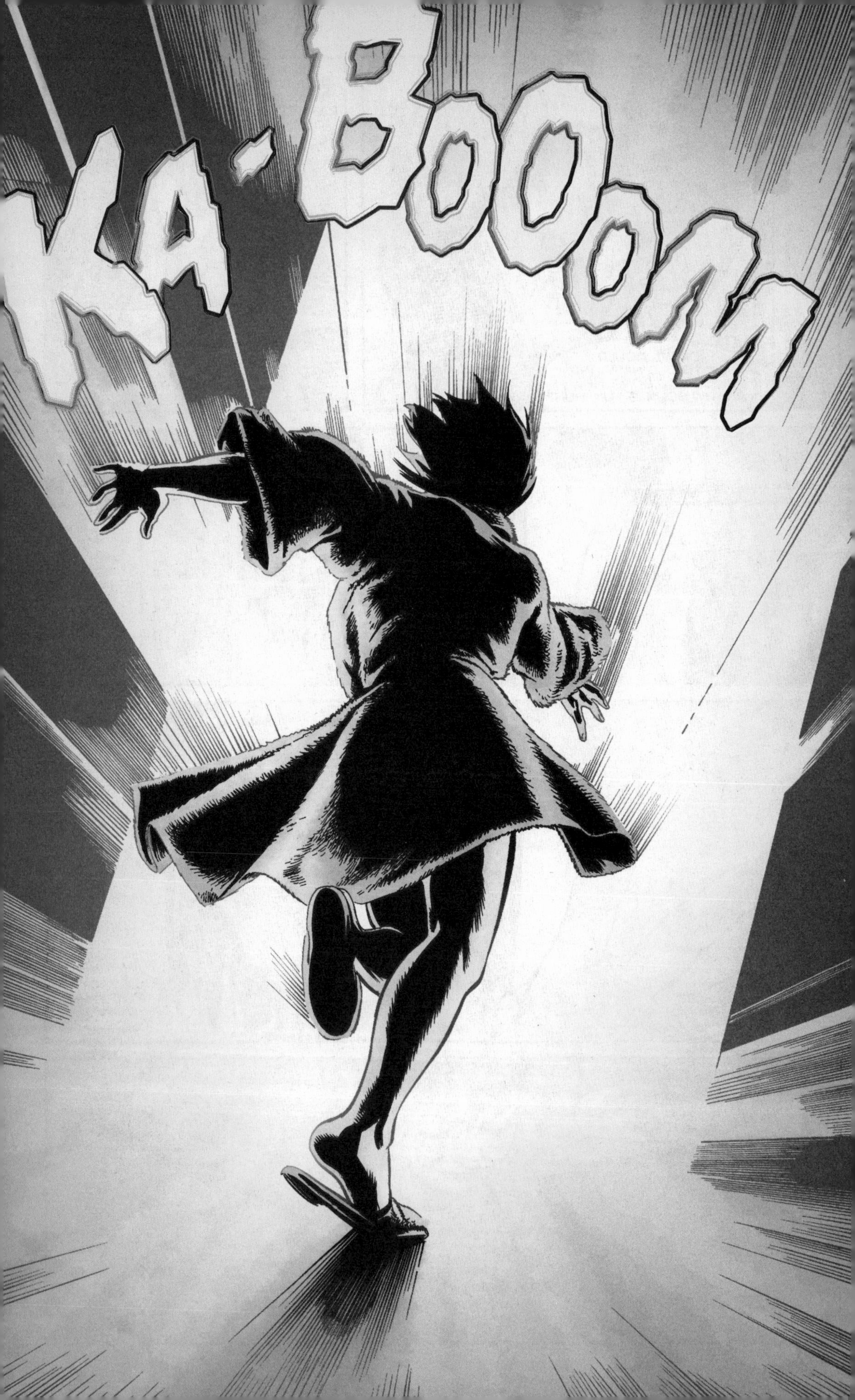
KA-BOOOM

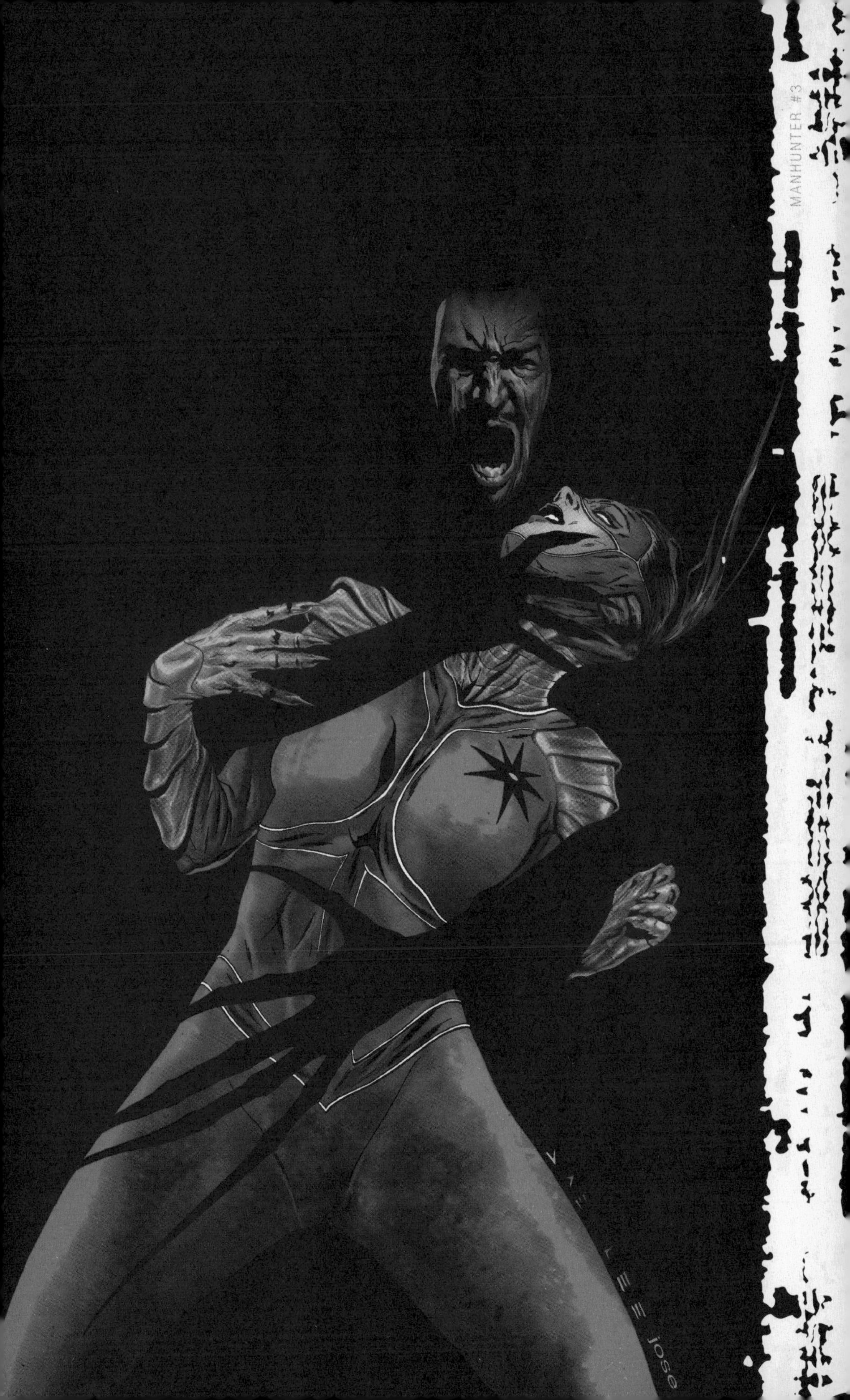
MANHUNTER #3

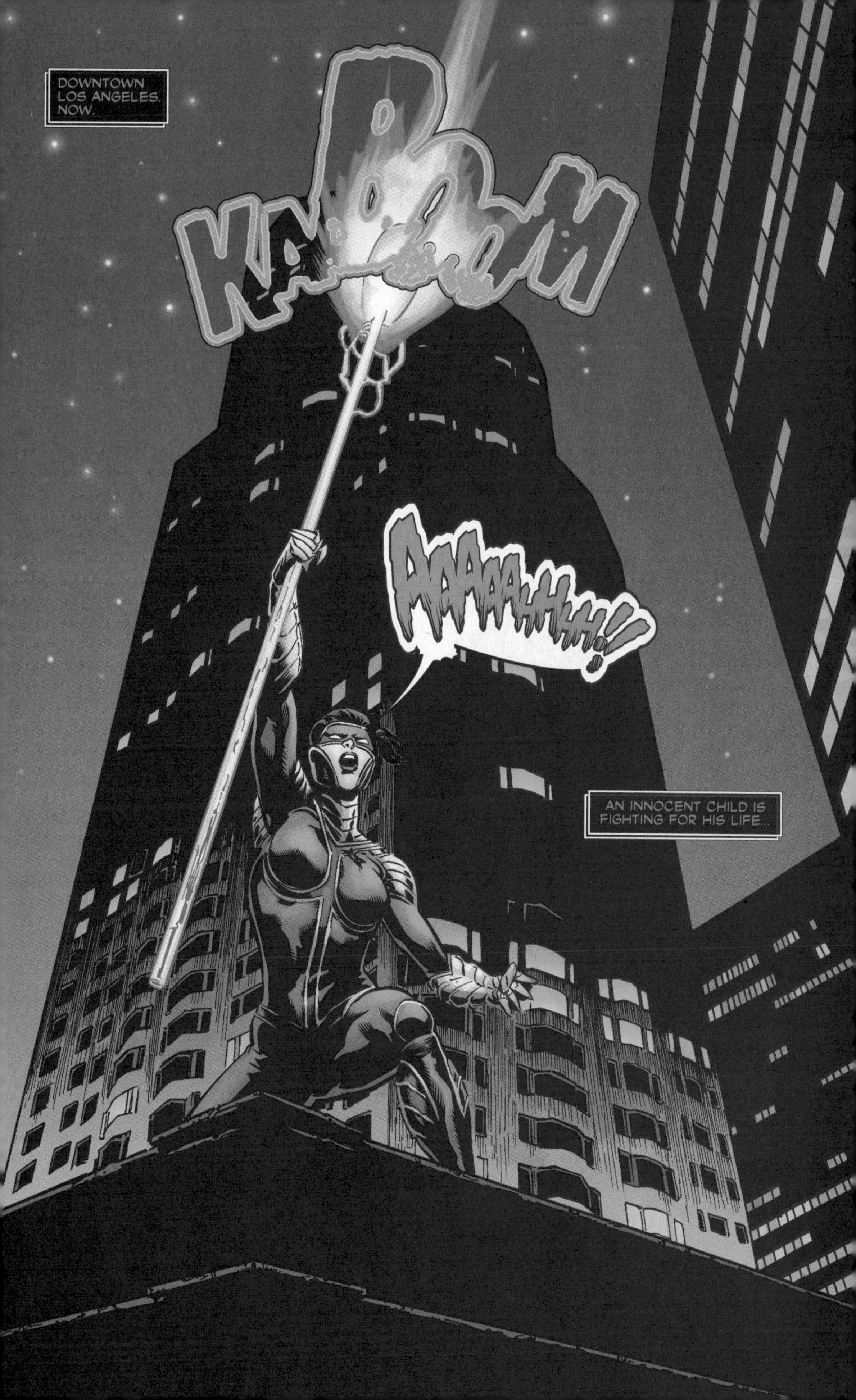
DOWNTOWN LOS ANGELES. NOW.
AAAAAHHHH!!
AN INNOCENT CHILD IS FIGHTING FOR HIS LIFE...

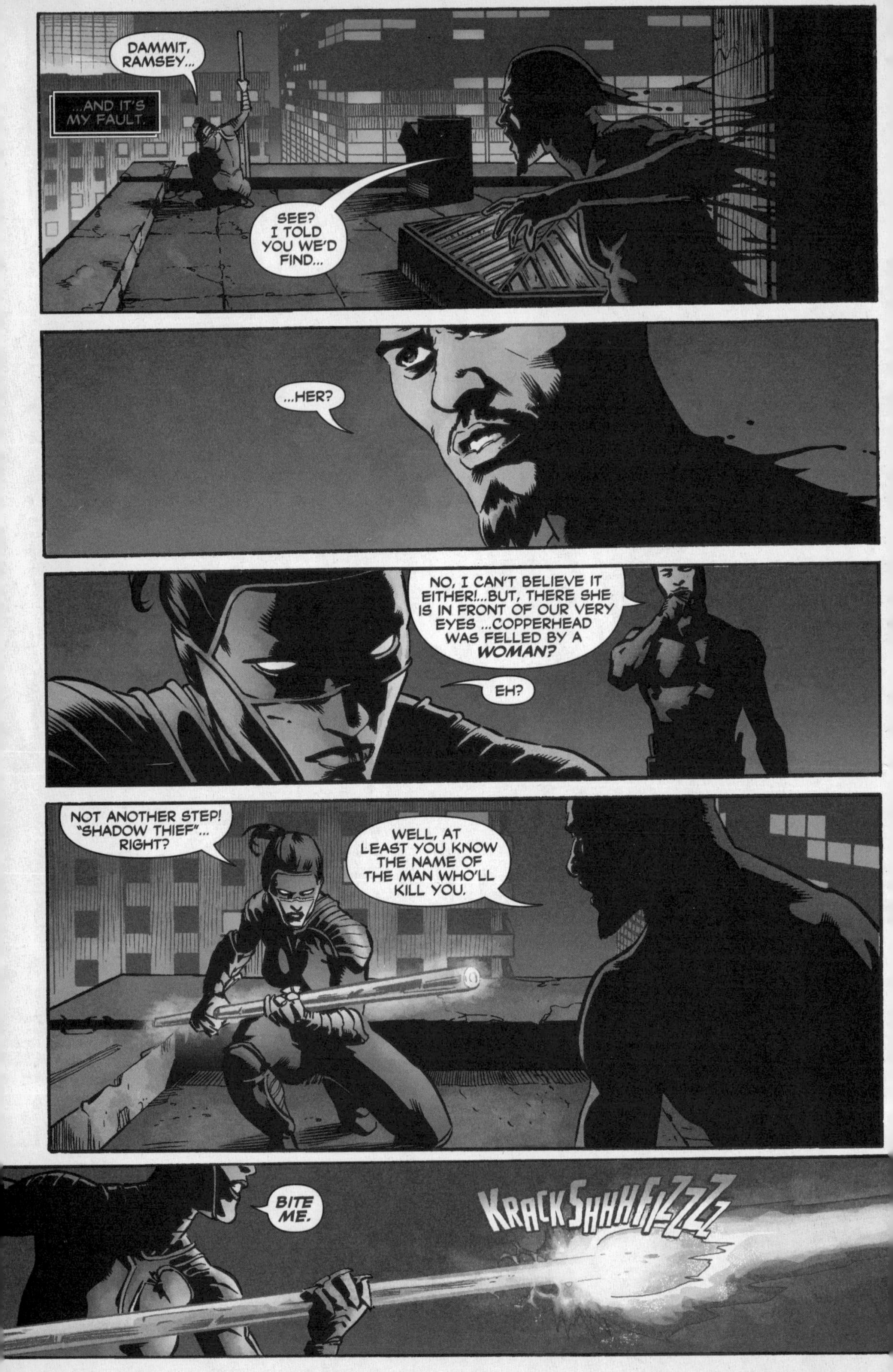
DAMMIT, RAMSEY...
...AND IT'S MY FAULT.
SEE? I TOLD YOU WE'D FIND...
...HER?
NO, I CAN'T BELIEVE IT EITHER!...BUT, THERE SHE IS IN FRONT OF OUR VERY EYES ...COPPERHEAD WAS FELLED BY A *WOMAN?*
EH?
NOT ANOTHER STEP! "SHADOW THIEF"... RIGHT?
WELL, AT LEAST YOU KNOW THE NAME OF THE MAN WHO'LL KILL YOU.
BITE ME.
KRACKSHHHFIZZZZ

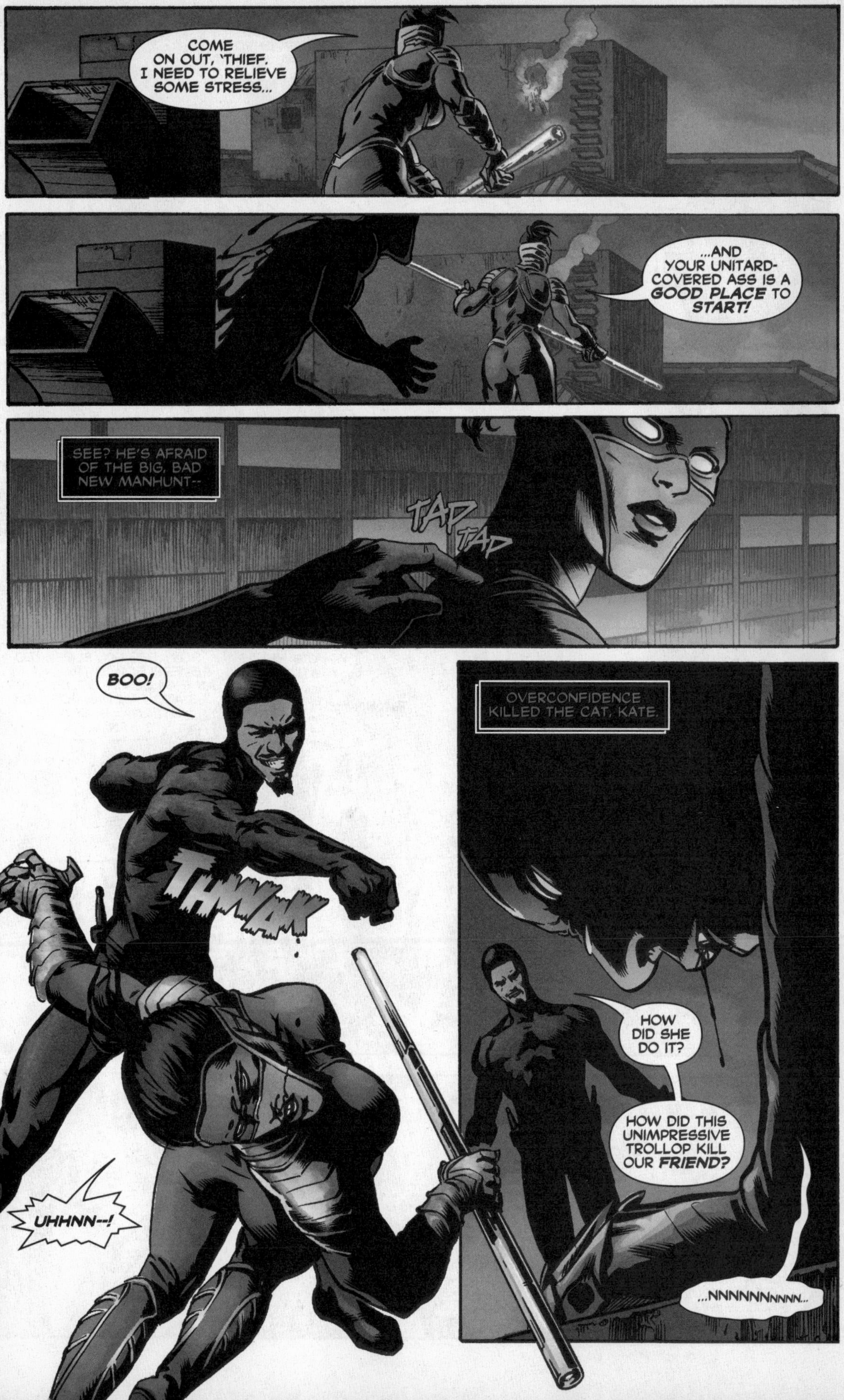
COME ON OUT, 'THIEF. I NEED TO RELIEVE SOME STRESS...
...AND YOUR UNITARD-COVERED ASS IS A GOOD PLACE TO START!
SEE? HE'S AFRAID OF THE BIG, BAD NEW MANHUNT--
TAP TAP
BOO!
THWAK
UHHNN--!
OVERCONFIDENCE KILLED THE CAT, KATE.
HOW DID SHE DO IT?
HOW DID THIS UNIMPRESSIVE TROLLOP KILL OUR FRIEND?
...NNNNNNnnnn...

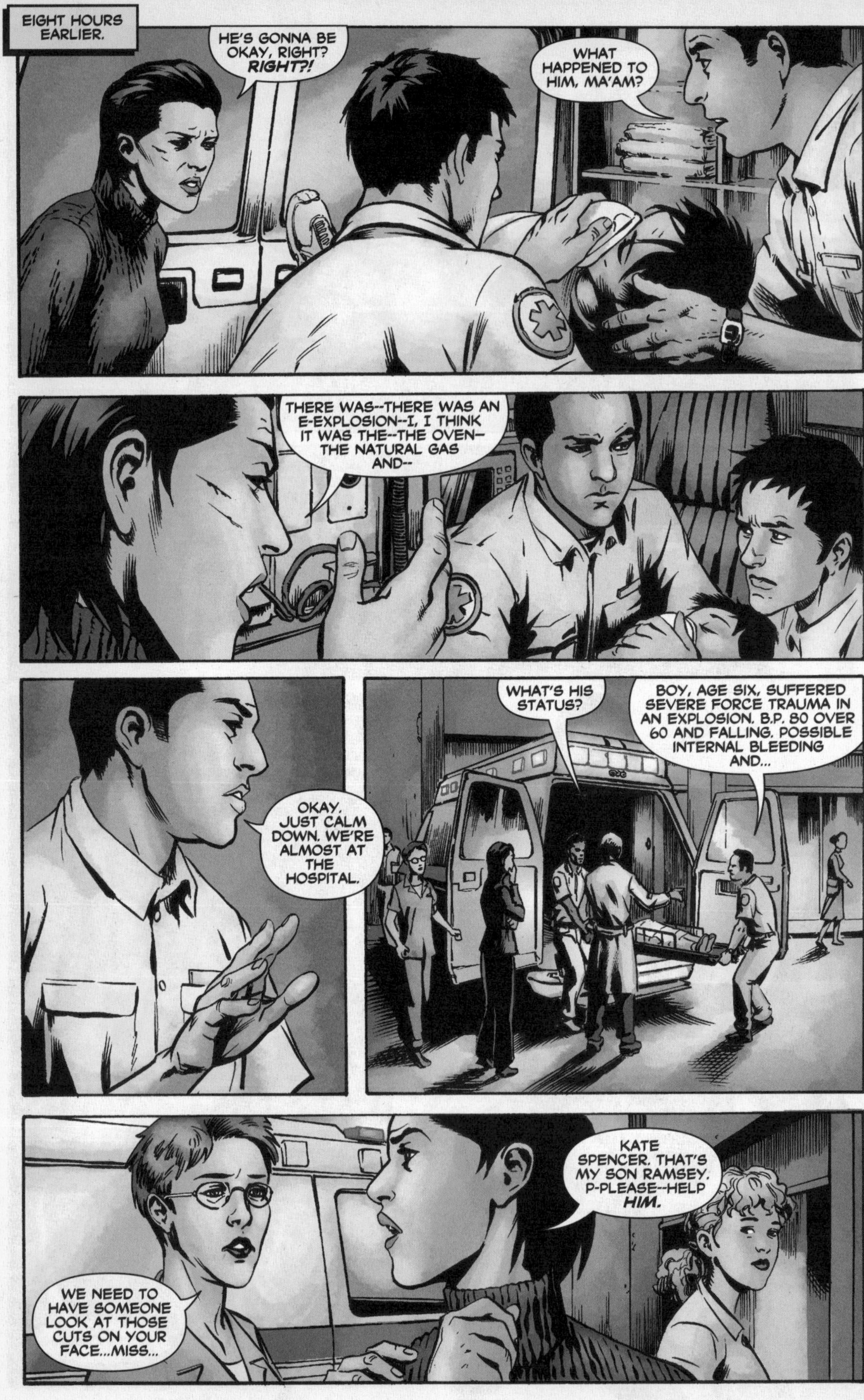
EIGHT HOURS EARLIER.
HE'S GONNA BE OKAY, RIGHT? RIGHT?!
WHAT HAPPENED TO HIM, MA'AM?
THERE WAS--THERE WAS AN E-EXPLOSION--I, I THINK IT WAS THE--THE OVEN-- THE NATURAL GAS AND--
OKAY. JUST CALM DOWN. WE'RE ALMOST AT THE HOSPITAL.
WHAT'S HIS STATUS?
BOY, AGE SIX, SUFFERED SEVERE FORCE TRAUMA IN AN EXPLOSION. B.P. 80 OVER 60 AND FALLING. POSSIBLE INTERNAL BLEEDING AND...
WE NEED TO HAVE SOMEONE LOOK AT THOSE CUTS ON YOUR FACE...MISS...
KATE SPENCER. THAT'S MY SON RAMSEY. P-PLEASE--HELP HIM.

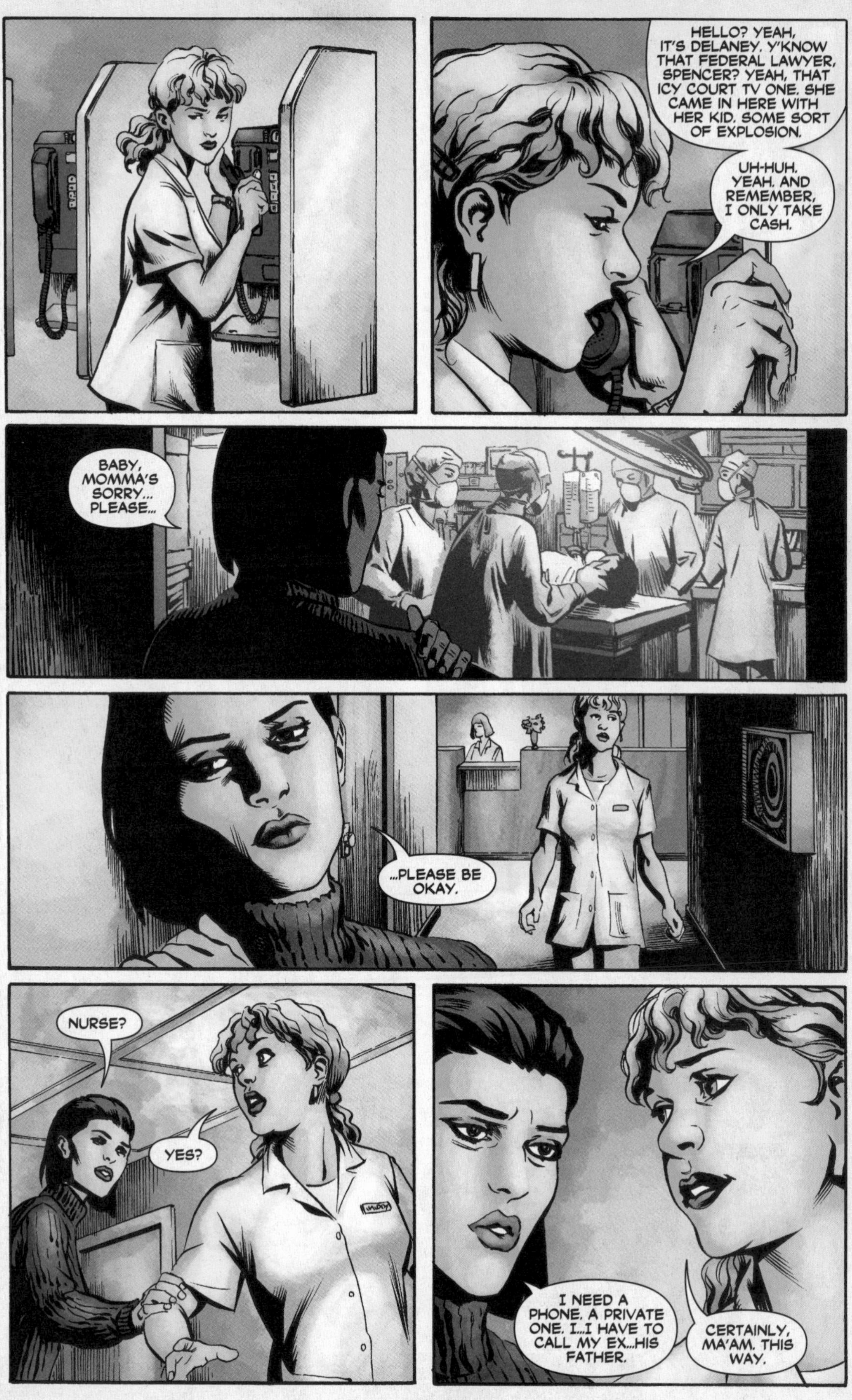
HELLO? YEAH, IT'S DELANEY. Y'KNOW THAT FEDERAL LAWYER, SPENCER? YEAH, THAT ICY COURT TV ONE. SHE CAME IN HERE WITH HER KID. SOME SORT OF EXPLOSION.
UH-HUH. YEAH. AND REMEMBER, I ONLY TAKE CASH.
BABY, MOMMA'S SORRY... PLEASE...
...PLEASE BE OKAY.
NURSE?
YES?
I NEED A PHONE. A PRIVATE ONE. I...I HAVE TO CALL MY EX...HIS FATHER.
CERTAINLY, MA'AM. THIS WAY.

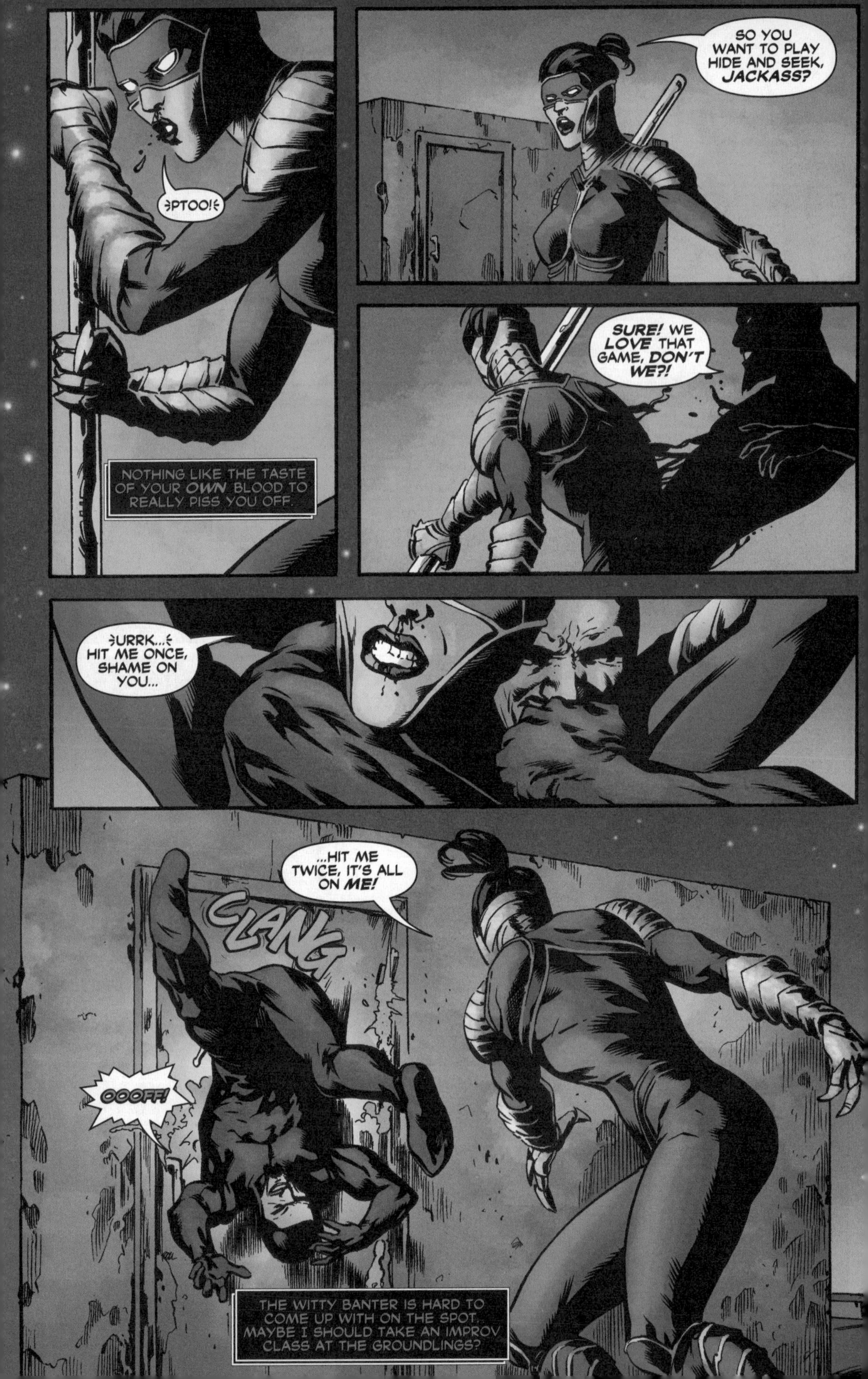

PTOO!
NOTHING LIKE THE TASTE OF YOUR OWN BLOOD TO REALLY PISS YOU OFF.
SO YOU WANT TO PLAY HIDE AND SEEK, JACKASS?
SURE! WE LOVE THAT GAME, DON'T WE?!
URRK... HIT ME ONCE, SHAME ON YOU...
...HIT ME TWICE, IT'S ALL ON ME!
CLANG
OOOFF!
THE WITTY BANTER IS HARD TO COME UP WITH ON THE SPOT. MAYBE I SHOULD TAKE AN IMPROV CLASS AT THE GROUNDLINGS?

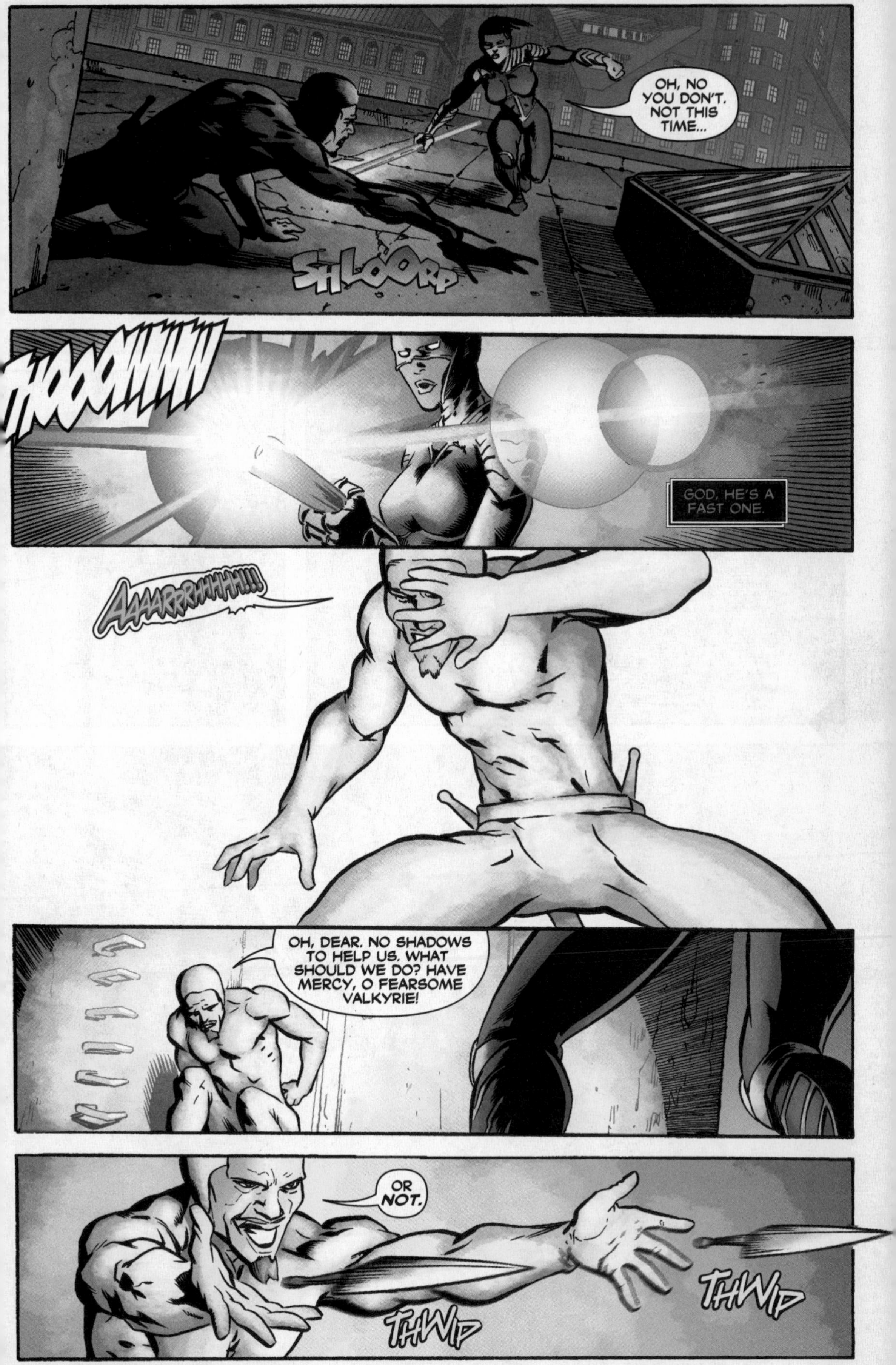
OH, NO YOU DON'T. NOT THIS TIME...
SHLOORP
THOOOMMM
GOD, HE'S A FAST ONE.
AAAARRRHHHHH!!!
OH, DEAR. NO SHADOWS TO HELP US. WHAT SHOULD WE DO? HAVE MERCY, O FEARSOME VALKYRIE!
OR NOT.
THWIP
THWIP

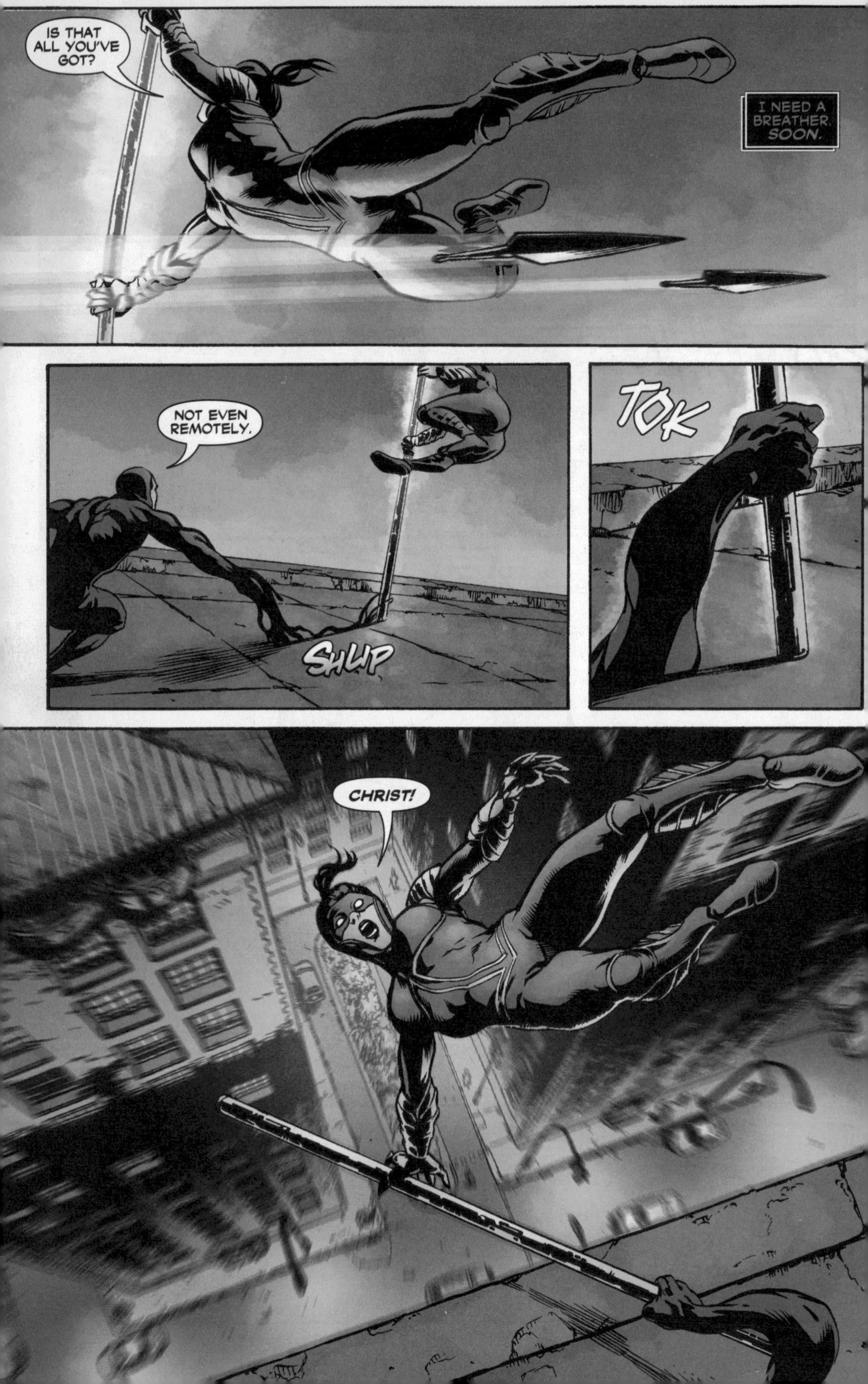
IS THAT ALL YOU'VE GOT?
I NEED A BREATHER. SOON.
NOT EVEN REMOTELY.
SHUP
TOK
CHRIST!

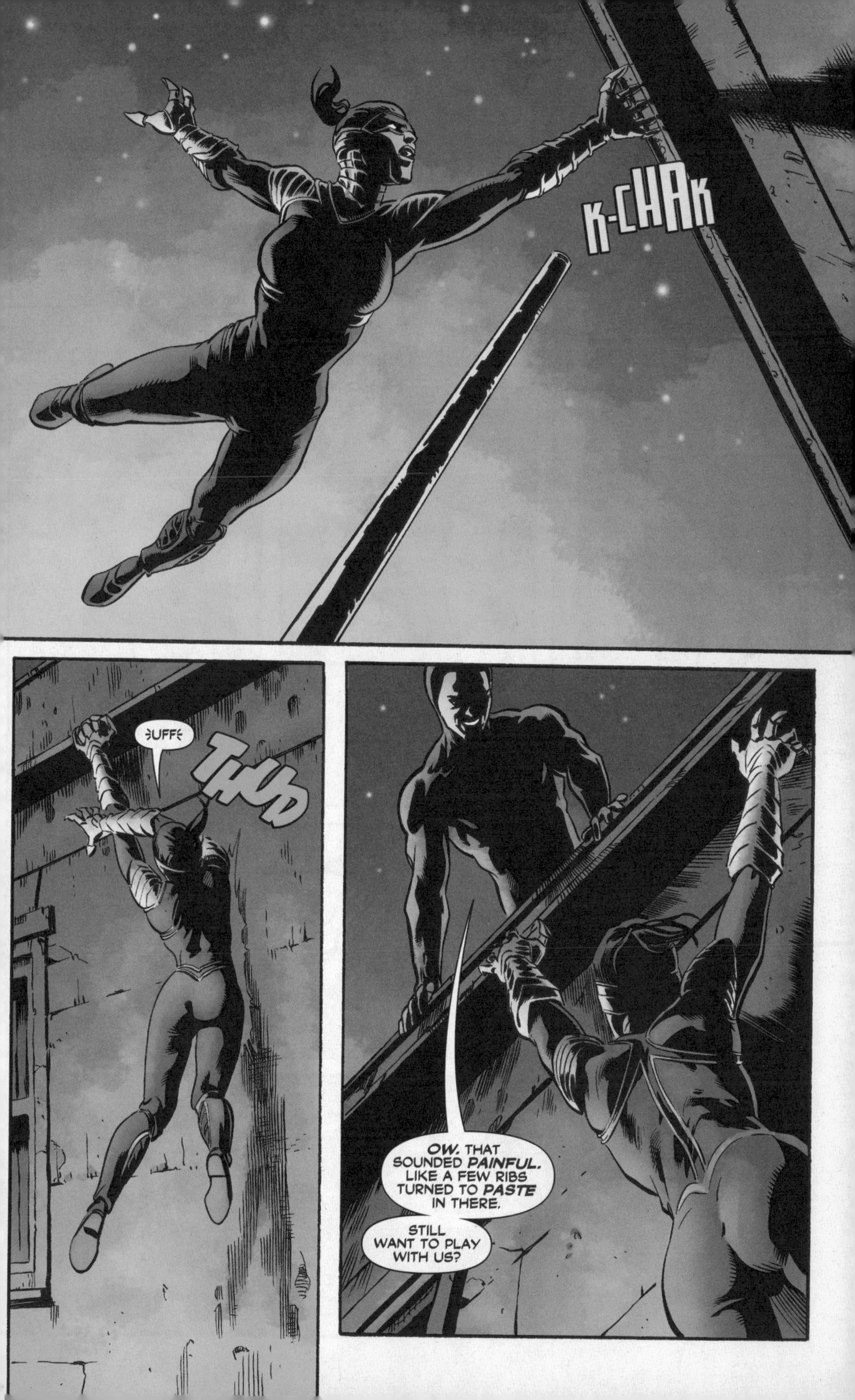
K-CHAK
UFF
THUD
OW. THAT SOUNDED PAINFUL. LIKE A FEW RIBS TURNED TO PASTE IN THERE.
STILL WANT TO PLAY WITH US?

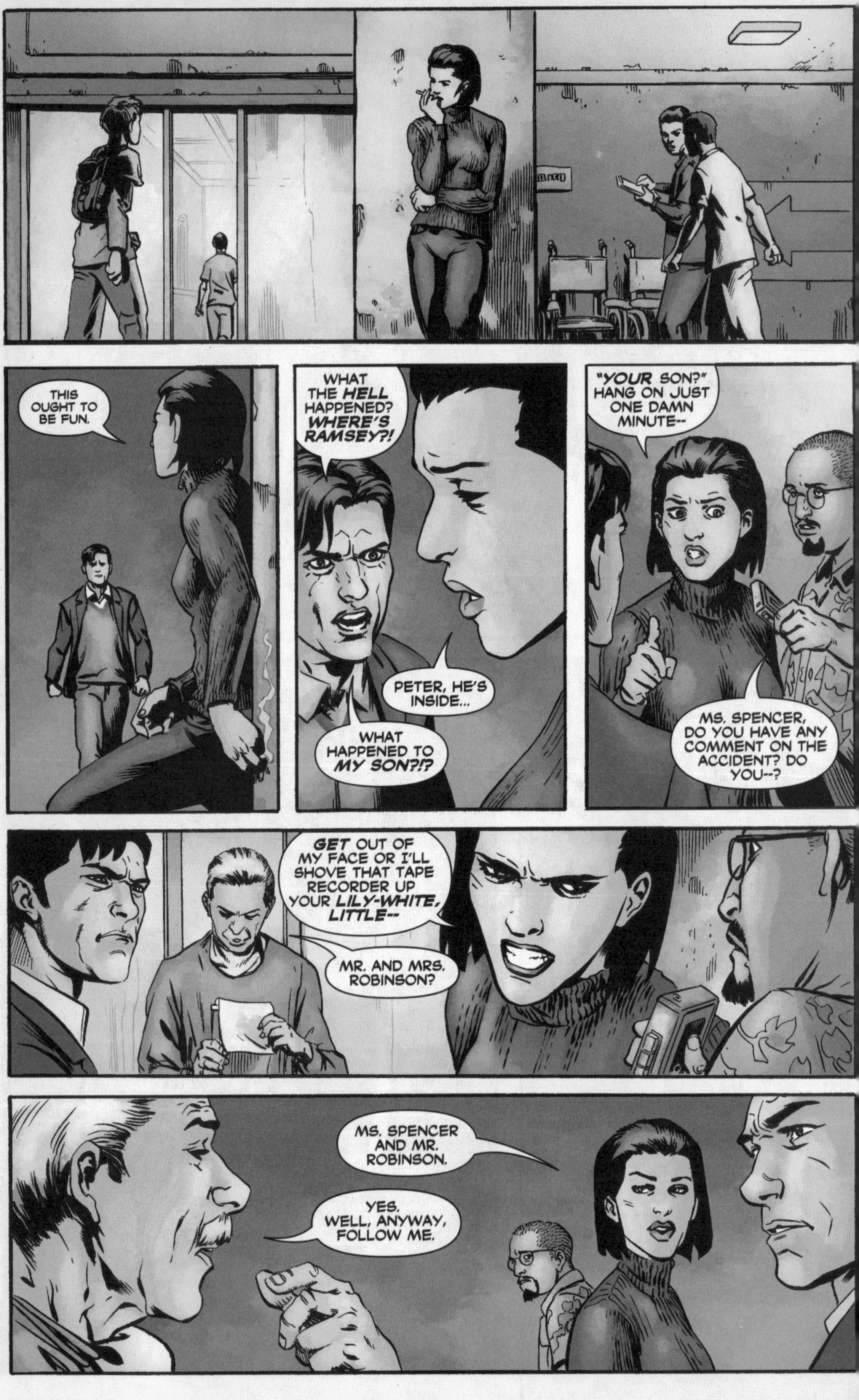
THIS OUGHT TO BE FUN.
WHAT THE HELL HAPPENED? WHERE'S RAMSEY?!
PETER, HE'S INSIDE...
WHAT HAPPENED TO MY SON?!?
"YOUR SON?" HANG ON JUST ONE DAMN MINUTE--
MS. SPENCER, DO YOU HAVE ANY COMMENT ON THE ACCIDENT? DO YOU--?
GET OUT OF MY FACE OR I'LL SHOVE THAT TAPE RECORDER UP YOUR LILY-WHITE, LITTLE--
MR. AND MRS. ROBINSON?
MS. SPENCER AND MR. ROBINSON.
YES. WELL, ANYWAY, FOLLOW ME.

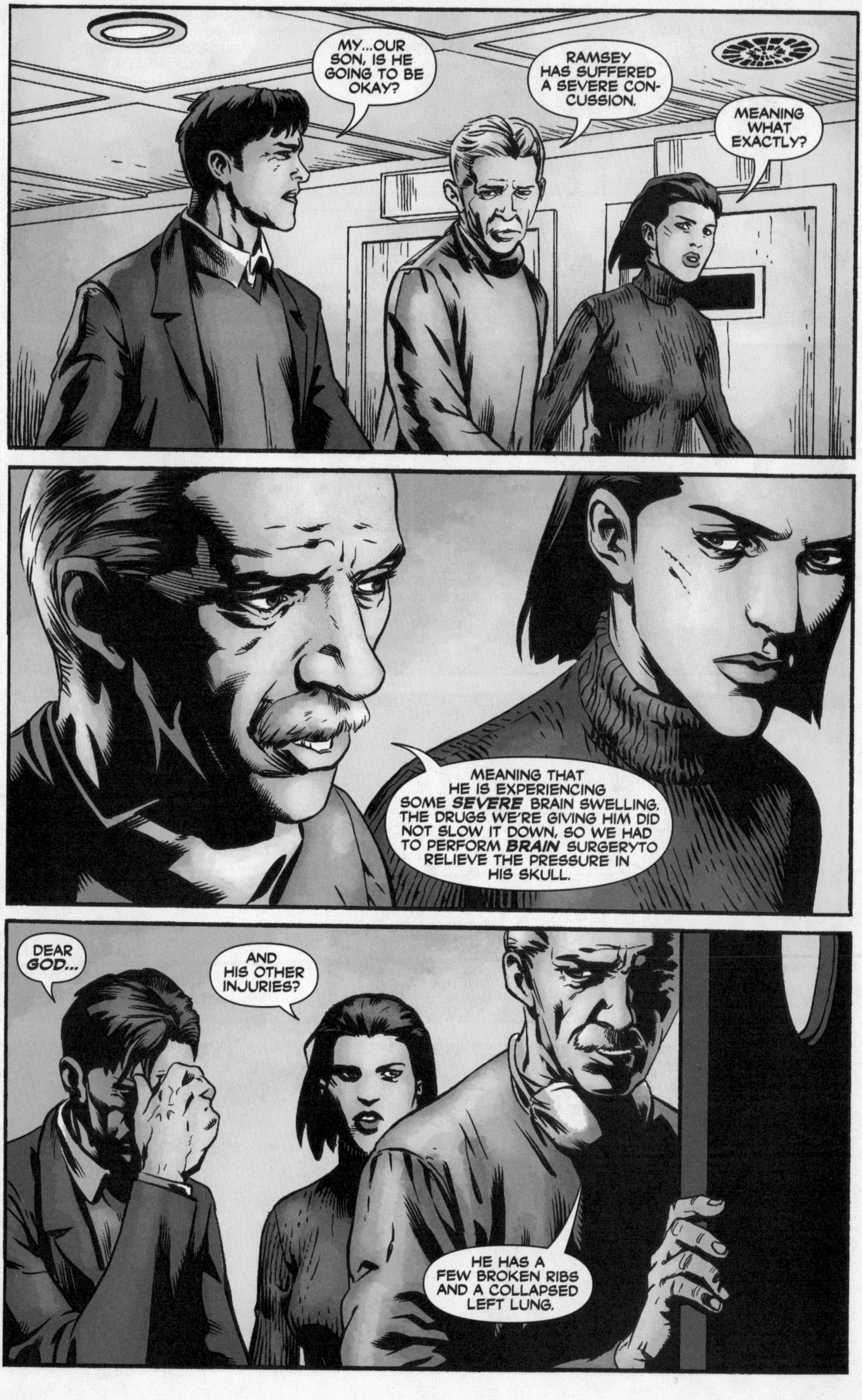
MY...OUR SON, IS HE GOING TO BE OKAY?
RAMSEY HAS SUFFERED A SEVERE CON-CUSSION.
MEANING WHAT EXACTLY?
MEANING THAT HE IS EXPERIENCING SOME *SEVERE* BRAIN SWELLING. THE DRUGS WE'RE GIVING HIM DID NOT SLOW IT DOWN, SO WE HAD TO PERFORM *BRAIN* SURGERYTO RELIEVE THE PRESSURE IN HIS SKULL.
DEAR *GOD...*
AND HIS OTHER INJURIES?
HE HAS A FEW BROKEN RIBS AND A COLLAPSED LEFT LUNG.

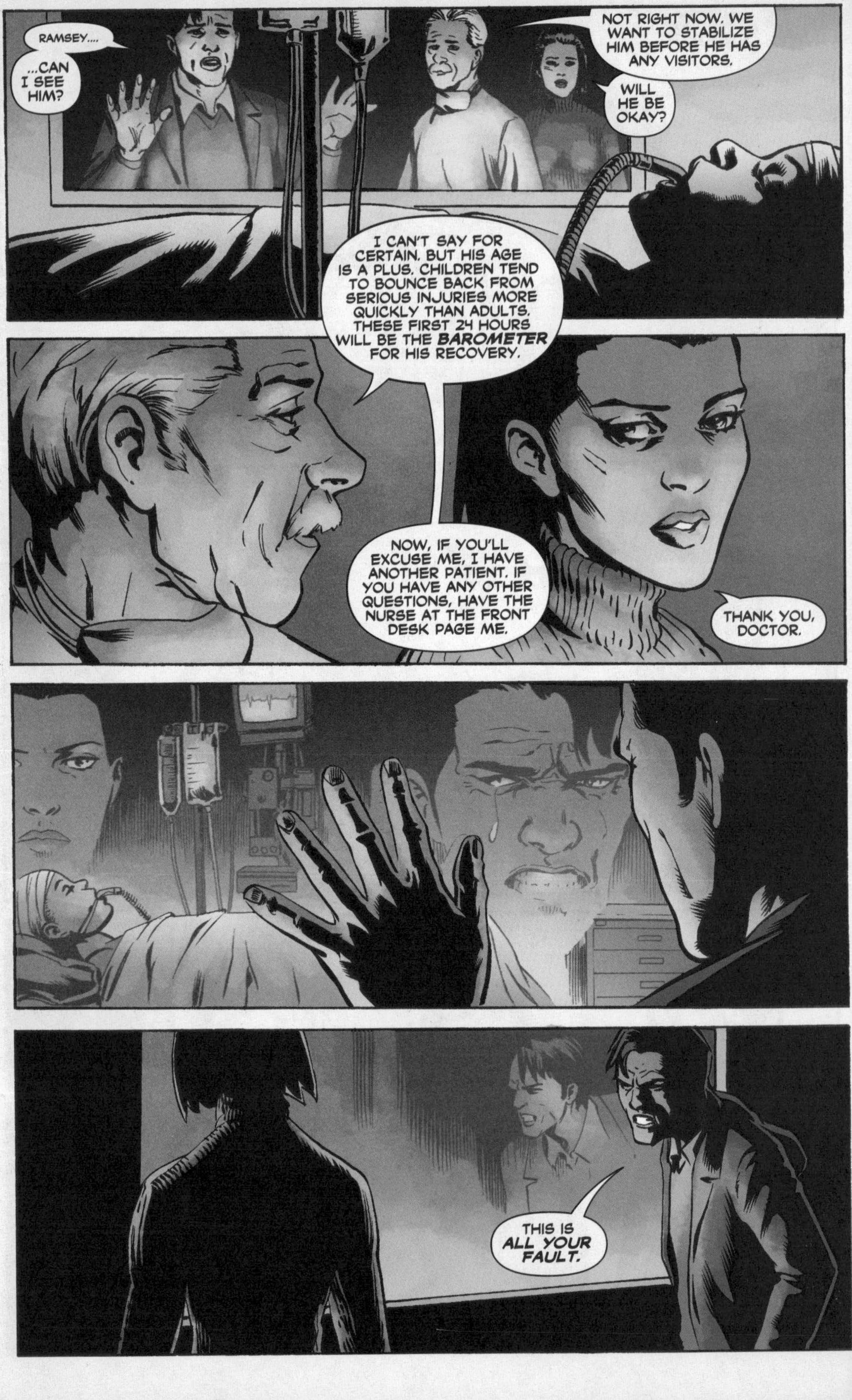
RAMSEY....
...CAN I SEE HIM?
NOT RIGHT NOW. WE WANT TO STABILIZE HIM BEFORE HE HAS ANY VISITORS.
WILL HE BE OKAY?
I CAN'T SAY FOR CERTAIN. BUT HIS AGE IS A PLUS. CHILDREN TEND TO BOUNCE BACK FROM SERIOUS INJURIES MORE QUICKLY THAN ADULTS. THESE FIRST 24 HOURS WILL BE THE BAROMETER FOR HIS RECOVERY.
NOW, IF YOU'LL EXCUSE ME, I HAVE ANOTHER PATIENT. IF YOU HAVE ANY OTHER QUESTIONS, HAVE THE NURSE AT THE FRONT DESK PAGE ME.
THANK YOU, DOCTOR.
THIS IS ALL YOUR FAULT.

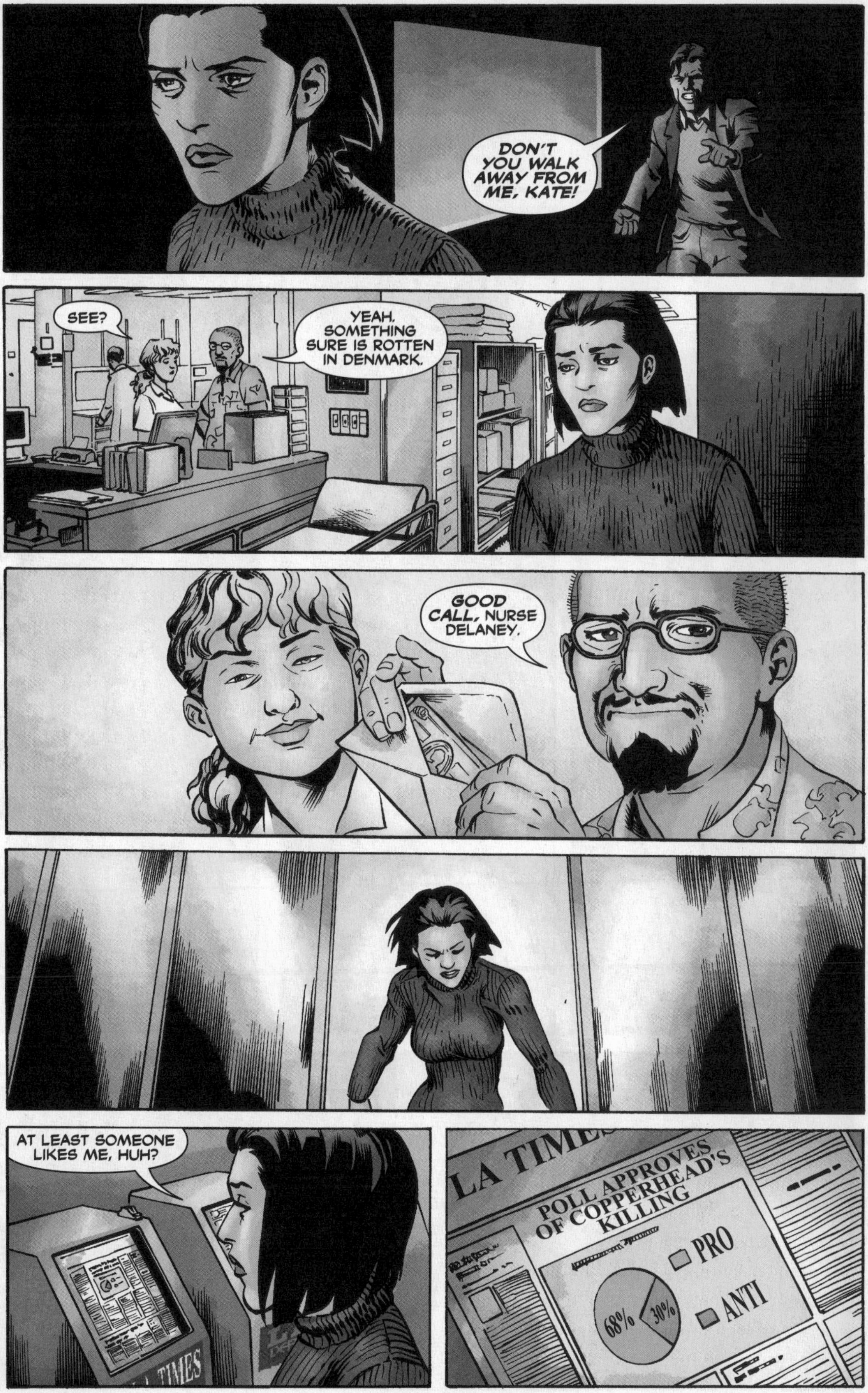
DON'T YOU WALK AWAY FROM ME, KATE!
SEE?
YEAH. SOMETHING SURE IS ROTTEN IN DENMARK.
GOOD CALL, NURSE DELANEY.
AT LEAST SOMEONE LIKES ME, HUH?
LA TIMES
POLL APPROVES OF COPPERHEAD'S KILLING
PRO
ANTI
68%
30%
LA TIMES

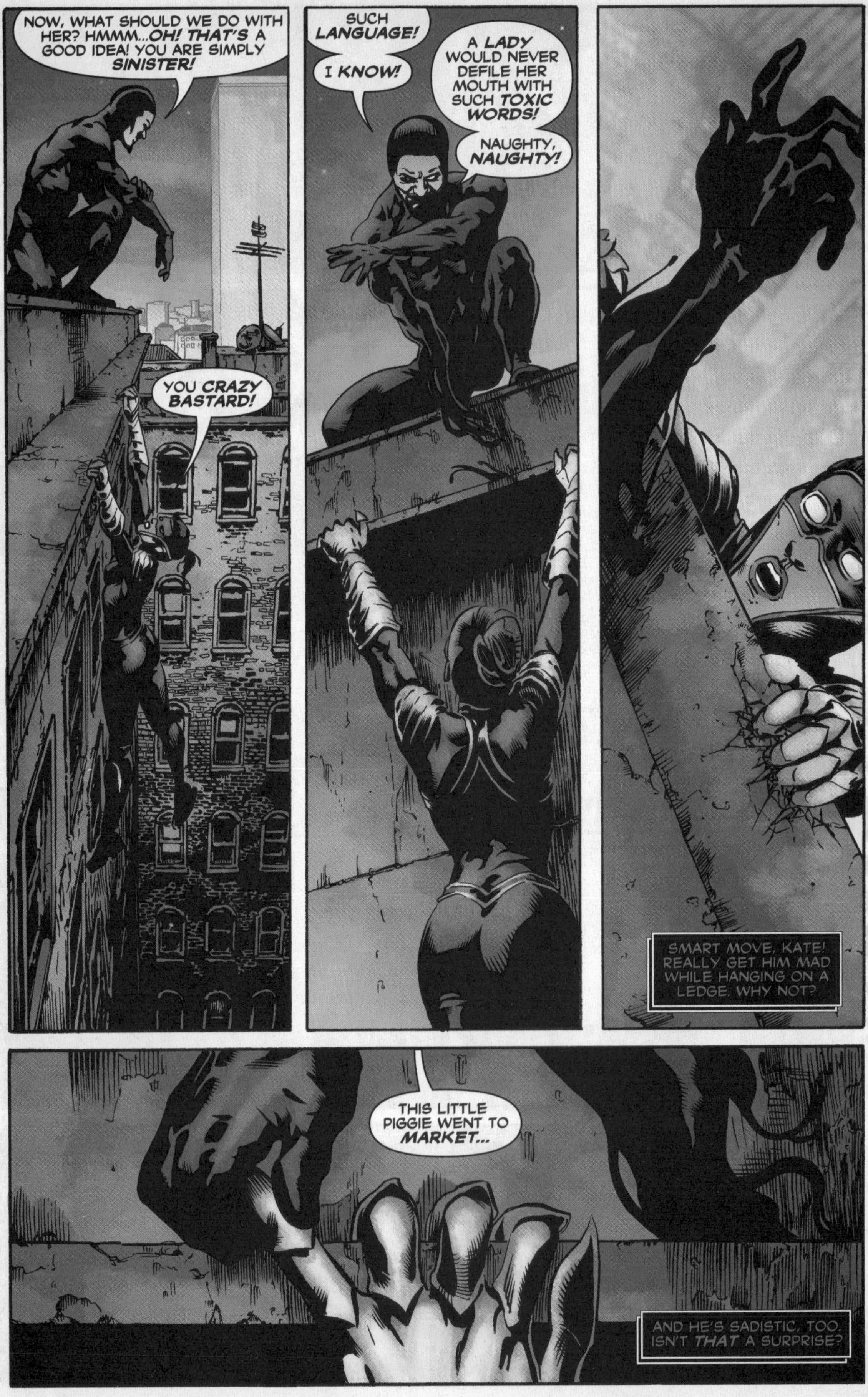
NOW, WHAT SHOULD WE DO WITH HER? HMMM...OH! THAT'S A GOOD IDEA! YOU ARE SIMPLY SINISTER!
YOU CRAZY BASTARD!
SUCH LANGUAGE!
I KNOW!
A LADY WOULD NEVER DEFILE HER MOUTH WITH SUCH TOXIC WORDS!
NAUGHTY, NAUGHTY!
SMART MOVE, KATE! REALLY GET HIM MAD WHILE HANGING ON A LEDGE. WHY NOT?
THIS LITTLE PIGGIE WENT TO MARKET...
AND HE'S SADISTIC, TOO. ISN'T THAT A SURPRISE?

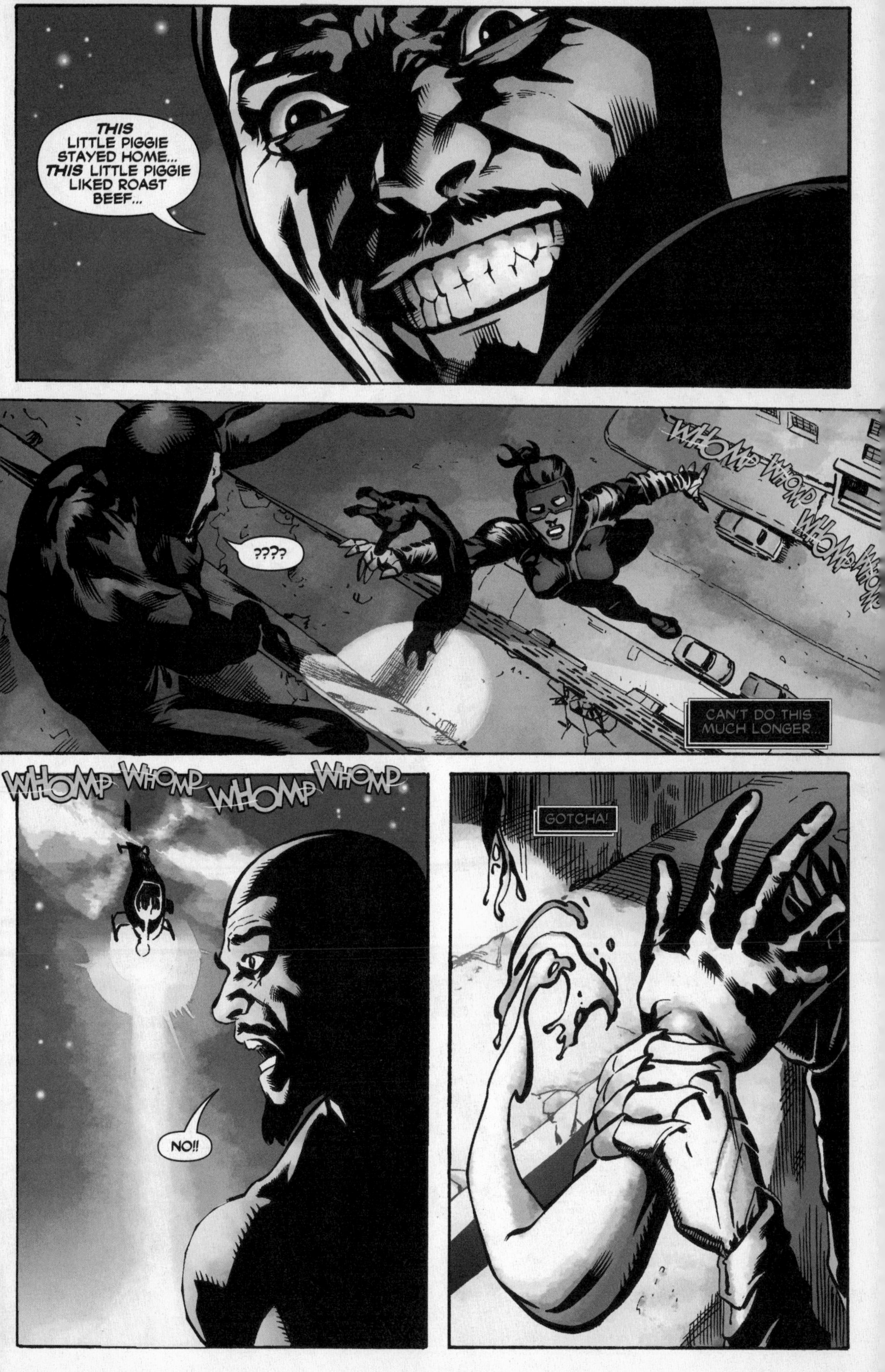
THIS LITTLE PIGGIE STAYED HOME... THIS LITTLE PIGGIE LIKED ROAST BEEF...
WHOMP WHOMP WHOMP WHOMP
????
CAN'T DO THIS MUCH LONGER...
WHOMP WHOMP WHOMP WHOMP
NO!!
GOTCHA!

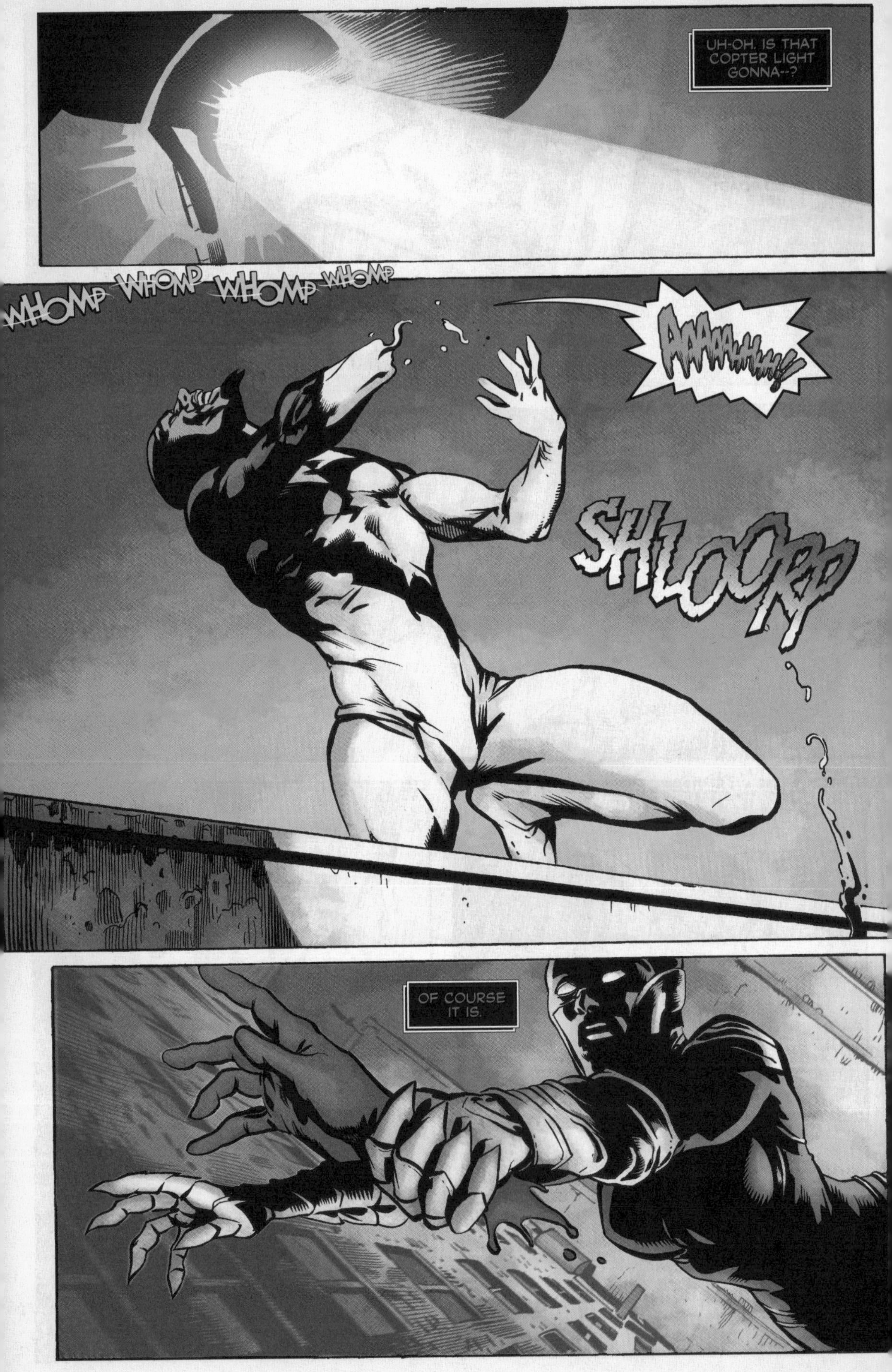
UH-OH. IS THAT COPTER LIGHT GONNA--?
WHOMP WHOMP WHOMP WHOMP
AAAAAHHHH!!
SHLOORP
OF COURSE IT IS.

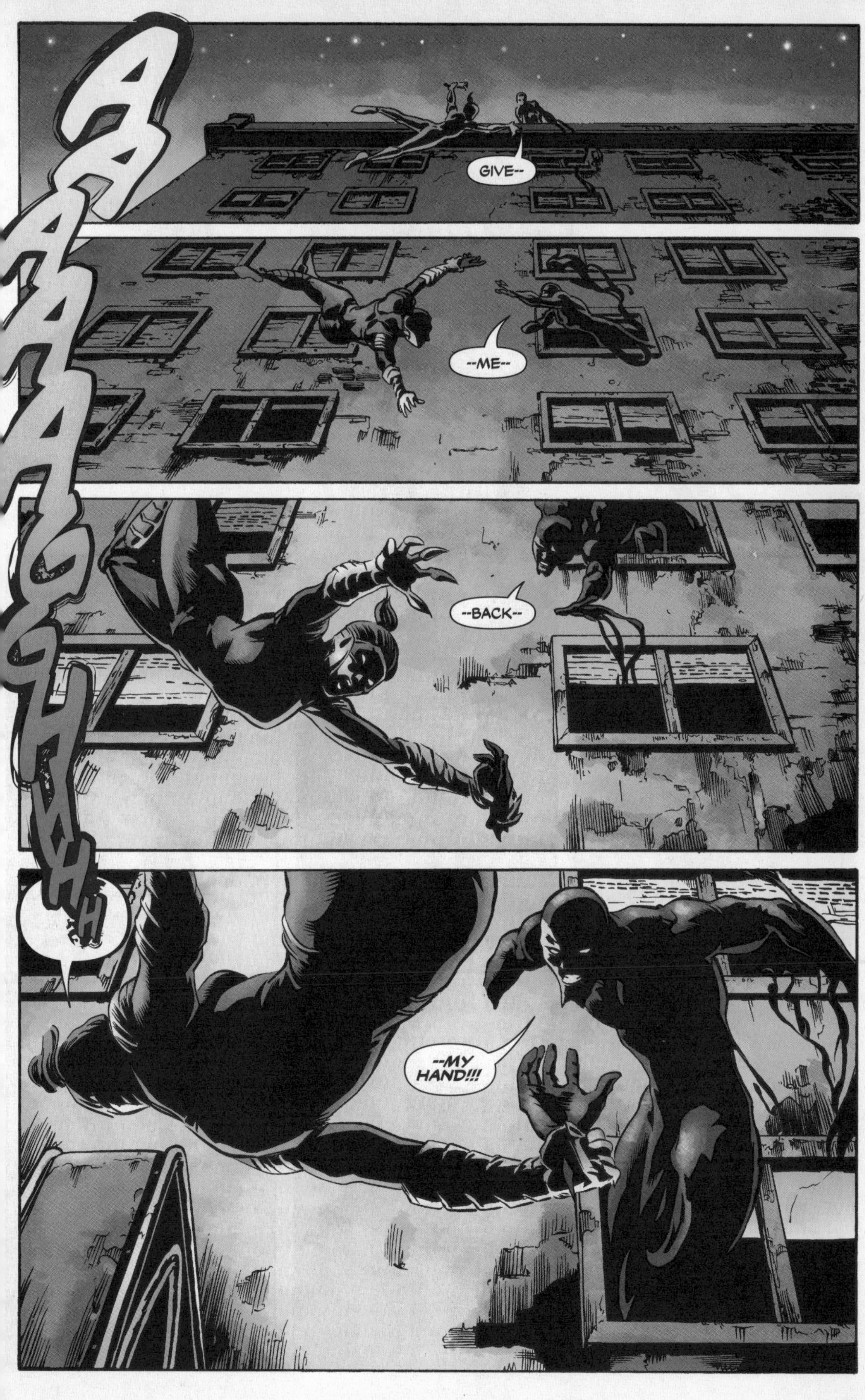
GIVE--
--ME--
--BACK--
--MY HAND!!!

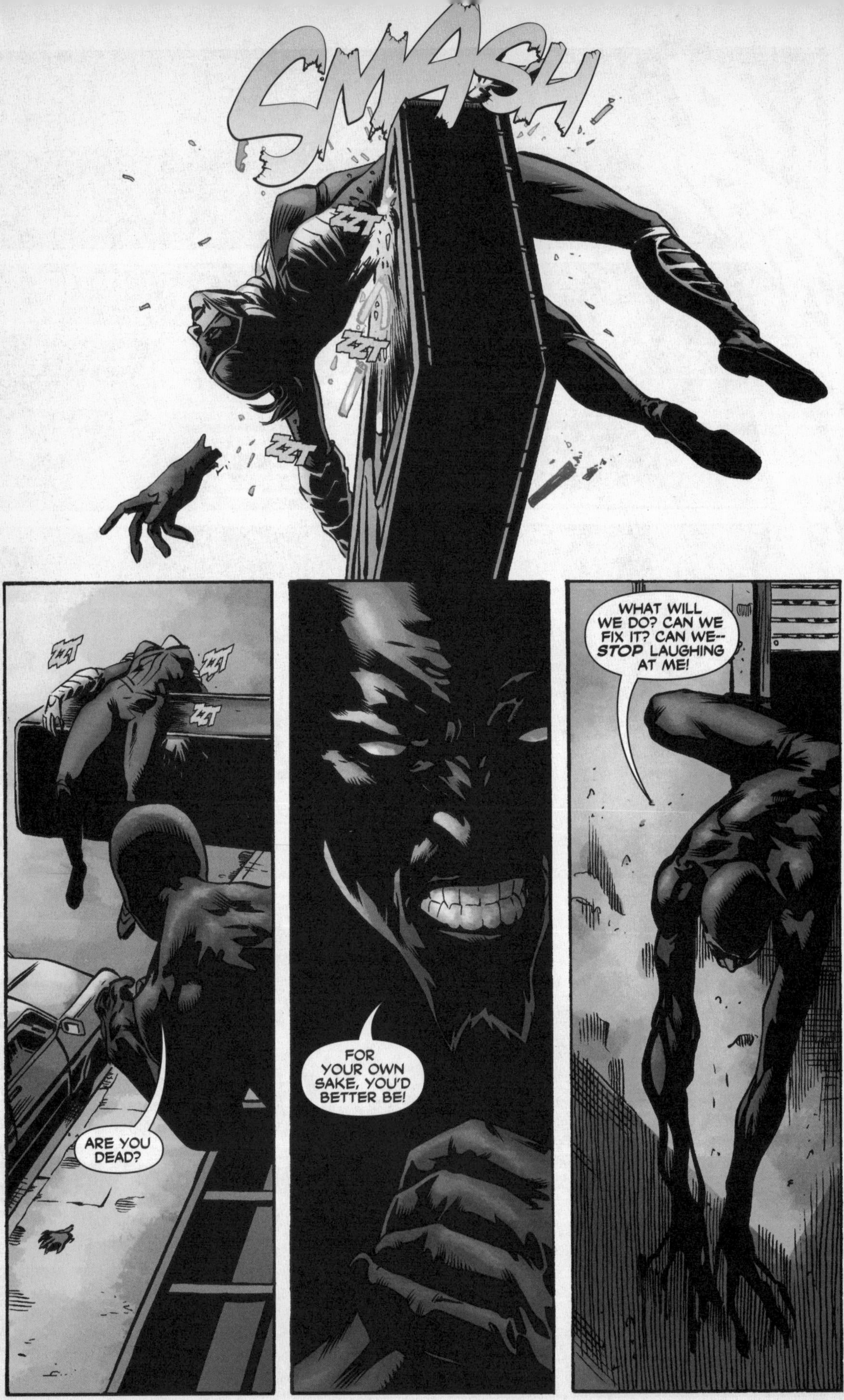
SMASH
ZZZT
ZZZT
ZZZT
ZZZT
ZZZT
ZZZT
ARE YOU DEAD?
FOR YOUR OWN SAKE, YOU'D BETTER BE!
WHAT WILL WE DO? CAN WE FIX IT? CAN WE-- STOP LAUGHING AT ME!

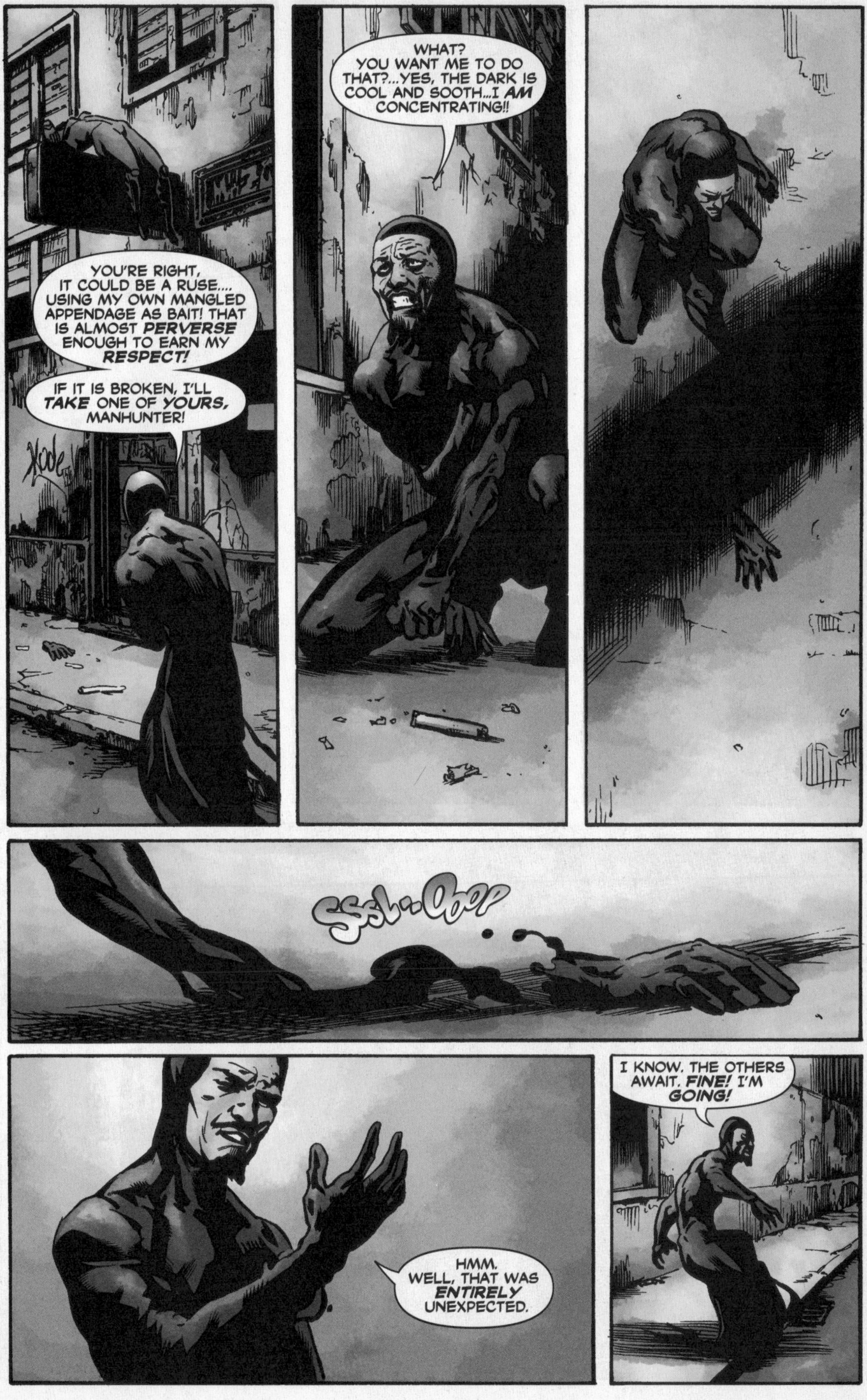
YOU'RE RIGHT, IT COULD BE A RUSE.... USING MY OWN MANGLED APPENDAGE AS BAIT! THAT IS ALMOST PERVERSE ENOUGH TO EARN MY RESPECT!
IF IT IS BROKEN, I'LL TAKE ONE OF YOURS, MANHUNTER!
WHAT? YOU WANT ME TO DO THAT?...YES, THE DARK IS COOL AND SOOTH...I AM CONCENTRATING!!
SSSL-OOOP
HMM. WELL, THAT WAS ENTIRELY UNEXPECTED.
I KNOW. THE OTHERS AWAIT. FINE! I'M GOING!

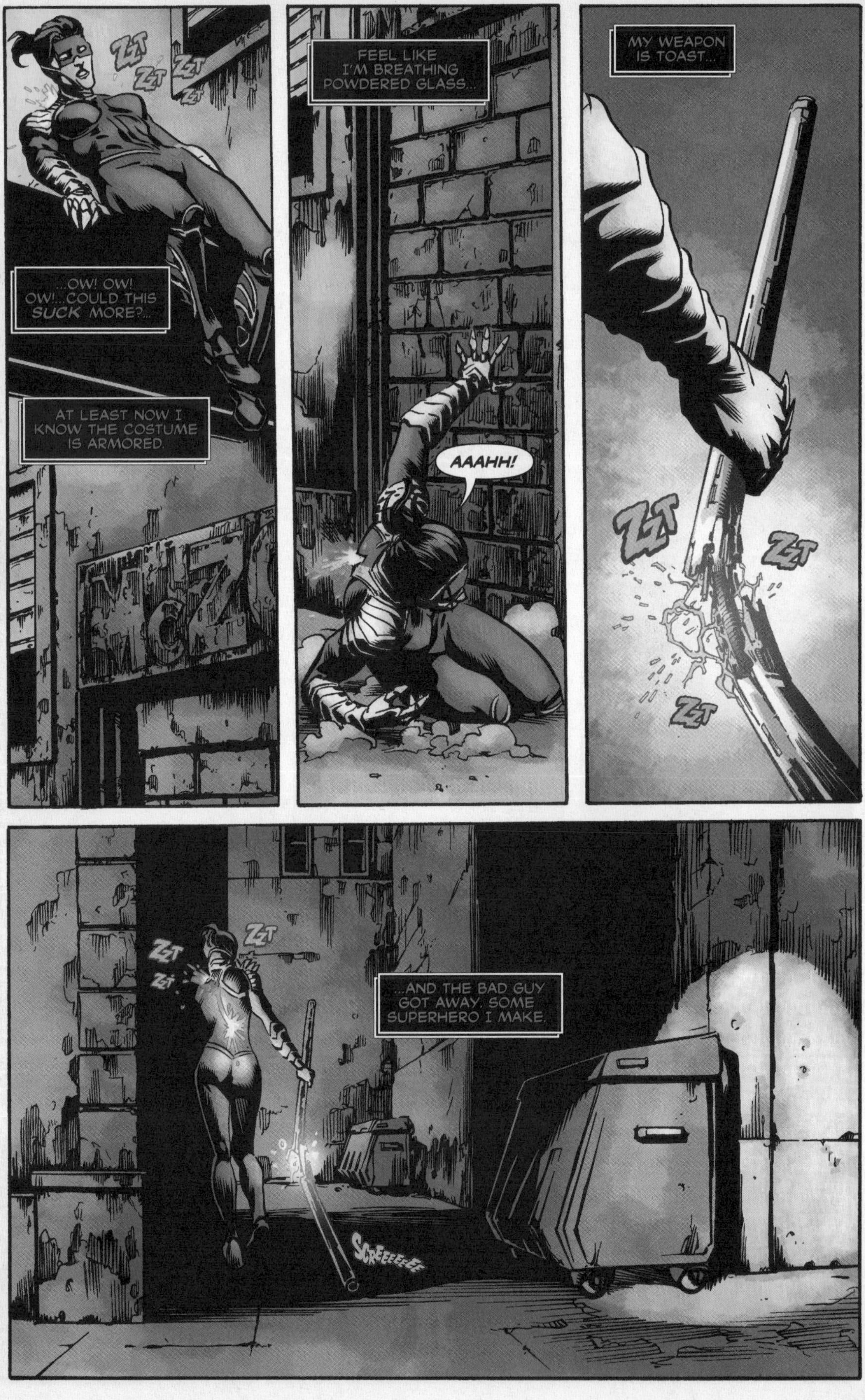
ZZT
ZZT
ZZT
ZZT
...OW! OW! OW!...COULD THIS SUCK MORE?...
AT LEAST NOW I KNOW THE COSTUME IS ARMORED.
FEEL LIKE I'M BREATHING POWDERED GLASS...
AAAHH!
MY WEAPON IS TOAST...
ZZT
ZZT
ZZT
ZZT
ZZT
ZZT
...AND THE BAD GUY GOT AWAY. SOME SUPERHERO I MAKE.
SCREEEEEEE

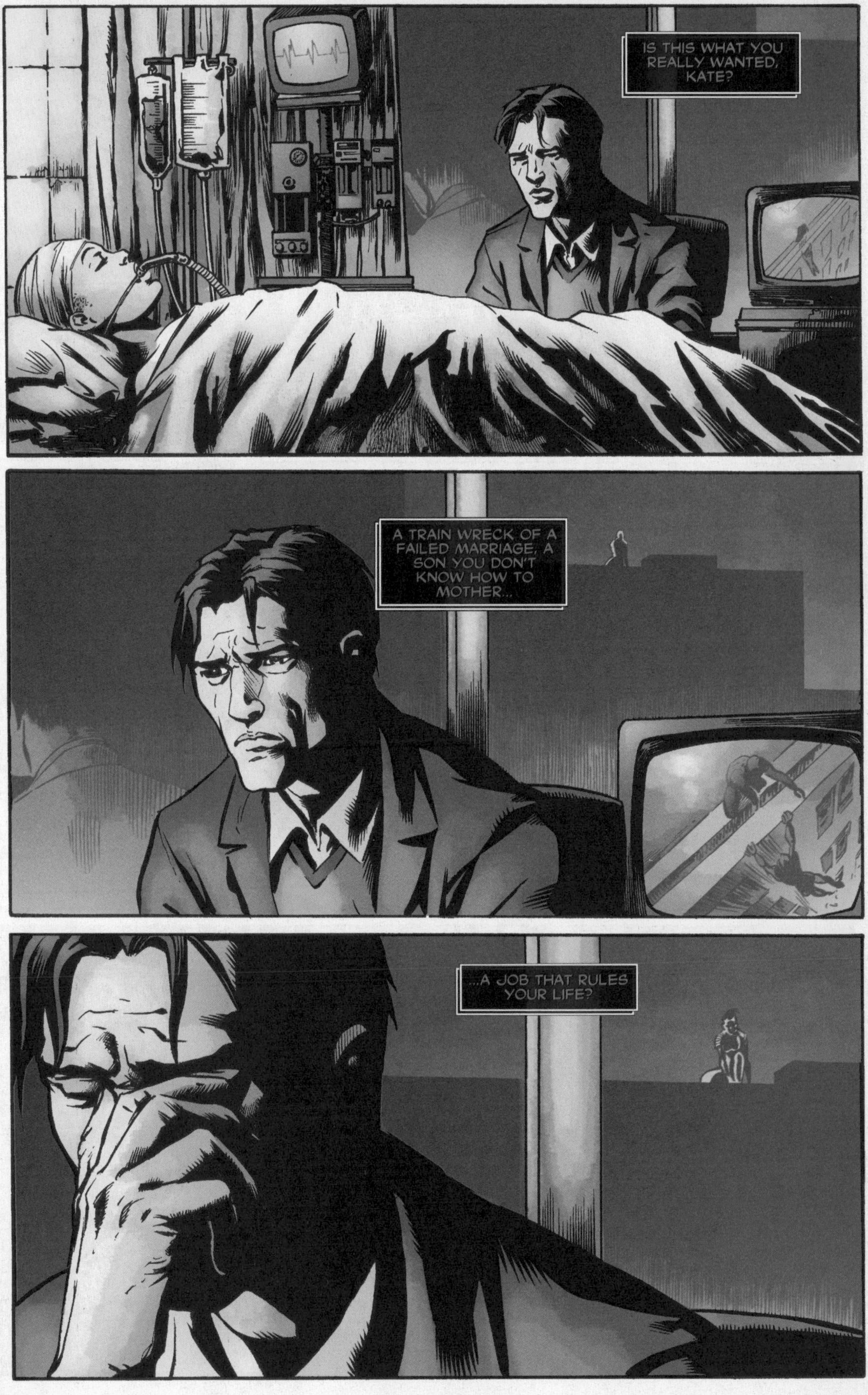
IS THIS WHAT YOU REALLY WANTED, KATE?
A TRAIN WRECK OF A FAILED MARRIAGE, A SON YOU DON'T KNOW HOW TO MOTHER...
...A JOB THAT RULES YOUR LIFE?

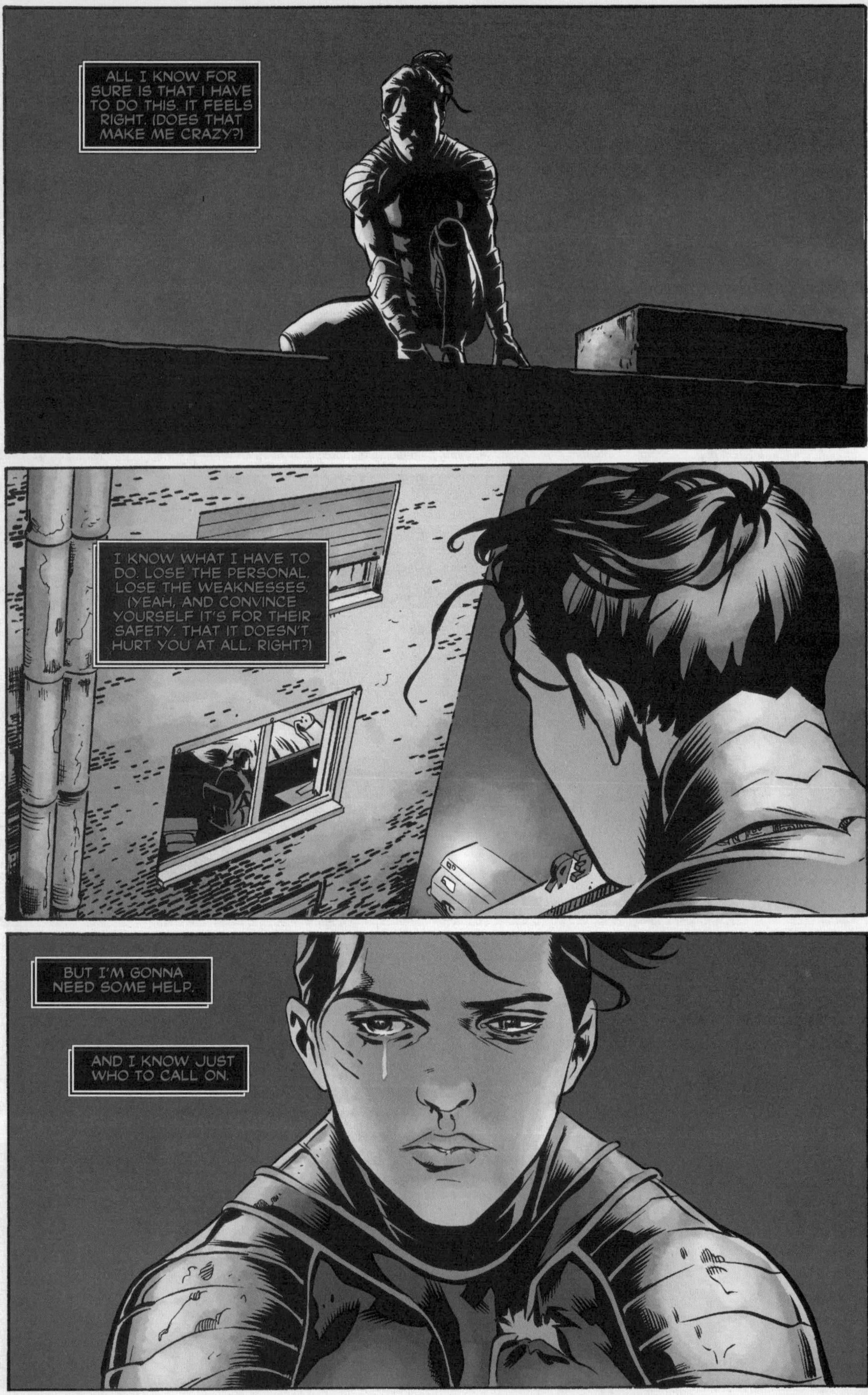
ALL I KNOW FOR SURE IS THAT I HAVE TO DO THIS. IT FEELS RIGHT. (DOES THAT MAKE ME CRAZY?)
I KNOW WHAT I HAVE TO DO. LOSE THE PERSONAL. LOSE THE WEAKNESSES. (YEAH, AND CONVINCE YOURSELF IT'S FOR THEIR SAFETY. THAT IT DOESN'T HURT YOU AT ALL, RIGHT?)
BUT I'M GONNA NEED SOME HELP.
AND I KNOW JUST WHO TO CALL ON.

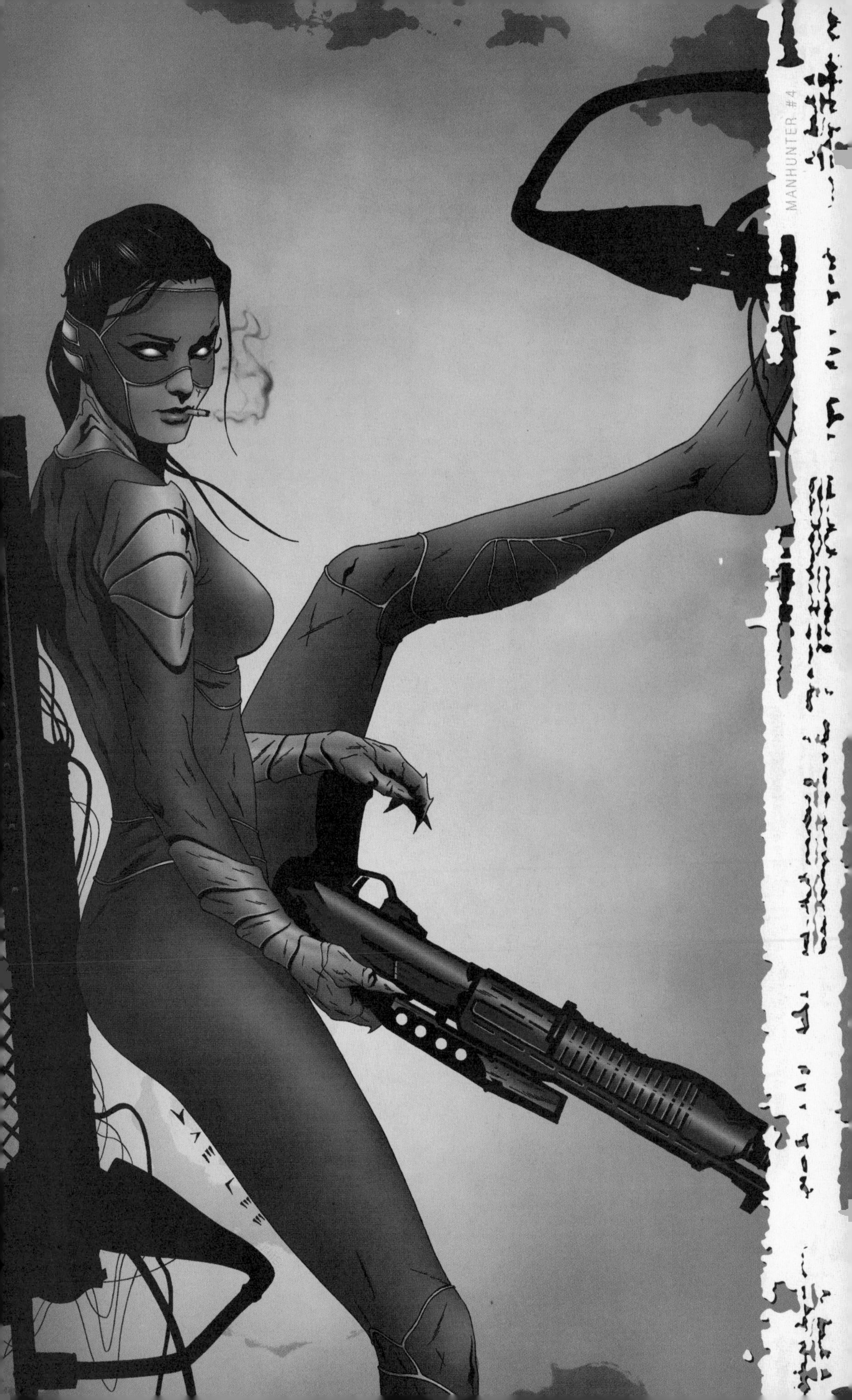
MANHUNTER #4

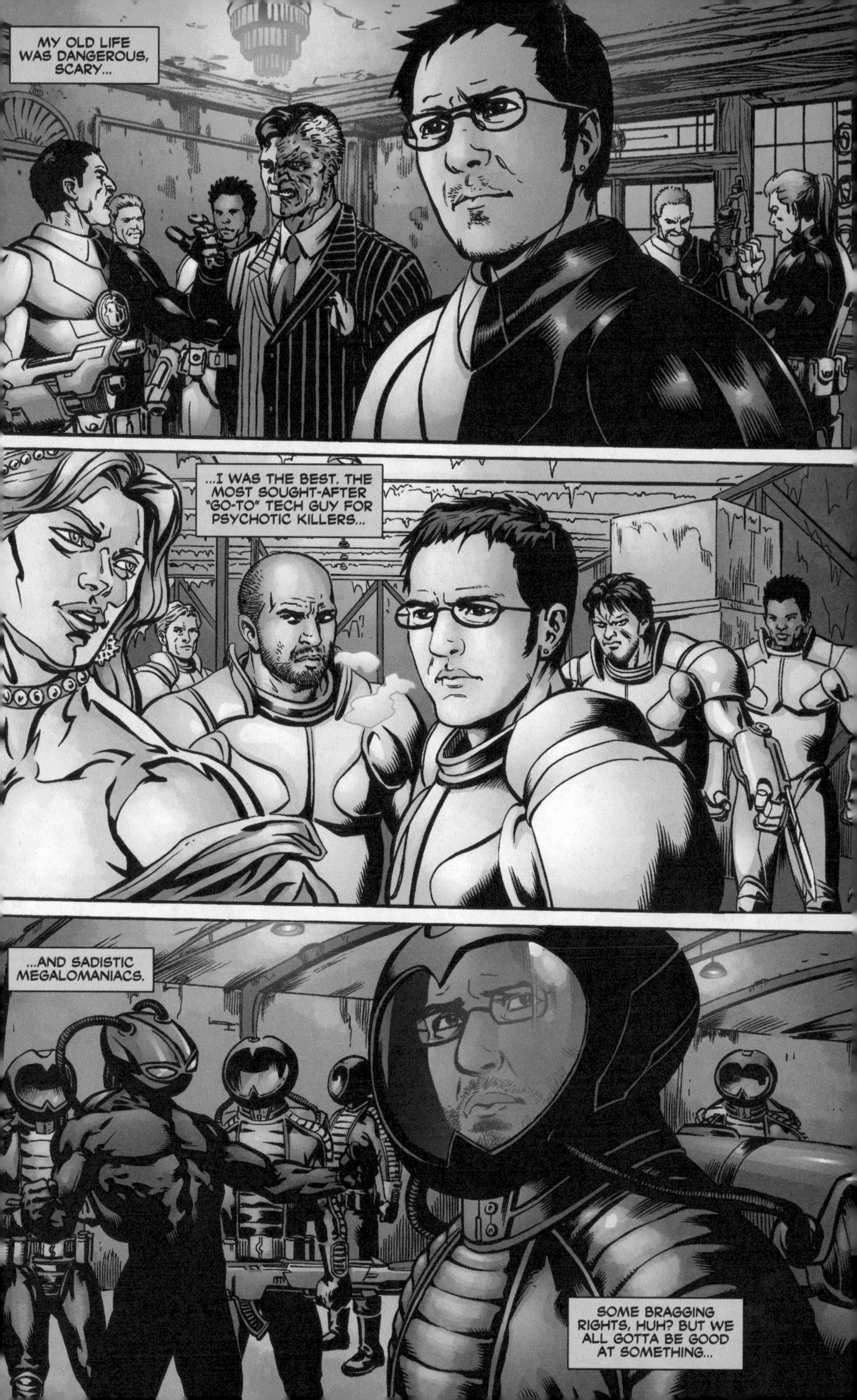
MY OLD LIFE WAS DANGEROUS, SCARY...
...I WAS THE BEST. THE MOST SOUGHT-AFTER "GO-TO" TECH GUY FOR PSYCHOTIC KILLERS...
...AND SADISTIC MEGALOMANIACS.
SOME BRAGGING RIGHTS, HUH? BUT WE ALL GOTTA BE GOOD AT SOMETHING...

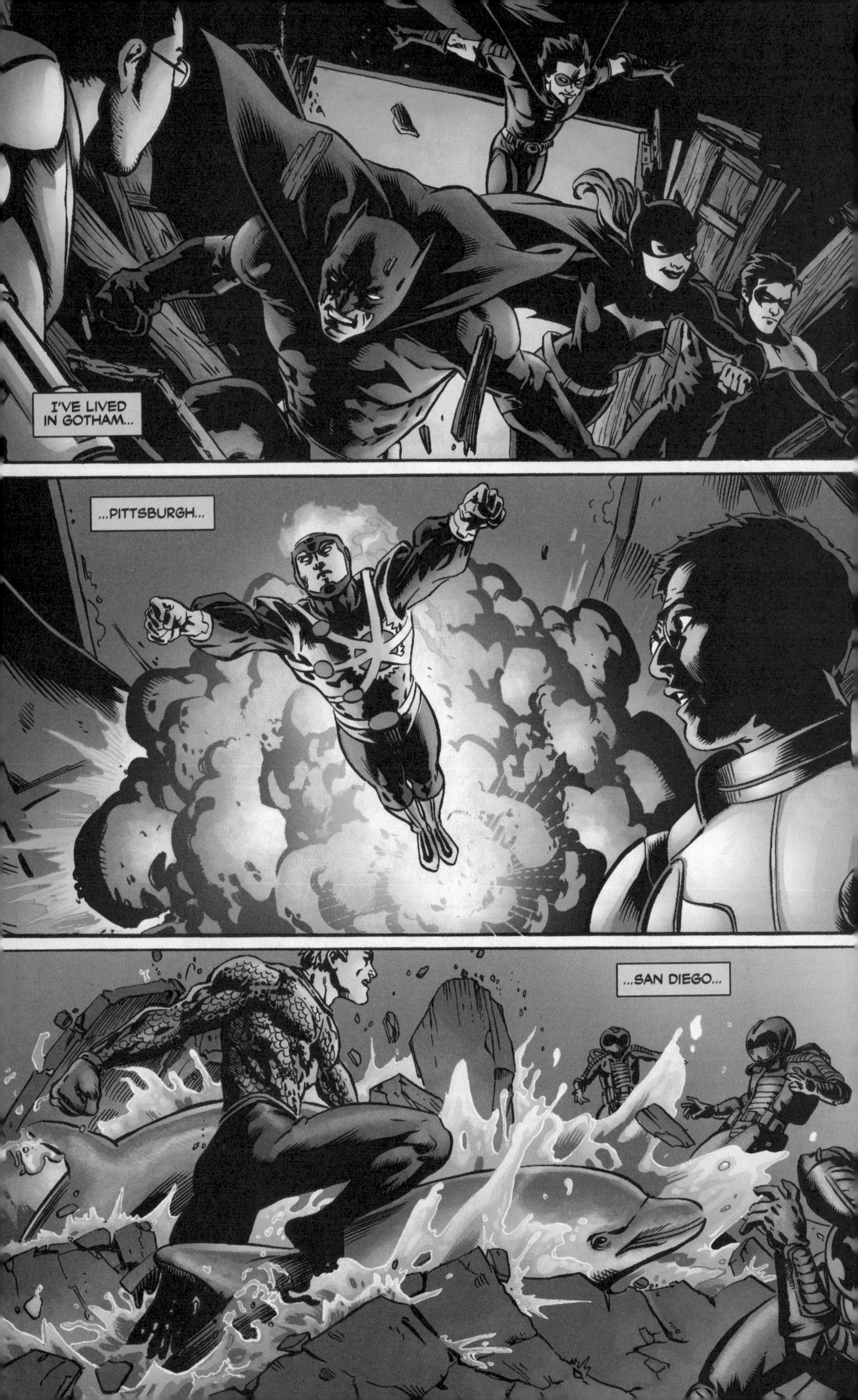
I'VE LIVED
IN GOTHAM...
...PITTSBURGH...
...SAN DIEGO...

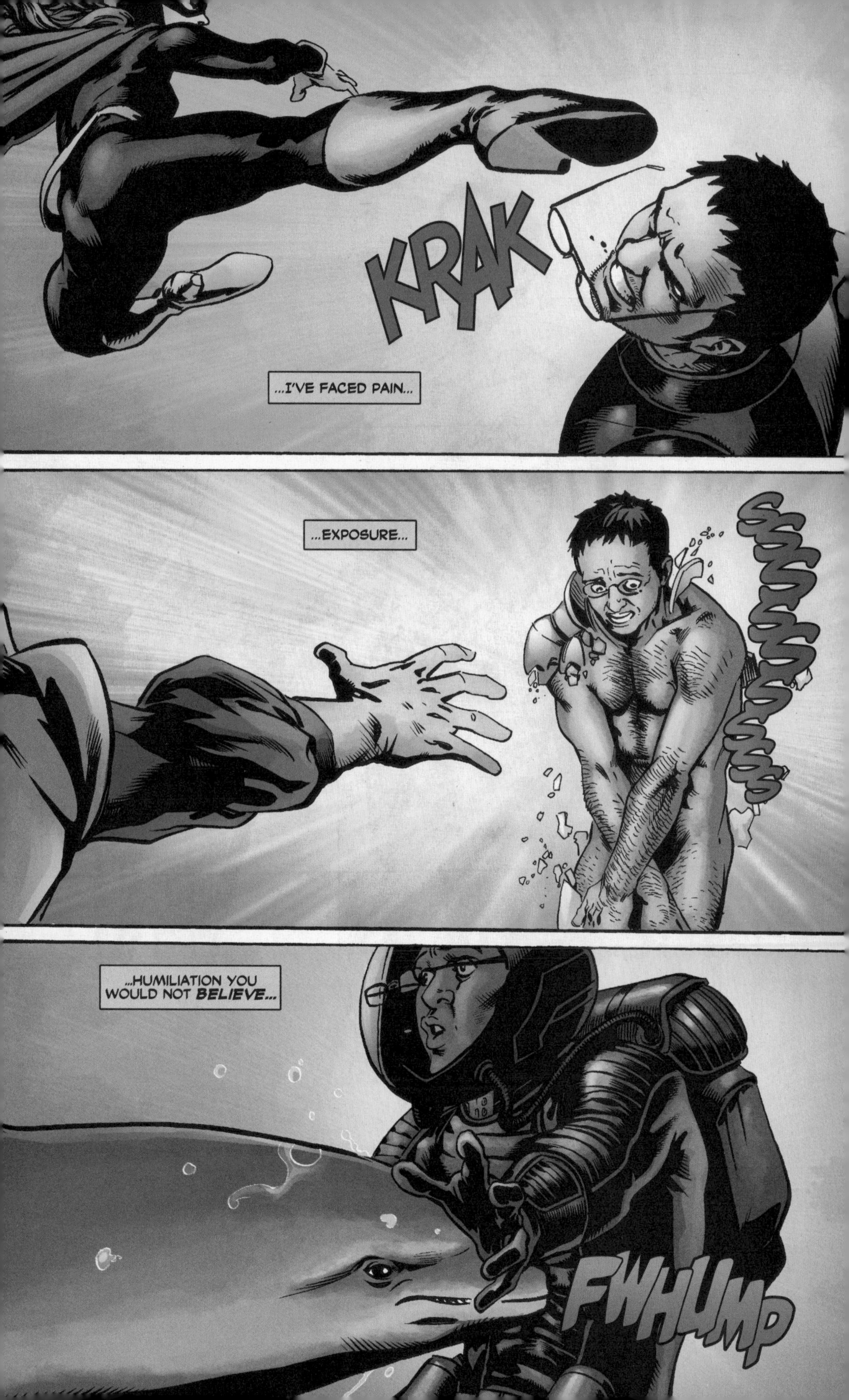
KRAK
...I'VE FACED PAIN...
...EXPOSURE...
SSSSSSSSSSSS
...HUMILIATION YOU WOULD NOT BELIEVE...
FWHUMP

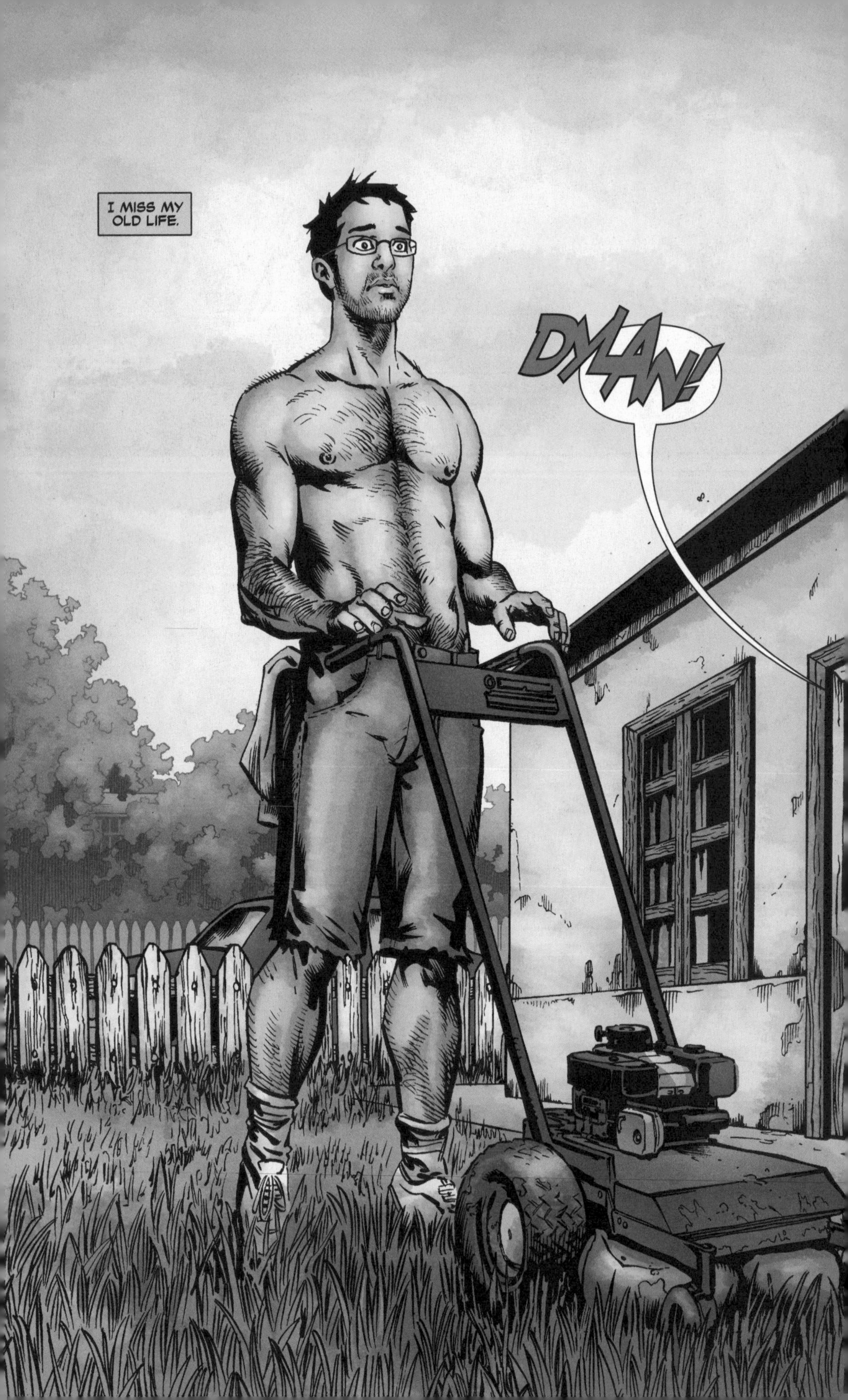
I MISS MY OLD LIFE.
DYLAN!

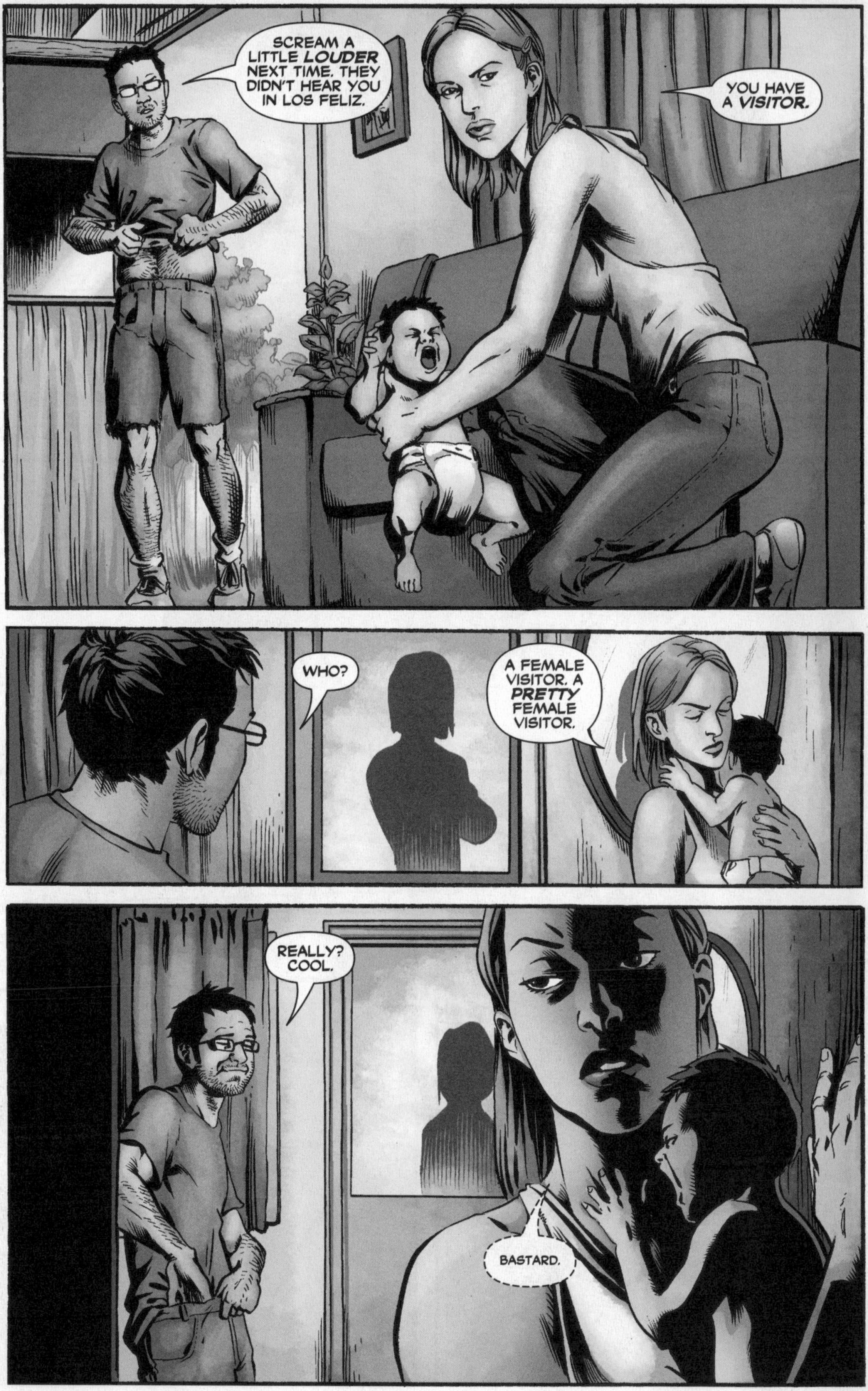
SCREAM A LITTLE LOUDER NEXT TIME. THEY DIDN'T HEAR YOU IN LOS FELIZ.
YOU HAVE A VISITOR.
WHO?
A FEMALE VISITOR. A PRETTY FEMALE VISITOR.
REALLY? COOL.
BASTARD.

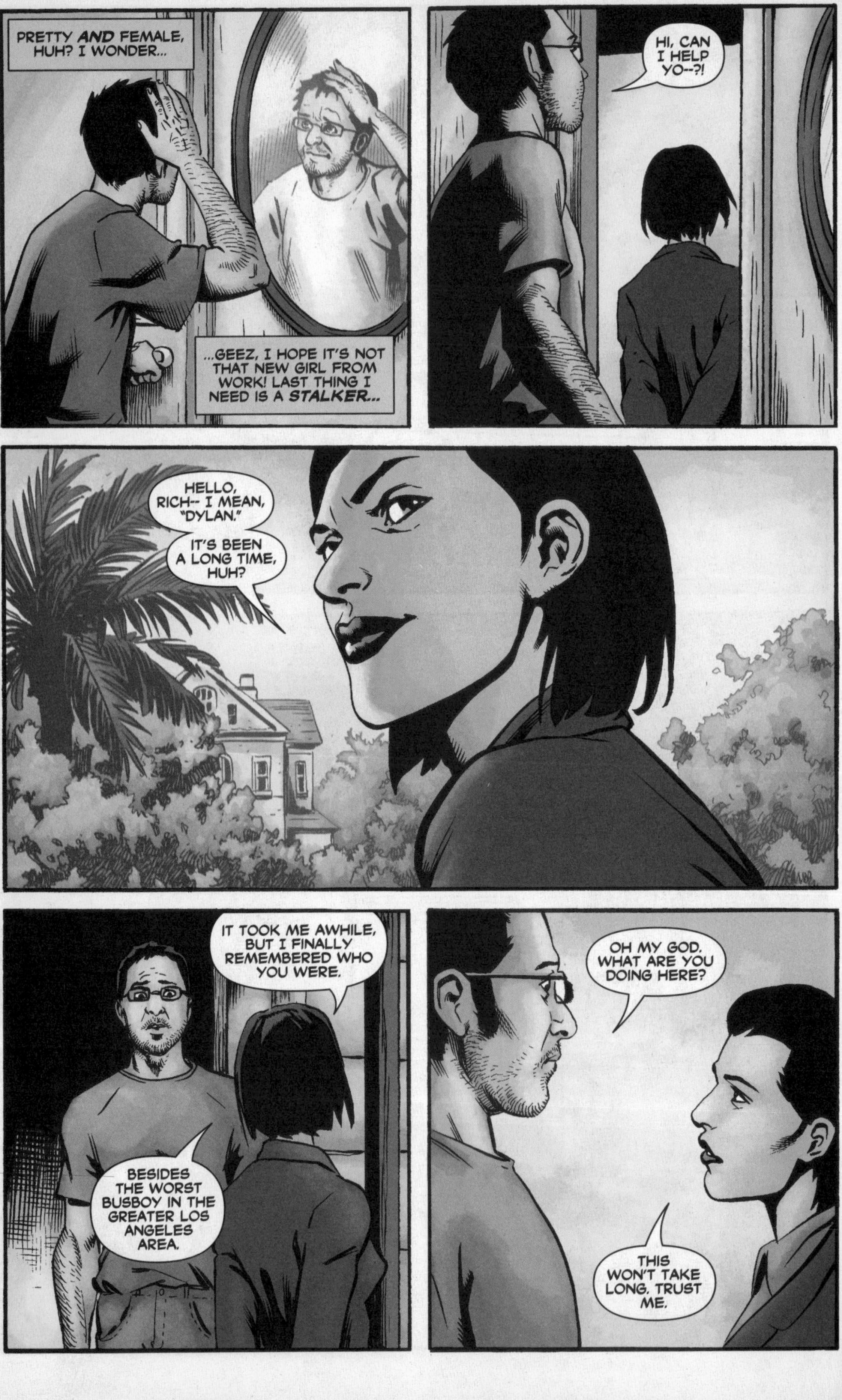
PRETTY AND FEMALE, HUH? I WONDER...
...GEEZ, I HOPE IT'S NOT THAT NEW GIRL FROM WORK! LAST THING I NEED IS A STALKER...
HI, CAN I HELP YO--?!
HELLO, RICH-- I MEAN, "DYLAN."
IT'S BEEN A LONG TIME, HUH?
IT TOOK ME AWHILE, BUT I FINALLY REMEMBERED WHO YOU WERE.
BESIDES THE WORST BUSBOY IN THE GREATER LOS ANGELES AREA.
OH MY GOD. WHAT ARE YOU DOING HERE?
THIS WON'T TAKE LONG. TRUST ME.

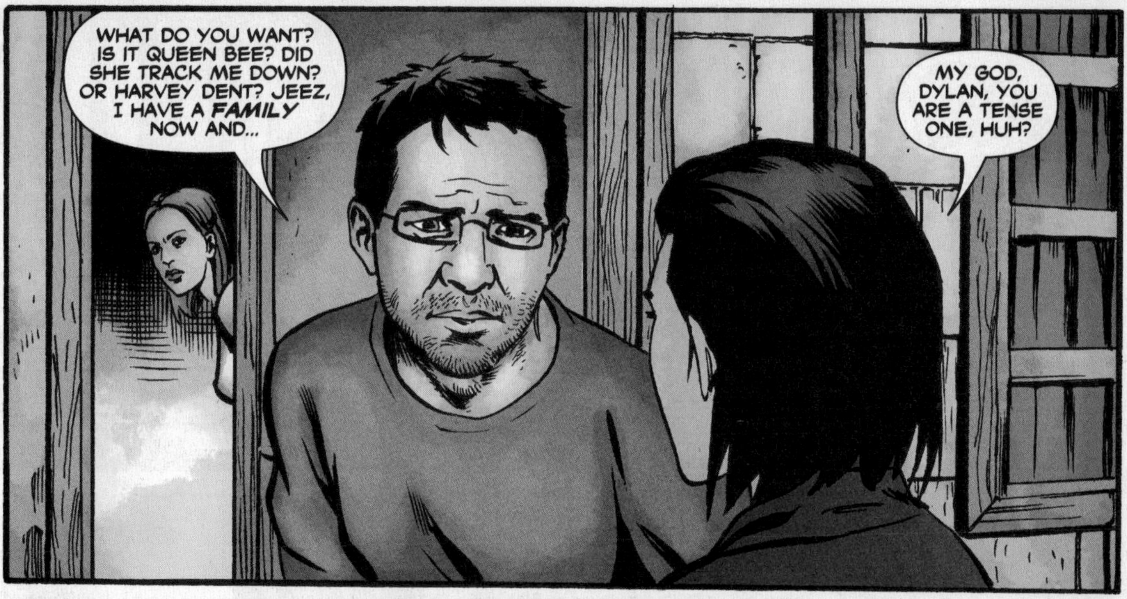
WHAT DO YOU WANT? IS IT QUEEN BEE? DID SHE TRACK ME DOWN? OR HARVEY DENT? JEEZ, I HAVE A FAMILY NOW AND...
MY GOD, DYLAN, YOU ARE A TENSE ONE, HUH?

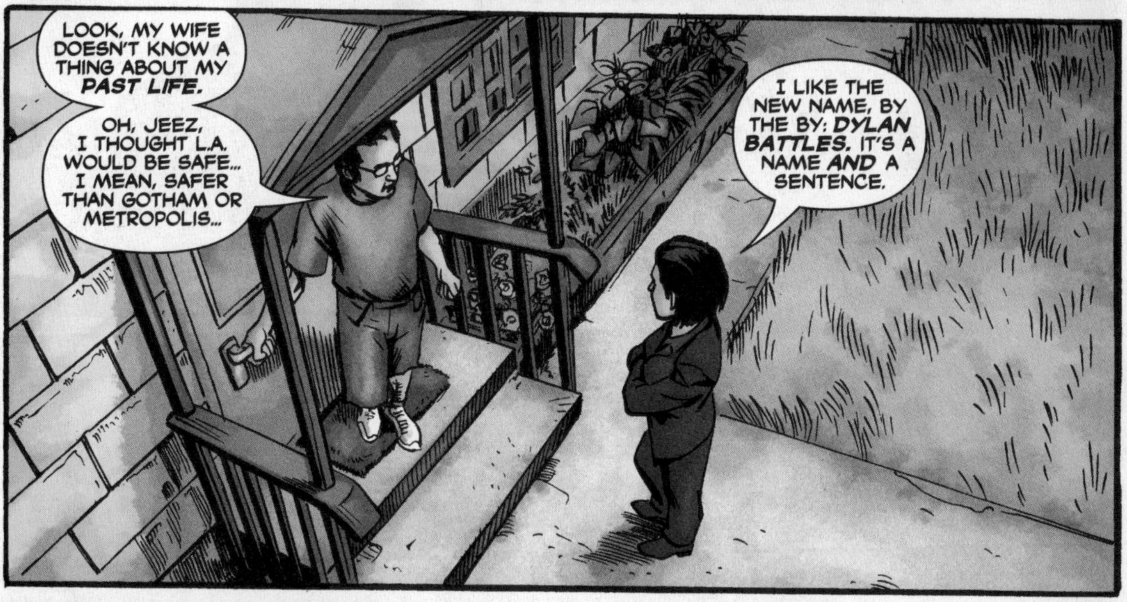
LOOK, MY WIFE DOESN'T KNOW A THING ABOUT MY PAST LIFE.
OH, JEEZ, I THOUGHT L.A. WOULD BE SAFE... I MEAN, SAFER THAN GOTHAM OR METROPOLIS...
I LIKE THE NEW NAME, BY THE BY: DYLAN BATTLES. IT'S A NAME AND A SENTENCE.

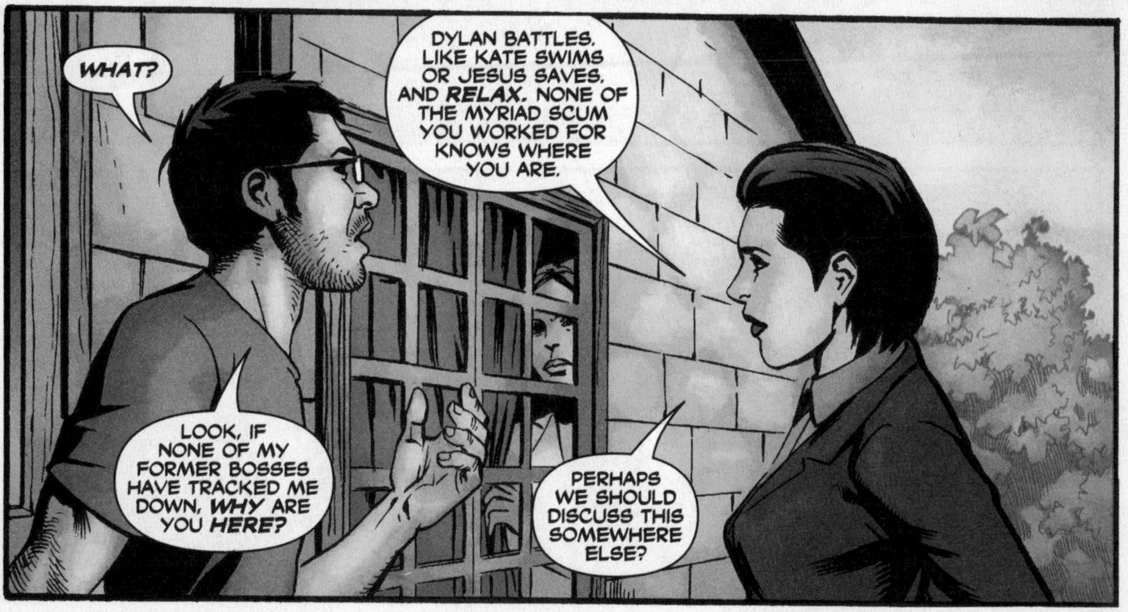
WHAT?
DYLAN BATTLES. LIKE KATE SWIMS OR JESUS SAVES. AND RELAX. NONE OF THE MYRIAD SCUM YOU WORKED FOR KNOWS WHERE YOU ARE.
LOOK, IF NONE OF MY FORMER BOSSES HAVE TRACKED ME DOWN, WHY ARE YOU HERE?
PERHAPS WE SHOULD DISCUSS THIS SOMEWHERE ELSE?

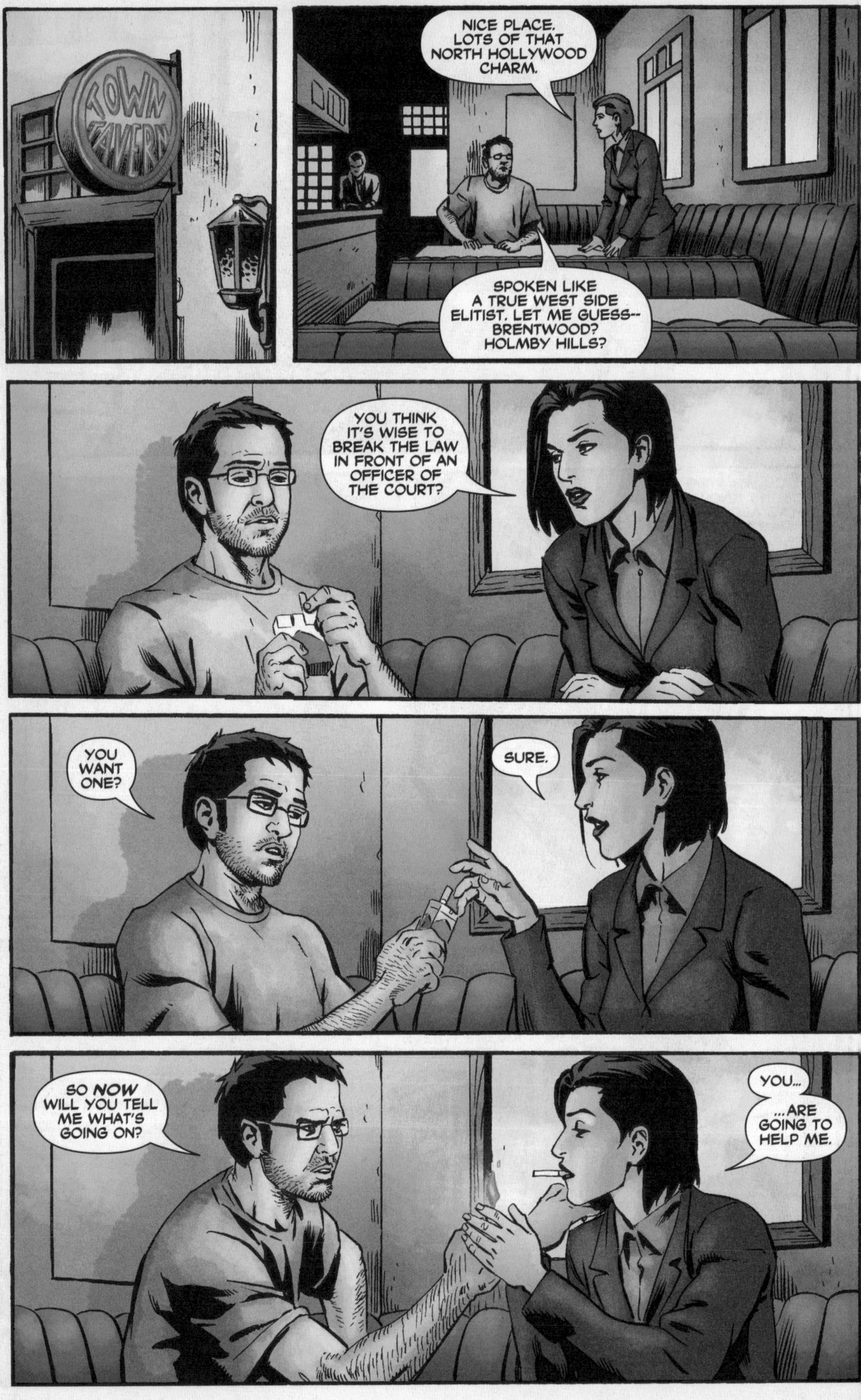
TOWN TAVERN
NICE PLACE. LOTS OF THAT NORTH HOLLYWOOD CHARM.
SPOKEN LIKE A TRUE WEST SIDE ELITIST. LET ME GUESS-- BRENTWOOD? HOLMBY HILLS?
YOU THINK IT'S WISE TO BREAK THE LAW IN FRONT OF AN OFFICER OF THE COURT?
YOU WANT ONE?
SURE.
SO *NOW* WILL YOU TELL ME WHAT'S GOING ON?
YOU...
...ARE GOING TO HELP ME.

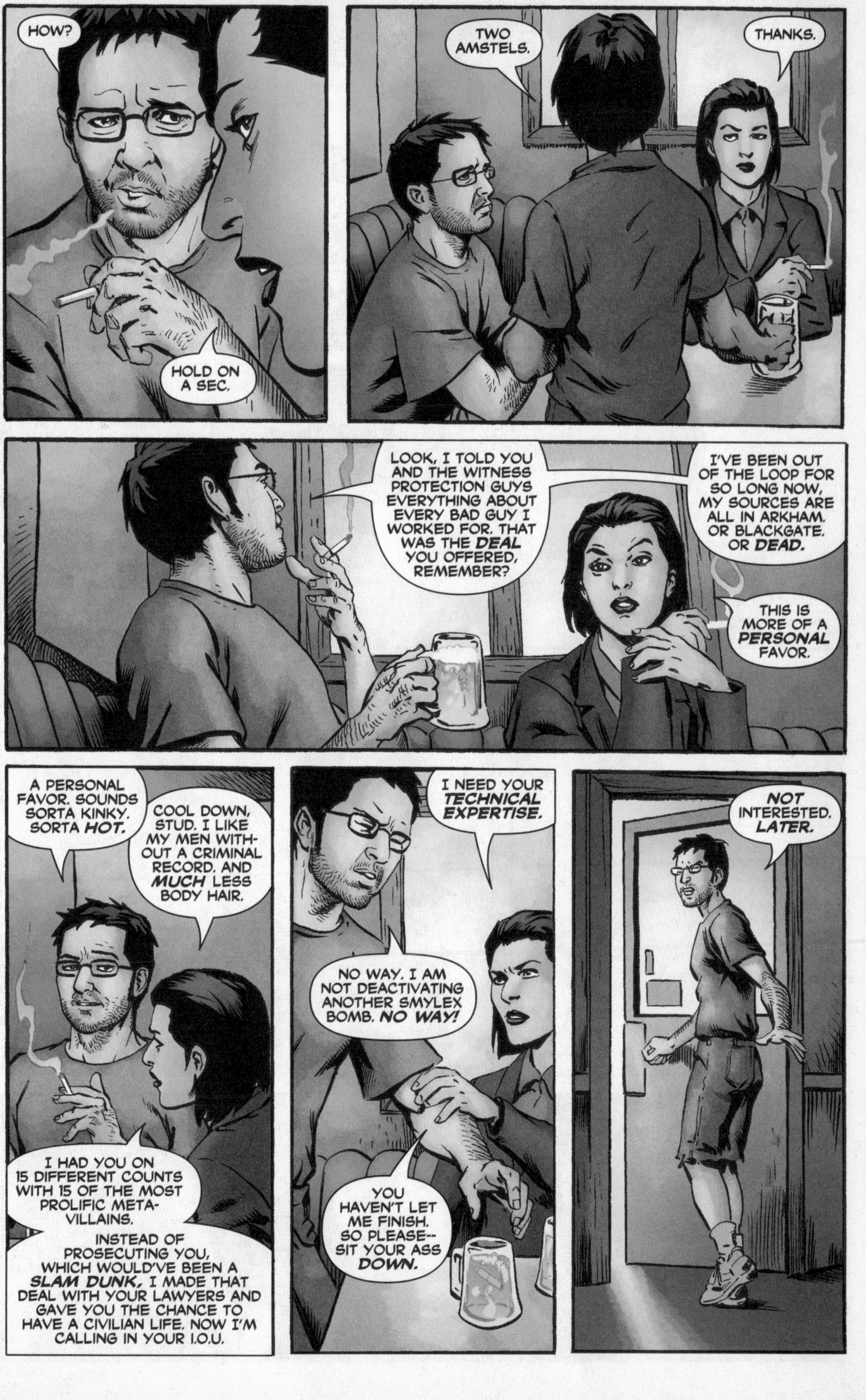
HOW?
HOLD ON A SEC.
TWO AMSTELS.
THANKS.
LOOK, I TOLD YOU AND THE WITNESS PROTECTION GUYS EVERYTHING ABOUT EVERY BAD GUY I WORKED FOR. THAT WAS THE DEAL YOU OFFERED, REMEMBER?
I'VE BEEN OUT OF THE LOOP FOR SO LONG NOW, MY SOURCES ARE ALL IN ARKHAM. OR BLACKGATE. OR DEAD.
THIS IS MORE OF A PERSONAL FAVOR.
A PERSONAL FAVOR. SOUNDS SORTA KINKY. SORTA HOT.
COOL DOWN, STUD. I LIKE MY MEN WITHOUT A CRIMINAL RECORD. AND MUCH LESS BODY HAIR.
I HAD YOU ON 15 DIFFERENT COUNTS WITH 15 OF THE MOST PROLIFIC META-VILLAINS.
INSTEAD OF PROSECUTING YOU, WHICH WOULD'VE BEEN A SLAM DUNK, I MADE THAT DEAL WITH YOUR LAWYERS AND GAVE YOU THE CHANCE TO HAVE A CIVILIAN LIFE. NOW I'M CALLING IN YOUR I.O.U.
I NEED YOUR TECHNICAL EXPERTISE.
NO WAY. I AM NOT DEACTIVATING ANOTHER SMYLEX BOMB. NO WAY!
YOU HAVEN'T LET ME FINISH. SO PLEASE--SIT YOUR ASS DOWN.
NOT INTERESTED. LATER.

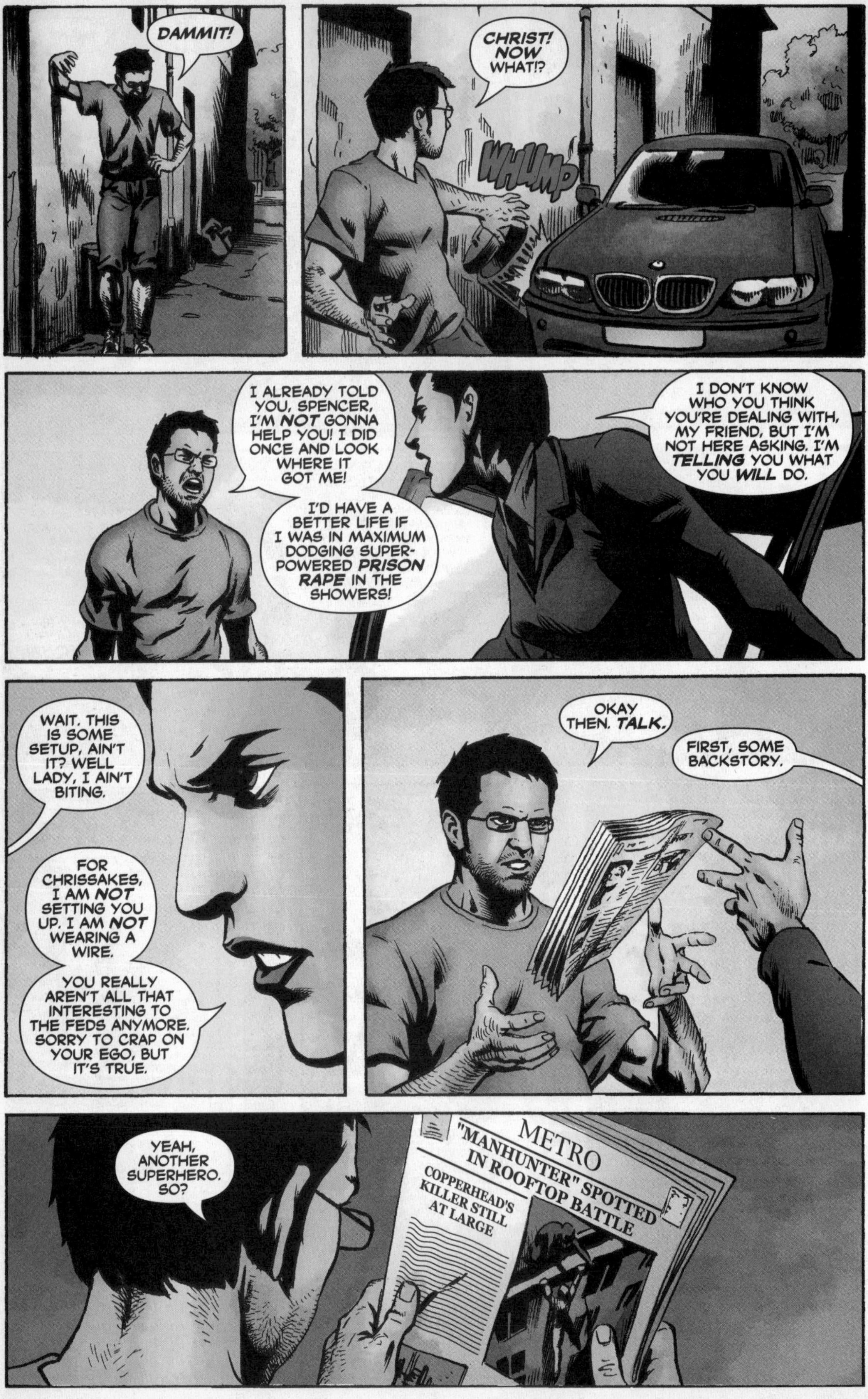
DAMMIT!
CHRIST! NOW WHAT!?
WHUMP
I ALREADY TOLD YOU, SPENCER, I'M NOT GONNA HELP YOU! I DID ONCE AND LOOK WHERE IT GOT ME!
I'D HAVE A BETTER LIFE IF I WAS IN MAXIMUM DODGING SUPER-POWERED PRISON RAPE IN THE SHOWERS!
I DON'T KNOW WHO YOU THINK YOU'RE DEALING WITH, MY FRIEND, BUT I'M NOT HERE ASKING. I'M TELLING YOU WHAT YOU WILL DO.
WAIT. THIS IS SOME SETUP, AIN'T IT? WELL LADY, I AIN'T BITING.
FOR CHRISSAKES, I AM NOT SETTING YOU UP. I AM NOT WEARING A WIRE.
YOU REALLY AREN'T ALL THAT INTERESTING TO THE FEDS ANYMORE. SORRY TO CRAP ON YOUR EGO, BUT IT'S TRUE.
OKAY THEN. TALK.
FIRST, SOME BACKSTORY.
YEAH, ANOTHER SUPERHERO. SO?
METRO
"MANHUNTER" SPOTTED IN ROOFTOP BATTLE
COPPERHEAD'S KILLER STILL AT LARGE

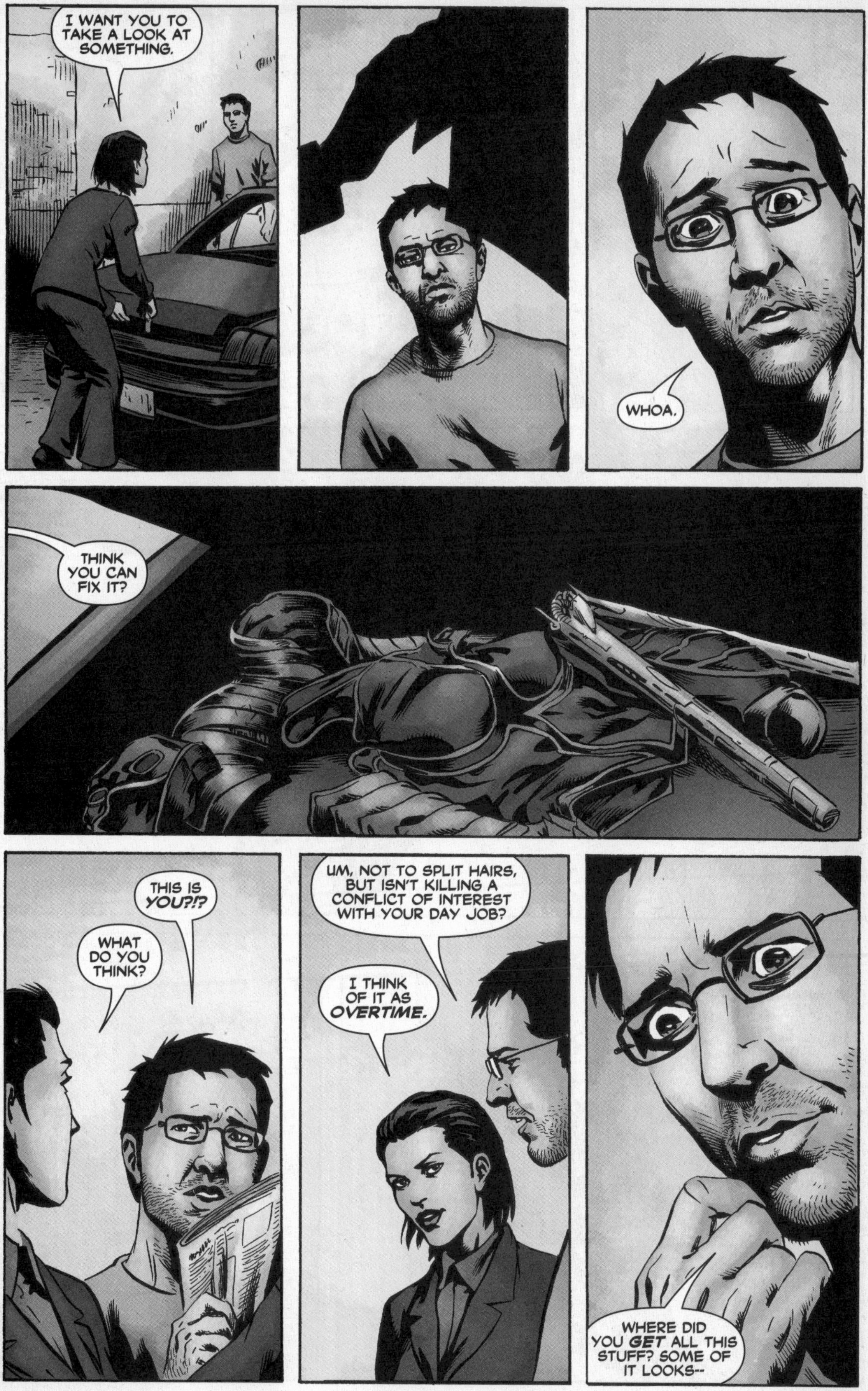
I WANT YOU TO TAKE A LOOK AT SOMETHING.
WHOA.
THINK YOU CAN FIX IT?
THIS IS *YOU?!?*
WHAT DO YOU THINK?
UM, NOT TO SPLIT HAIRS, BUT ISN'T KILLING A CONFLICT OF INTEREST WITH YOUR DAY JOB?
I THINK OF IT AS *OVERTIME.*
WHERE DID YOU *GET* ALL THIS STUFF? SOME OF IT LOOKS--

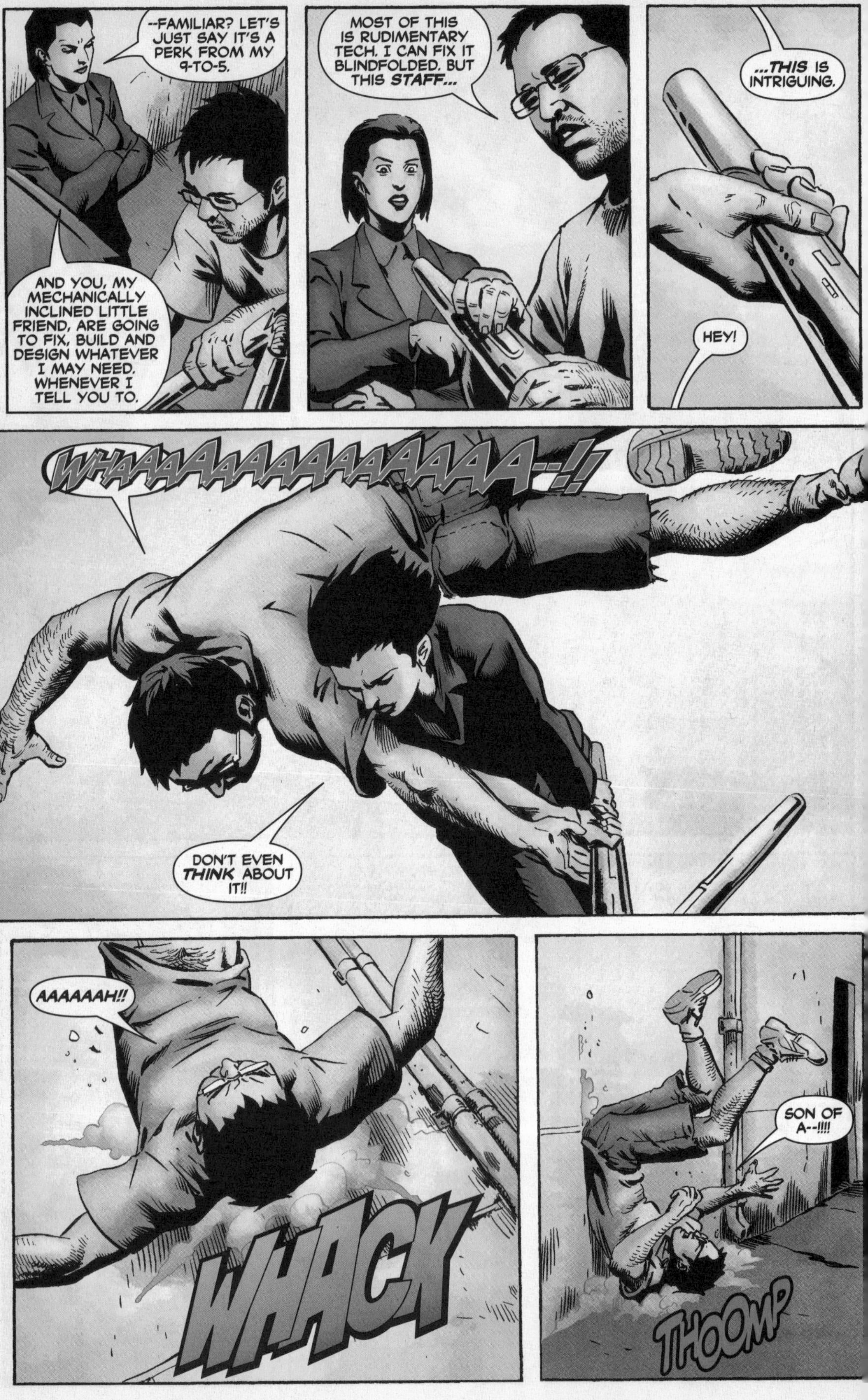
--FAMILIAR? LET'S JUST SAY IT'S A PERK FROM MY 9-TO-5.
AND YOU, MY MECHANICALLY INCLINED LITTLE FRIEND, ARE GOING TO FIX, BUILD AND DESIGN WHATEVER I MAY NEED. WHENEVER I TELL YOU TO.
MOST OF THIS IS RUDIMENTARY TECH. I CAN FIX IT BLINDFOLDED. BUT THIS STAFF...
...THIS IS INTRIGUING.
HEY!
WHAAAAAAAAAAAAAA--!!
DON'T EVEN THINK ABOUT IT!!
AAAAAAH!!
WHACK
SON OF A--!!!!
THOOMP

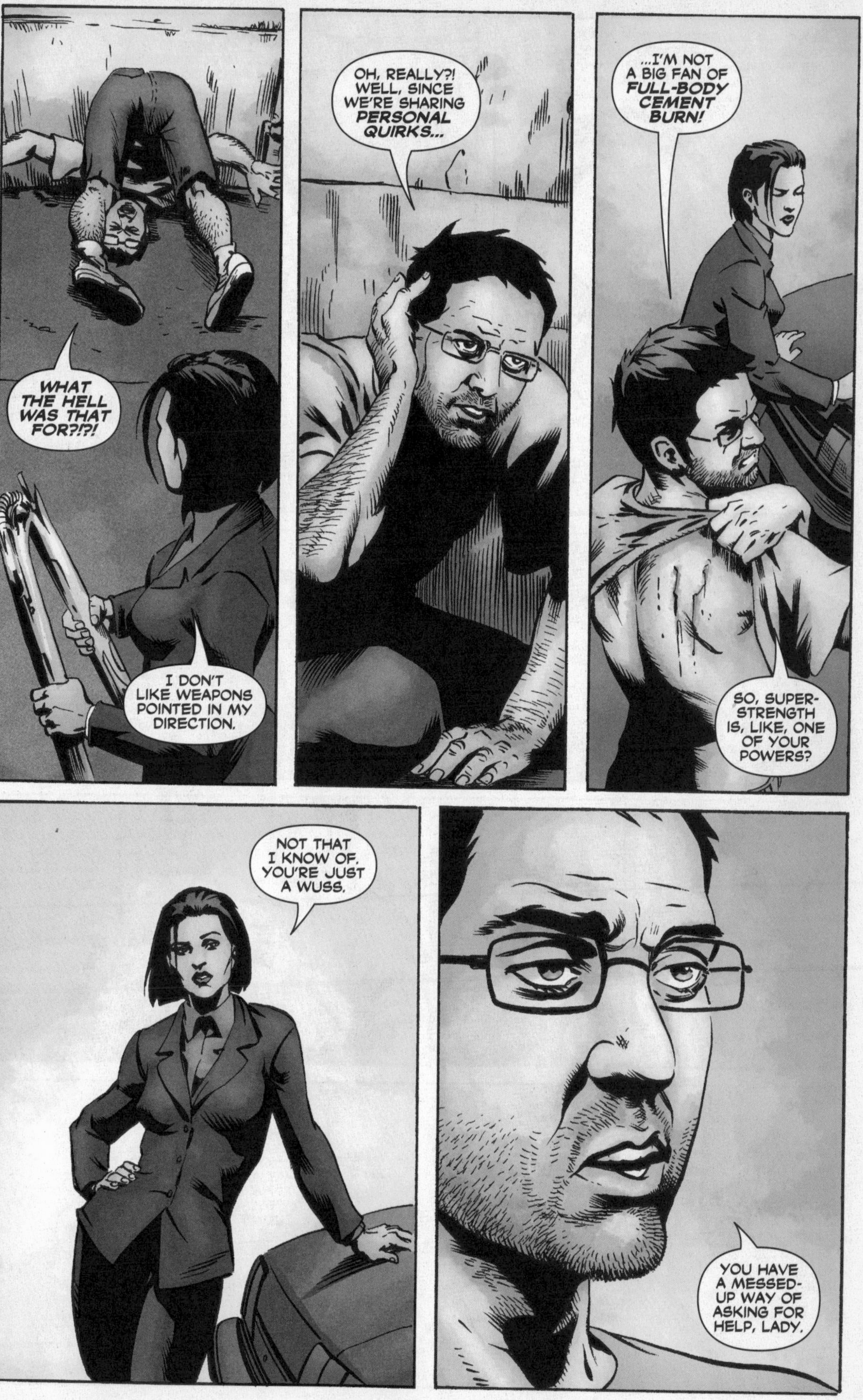
WHAT THE HELL WAS THAT FOR?!?!
I DON'T LIKE WEAPONS POINTED IN MY DIRECTION.
OH, REALLY?! WELL, SINCE WE'RE SHARING PERSONAL QUIRKS...
...I'M NOT A BIG FAN OF FULL-BODY CEMENT BURN!
SO, SUPER-STRENGTH IS, LIKE, ONE OF YOUR POWERS?
NOT THAT I KNOW OF. YOU'RE JUST A WUSS.
YOU HAVE A MESSED-UP WAY OF ASKING FOR HELP, LADY.

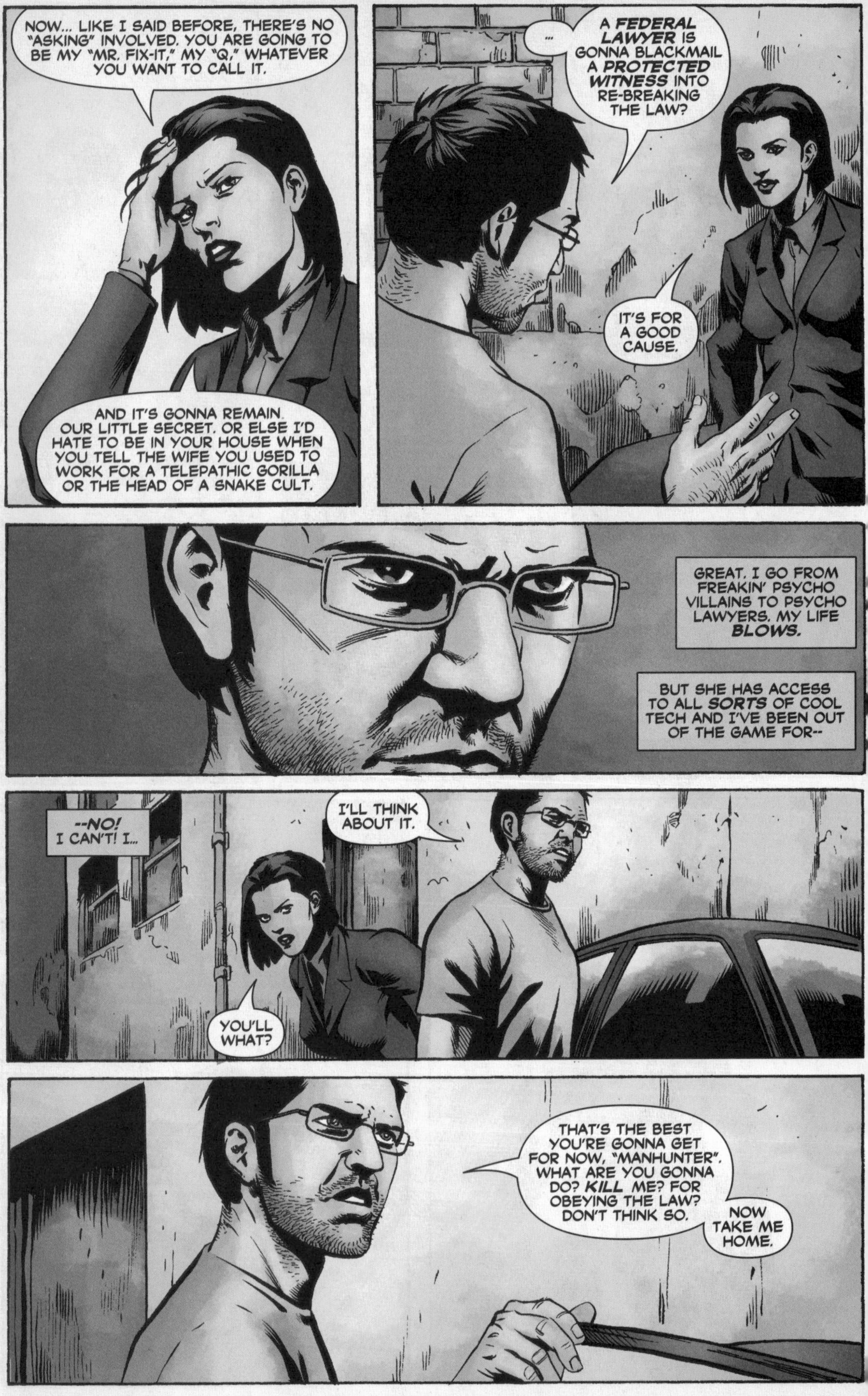
NOW... LIKE I SAID BEFORE, THERE'S NO "ASKING" INVOLVED. YOU ARE GOING TO BE MY "MR. FIX-IT," MY "Q," WHATEVER YOU WANT TO CALL IT.
AND IT'S GONNA REMAIN OUR LITTLE SECRET. OR ELSE I'D HATE TO BE IN YOUR HOUSE WHEN YOU TELL THE WIFE YOU USED TO WORK FOR A TELEPATHIC GORILLA OR THE HEAD OF A SNAKE CULT.
...
A *FEDERAL LAWYER* IS GONNA BLACKMAIL A *PROTECTED WITNESS* INTO RE-BREAKING THE LAW?
IT'S FOR A GOOD CAUSE.
GREAT. I GO FROM FREAKIN' PSYCHO VILLAINS TO PSYCHO LAWYERS. MY LIFE *BLOWS.*
BUT SHE HAS ACCESS TO ALL *SORTS* OF COOL TECH AND I'VE BEEN OUT OF THE GAME FOR--
--NO! I CAN'T! I...
I'LL THINK ABOUT IT.
YOU'LL WHAT?
THAT'S THE BEST YOU'RE GONNA GET FOR NOW, "MANHUNTER". WHAT ARE YOU GONNA DO? *KILL* ME? FOR OBEYING THE LAW? DON'T THINK SO.
NOW TAKE ME HOME.

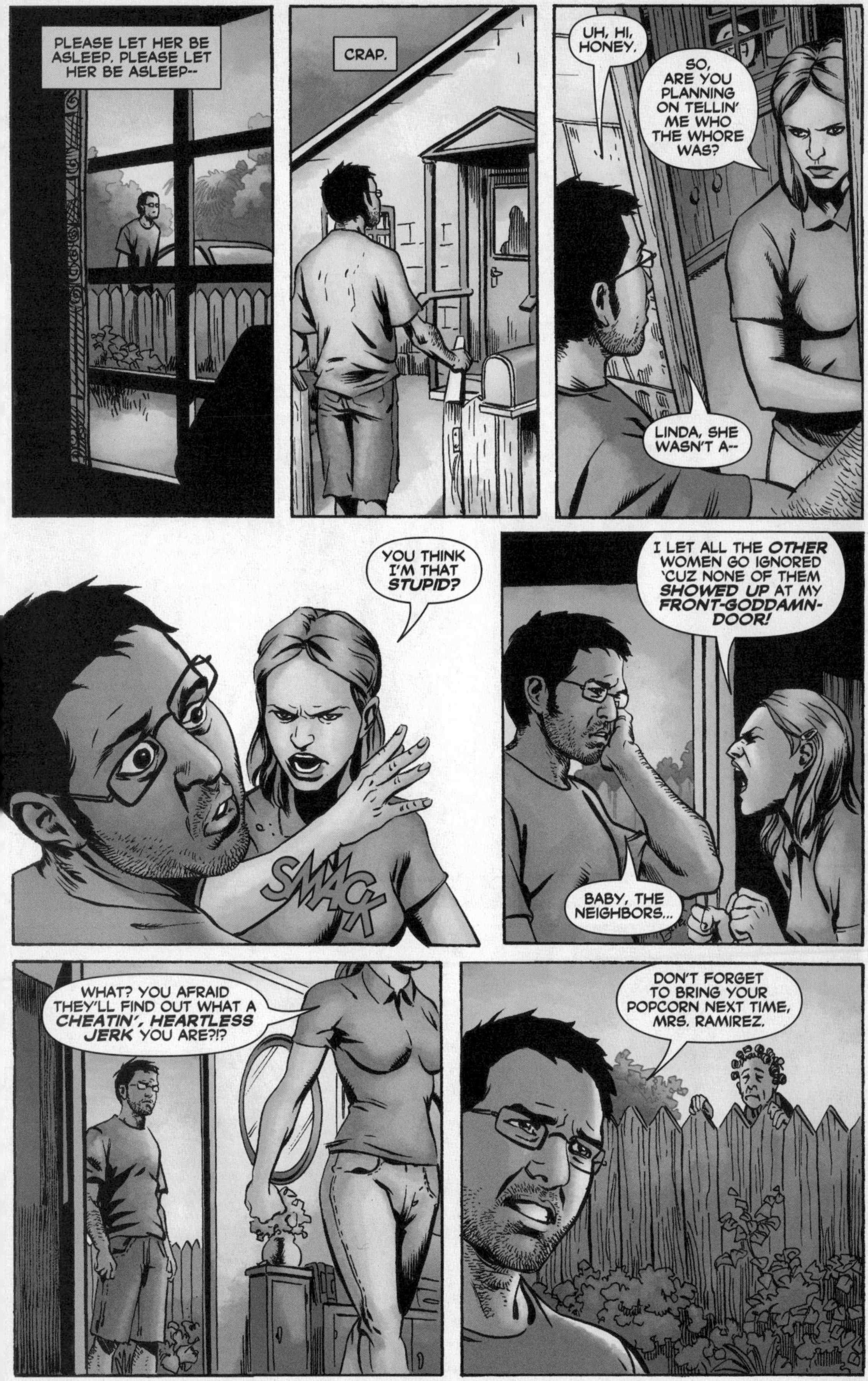
PLEASE LET HER BE ASLEEP. PLEASE LET HER BE ASLEEP--
CRAP.
UH, HI, HONEY.
SO, ARE YOU PLANNING ON TELLIN' ME WHO THE WHORE WAS?
LINDA, SHE WASN'T A--
YOU THINK I'M THAT STUPID?
SMACK
I LET ALL THE OTHER WOMEN GO IGNORED 'CUZ NONE OF THEM SHOWED UP AT MY FRONT-GODDAMN-DOOR!
BABY, THE NEIGHBORS...
WHAT? YOU AFRAID THEY'LL FIND OUT WHAT A CHEATIN', HEARTLESS JERK YOU ARE?!?
DON'T FORGET TO BRING YOUR POPCORN NEXT TIME, MRS. RAMIREZ.

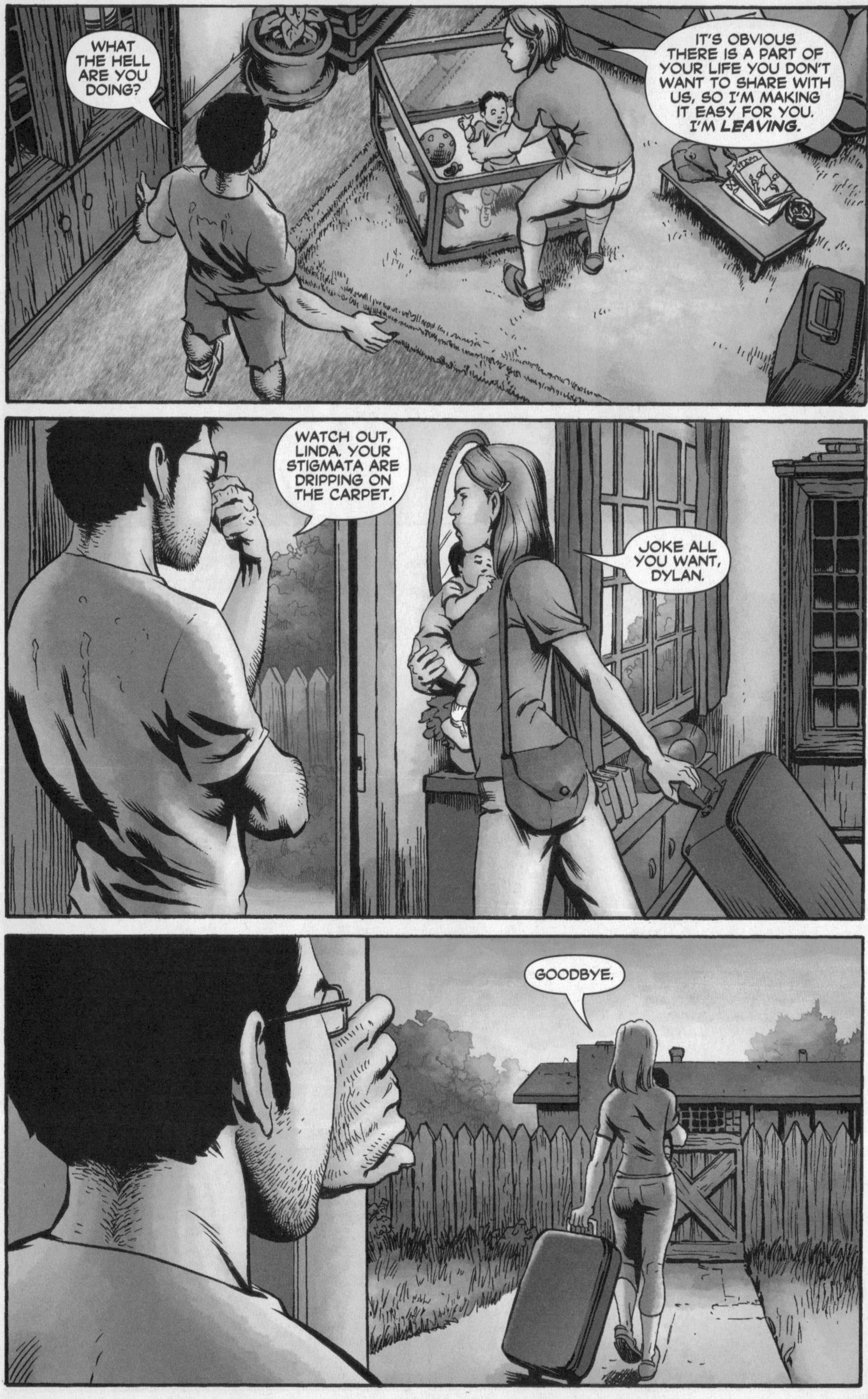
WHAT THE HELL ARE YOU DOING?
IT'S OBVIOUS THERE IS A PART OF YOUR LIFE YOU DON'T WANT TO SHARE WITH US, SO I'M MAKING IT EASY FOR YOU. I'M *LEAVING.*
WATCH OUT, LINDA. YOUR STIGMATA ARE DRIPPING ON THE CARPET.
JOKE ALL YOU WANT, DYLAN.
GOODBYE.

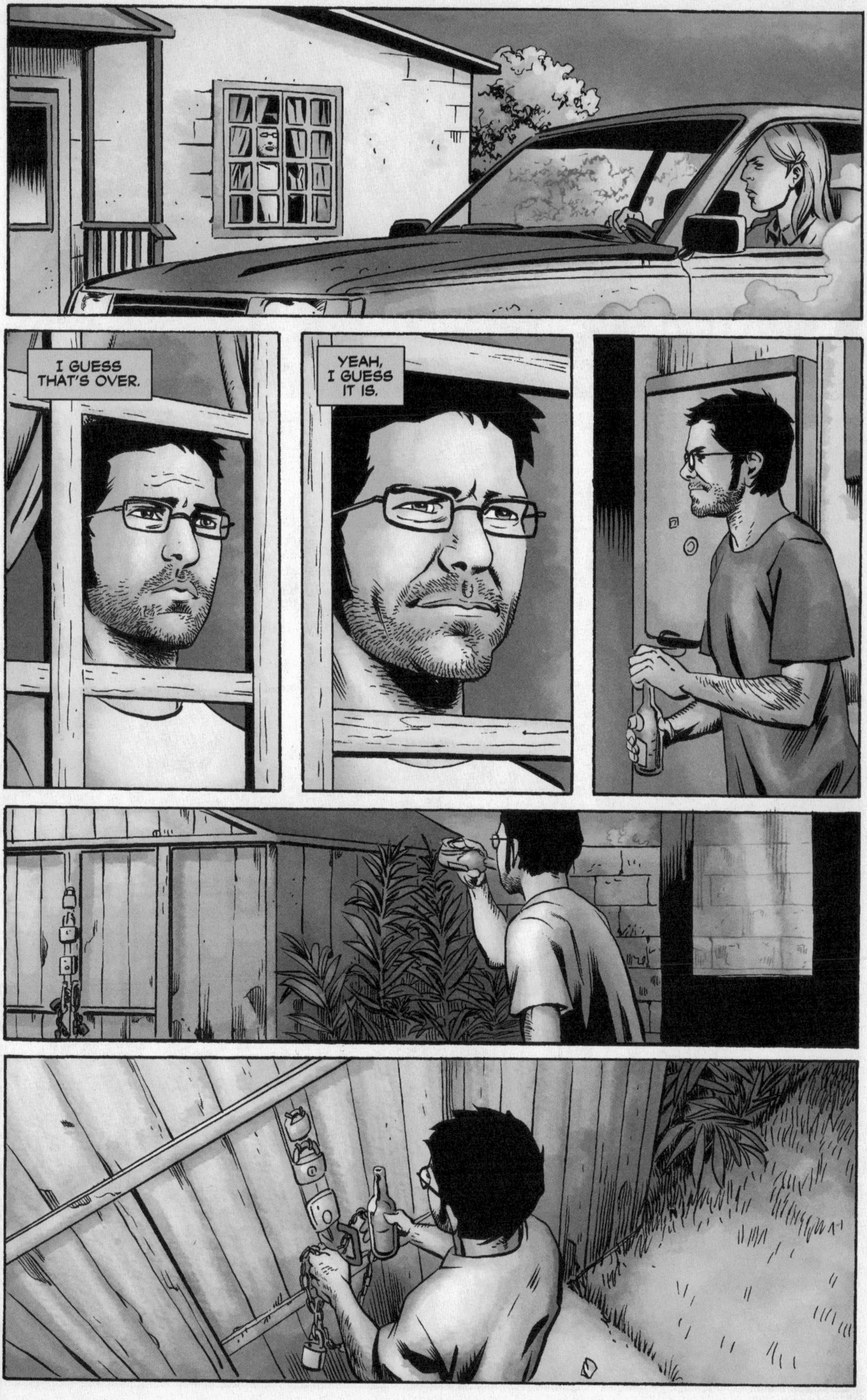
I GUESS THAT'S OVER.
YEAH, I GUESS IT IS.

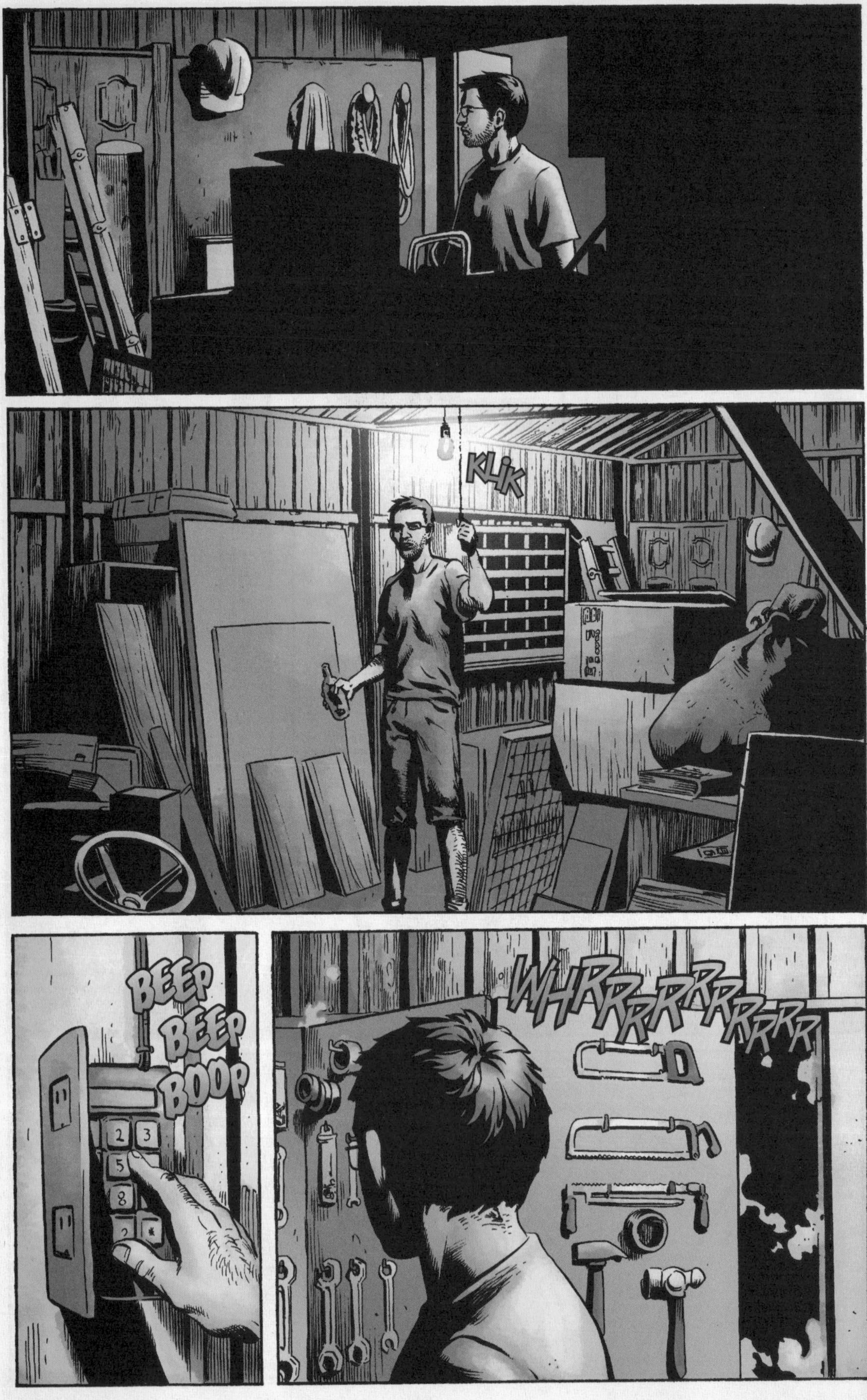
KLIK
BEEP
BEEP
BOOP
WHRRRRRRRRRRR

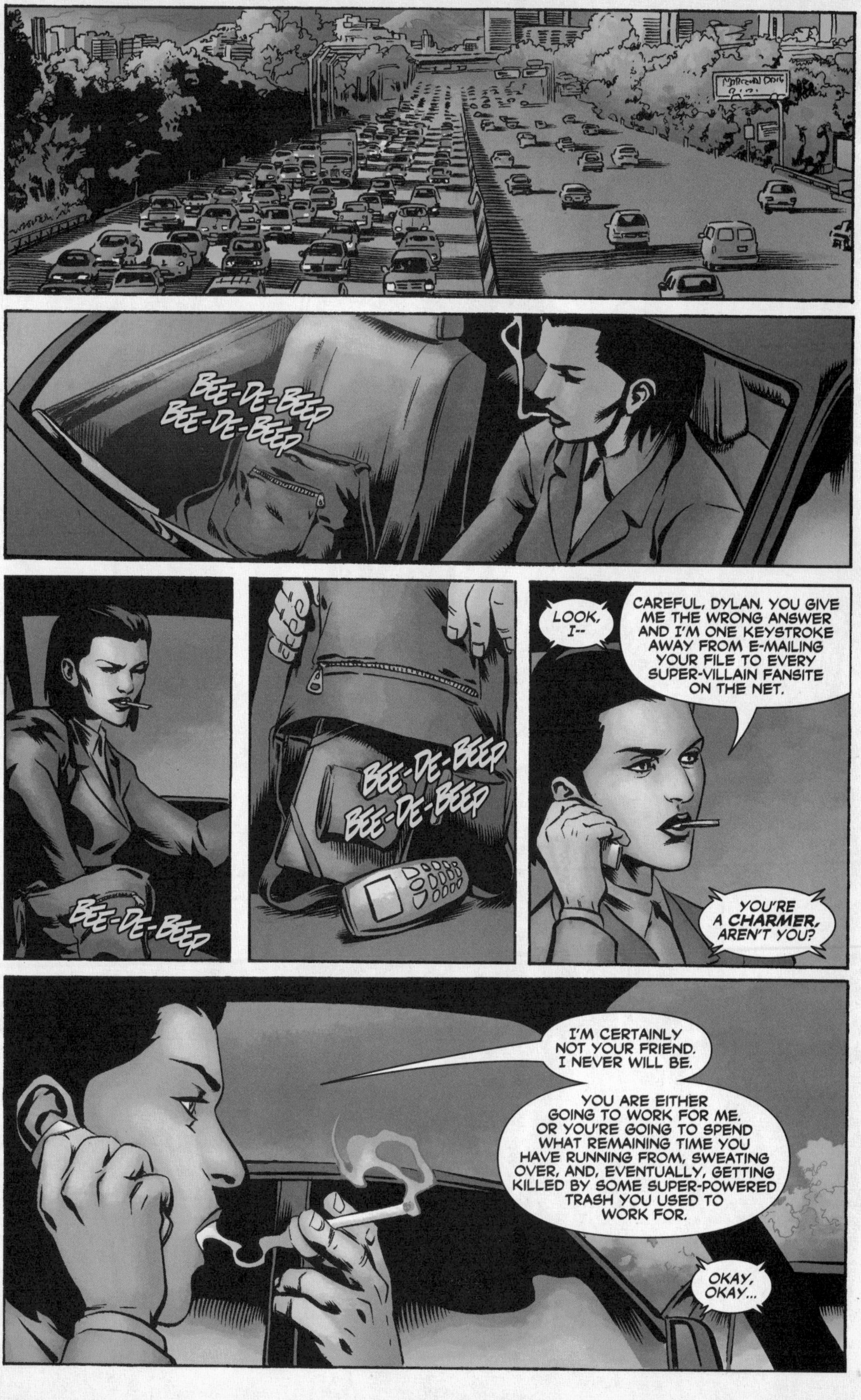
BEE-DE-BEEP
BEE-DE-BEEP
BEE-DE-BEEP
BEE-DE-BEEP
BEE-DE-BEEP
LOOK, I--
CAREFUL, DYLAN. YOU GIVE ME THE WRONG ANSWER AND I'M ONE KEYSTROKE AWAY FROM E-MAILING YOUR FILE TO EVERY SUPER-VILLAIN FANSITE ON THE NET.
YOU'RE A CHARMER, AREN'T YOU?
I'M CERTAINLY NOT YOUR FRIEND. I NEVER WILL BE.
YOU ARE EITHER GOING TO WORK FOR ME. OR YOU'RE GOING TO SPEND WHAT REMAINING TIME YOU HAVE RUNNING FROM, SWEATING OVER, AND, EVENTUALLY, GETTING KILLED BY SOME SUPER-POWERED TRASH YOU USED TO WORK FOR.
OKAY, OKAY...

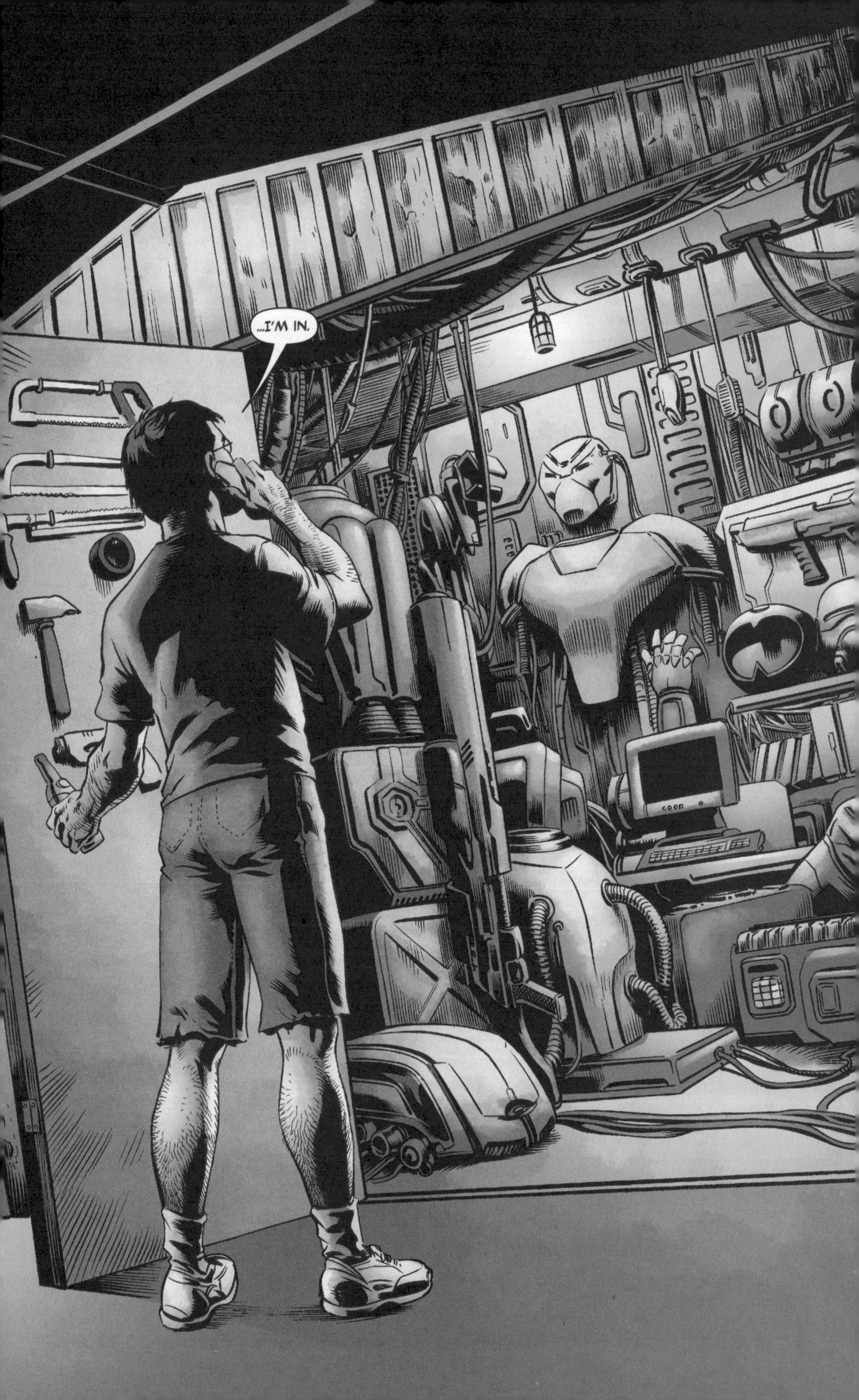
...I'M IN.

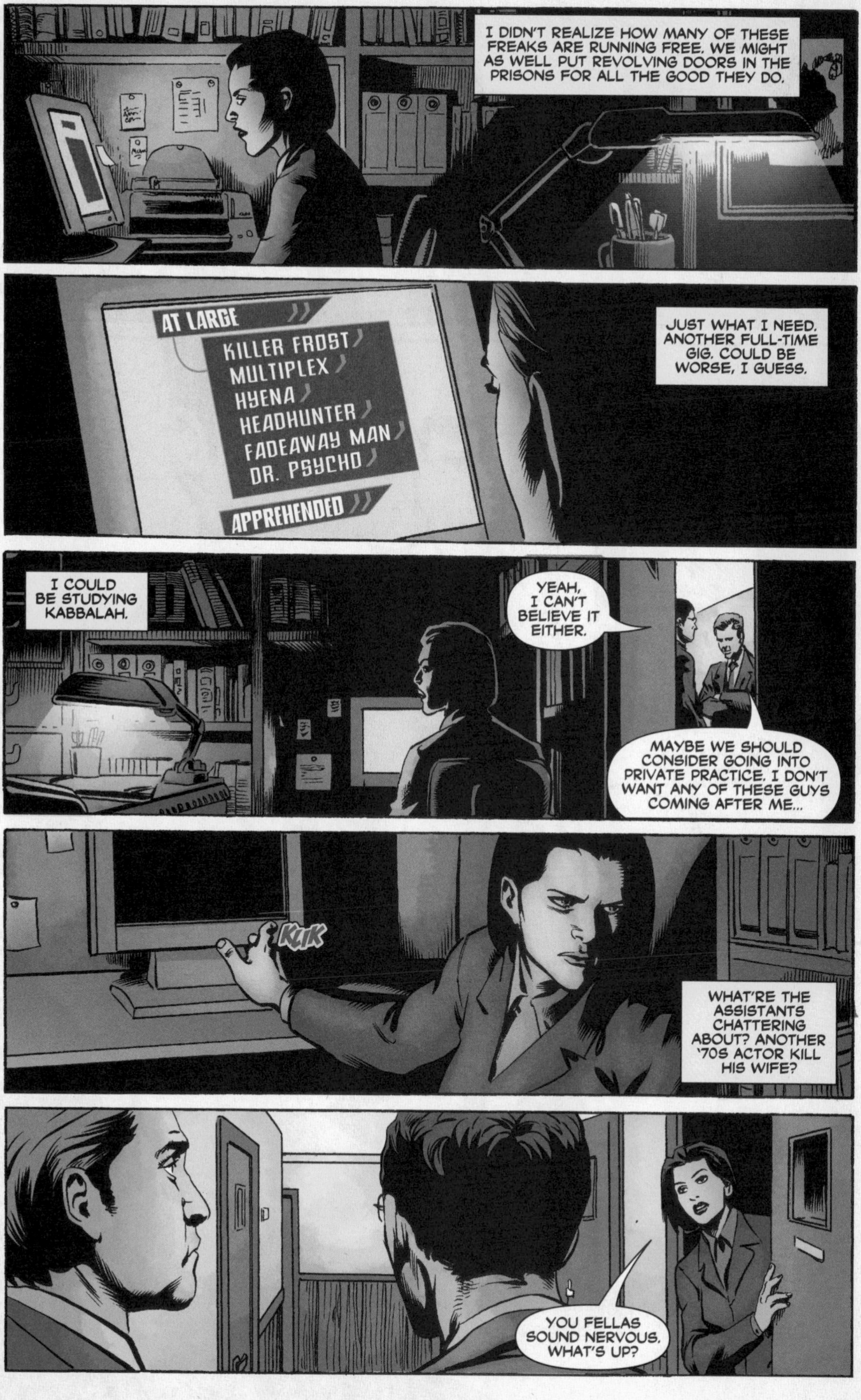
I DIDN'T REALIZE HOW MANY OF THESE FREAKS ARE RUNNING FREE. WE MIGHT AS WELL PUT REVOLVING DOORS IN THE PRISONS FOR ALL THE GOOD THEY DO.
AT LARGE
KILLER FROST
MULTIPLEX
HYENA
HEADHUNTER
FADEAWAY MAN
DR. PSYCHO
APPREHENDED
JUST WHAT I NEED. ANOTHER FULL-TIME GIG. COULD BE WORSE, I GUESS.
I COULD BE STUDYING KABBALAH.
YEAH, I CAN'T BELIEVE IT EITHER.
MAYBE WE SHOULD CONSIDER GOING INTO PRIVATE PRACTICE. I DON'T WANT ANY OF THESE GUYS COMING AFTER ME...
KLIK
WHAT'RE THE ASSISTANTS CHATTERING ABOUT? ANOTHER '70S ACTOR KILL HIS WIFE?
YOU FELLAS SOUND NERVOUS. WHAT'S UP?

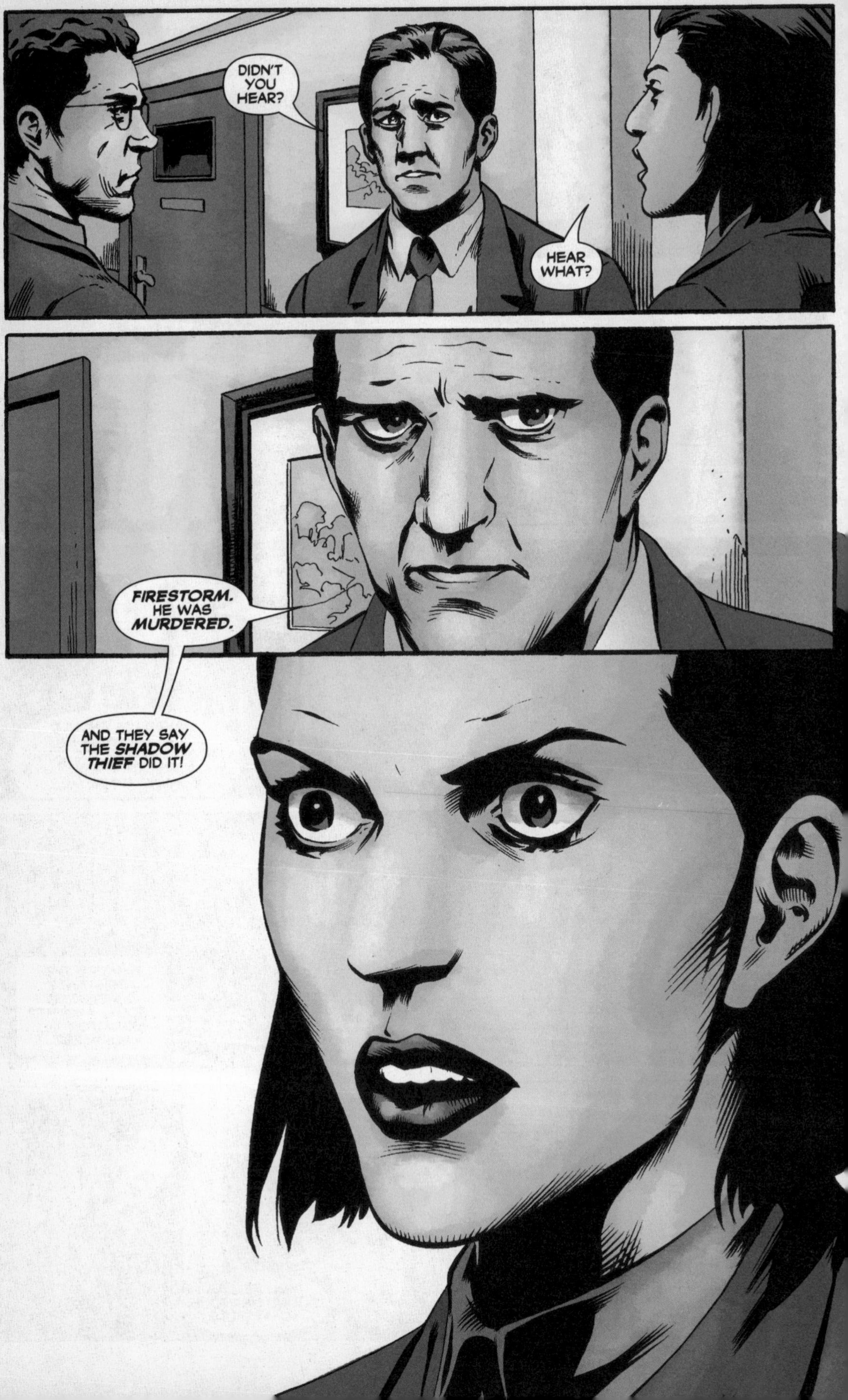
DIDN'T YOU HEAR?
HEAR WHAT?
FIRESTORM. HE WAS MURDERED.
AND THEY SAY THE SHADOW THIEF DID IT!

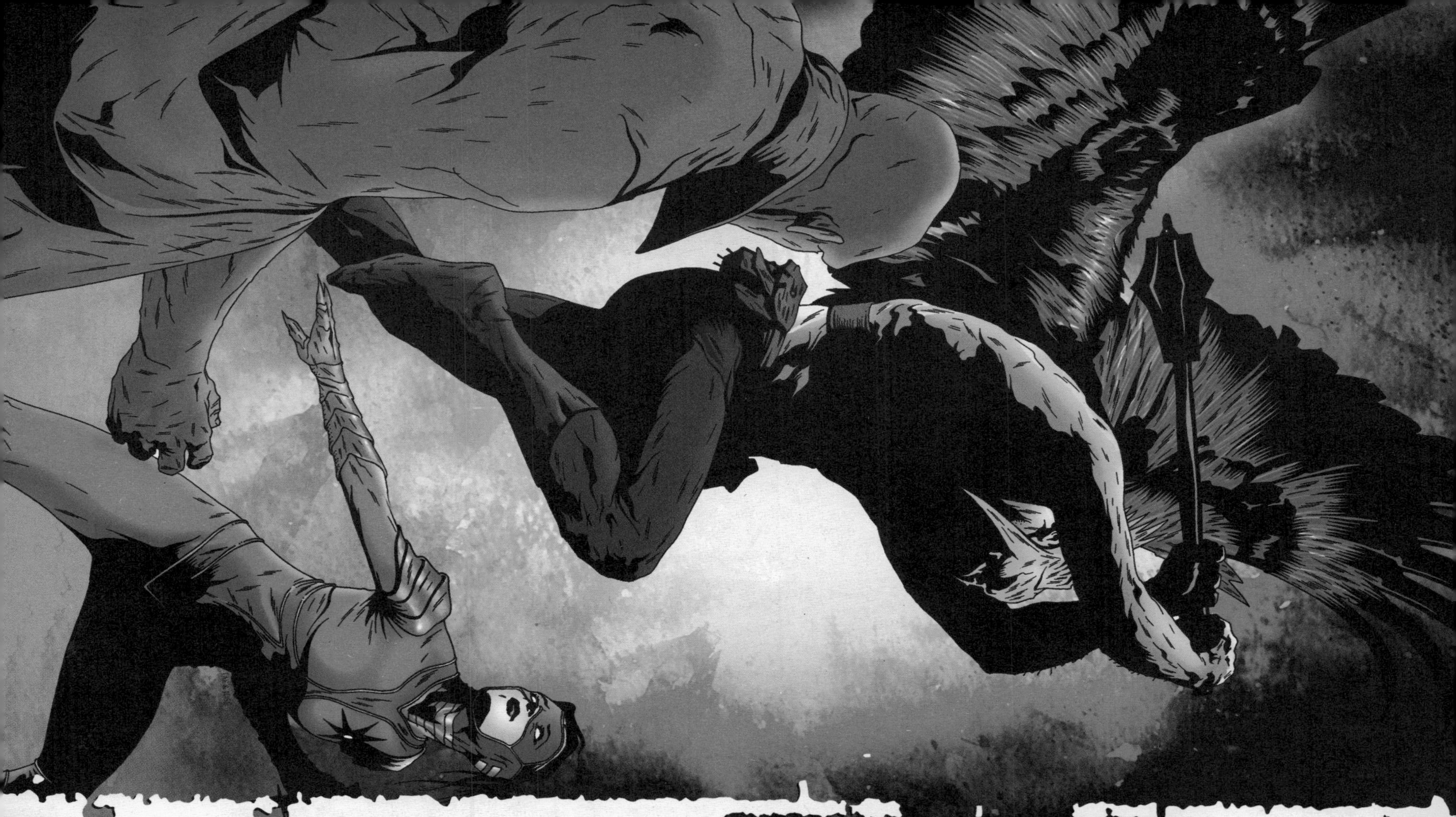

MANHUNTER #5

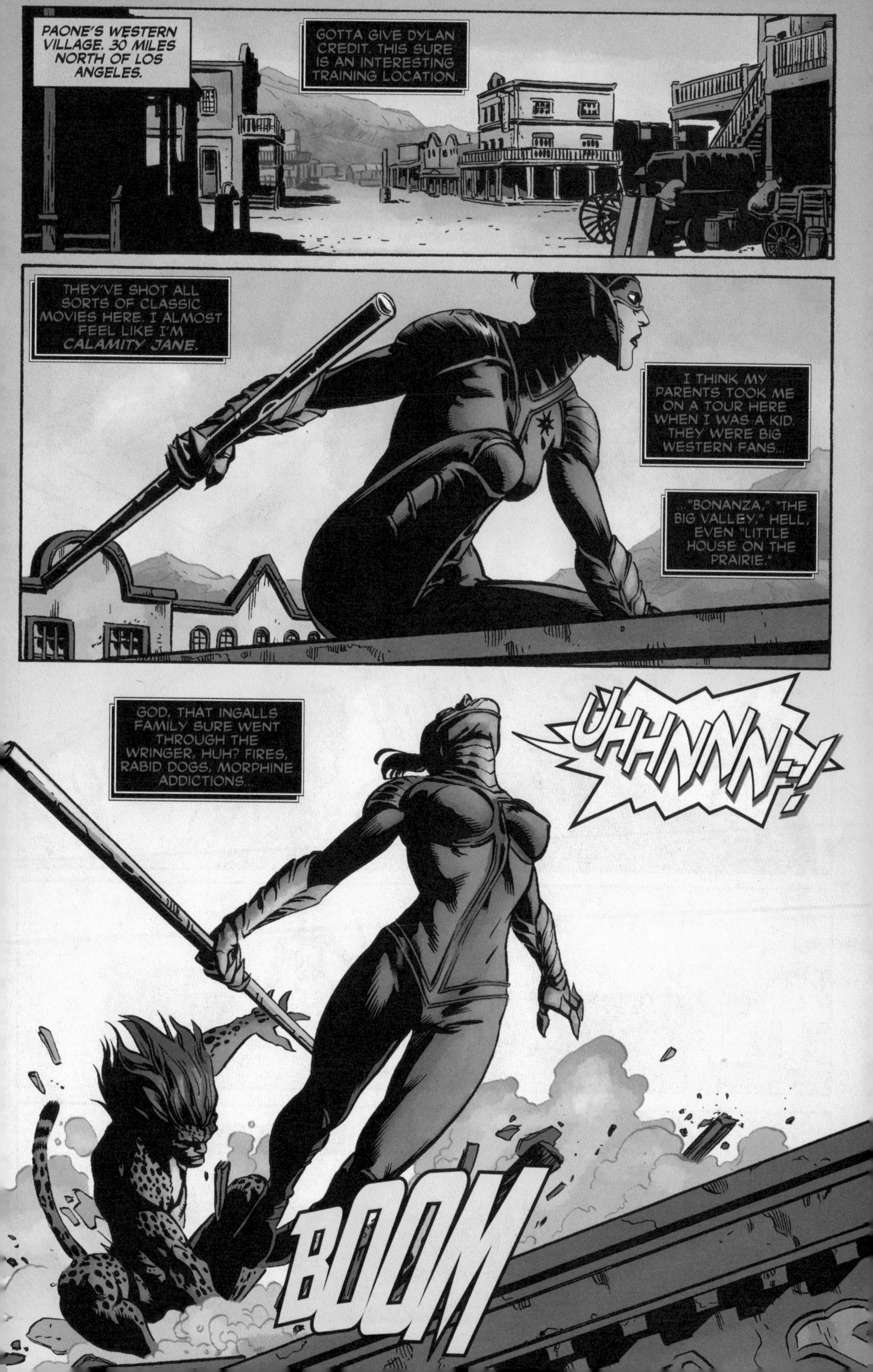
PAONE'S WESTERN VILLAGE. 30 MILES NORTH OF LOS ANGELES.
GOTTA GIVE DYLAN CREDIT. THIS SURE IS AN INTERESTING TRAINING LOCATION.
THEY'VE SHOT ALL SORTS OF CLASSIC MOVIES HERE. I ALMOST FEEL LIKE I'M *CALAMITY JANE.*
I THINK MY PARENTS TOOK ME ON A TOUR HERE WHEN I WAS A KID. THEY WERE BIG WESTERN FANS...
..."BONANZA," "THE BIG VALLEY," HELL, EVEN "LITTLE HOUSE ON THE PRAIRIE."
GOD, THAT INGALLS FAMILY SURE WENT THROUGH THE WRINGER, HUH? FIRES, RABID DOGS, MORPHINE ADDICTIONS...
UHHNNN--!
BOOM

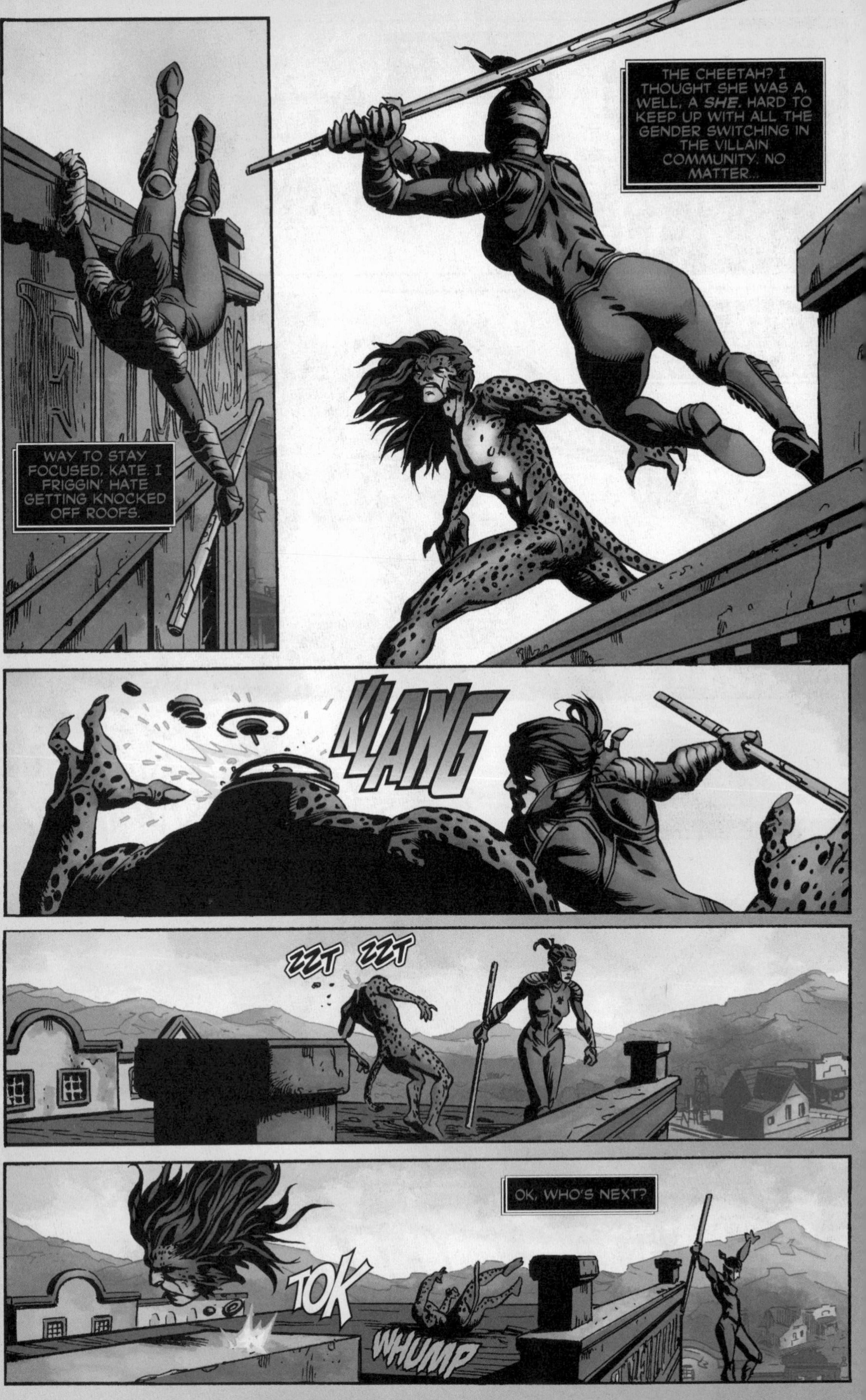
THE CHEETAH? I THOUGHT SHE WAS A, WELL, A SHE. HARD TO KEEP UP WITH ALL THE GENDER SWITCHING IN THE VILLAIN COMMUNITY. NO MATTER...
WAY TO STAY FOCUSED, KATE. I FRIGGIN' HATE GETTING KNOCKED OFF ROOFS.
KLANG
ZZT ZZT
OK, WHO'S NEXT?
TOK
WHUMP

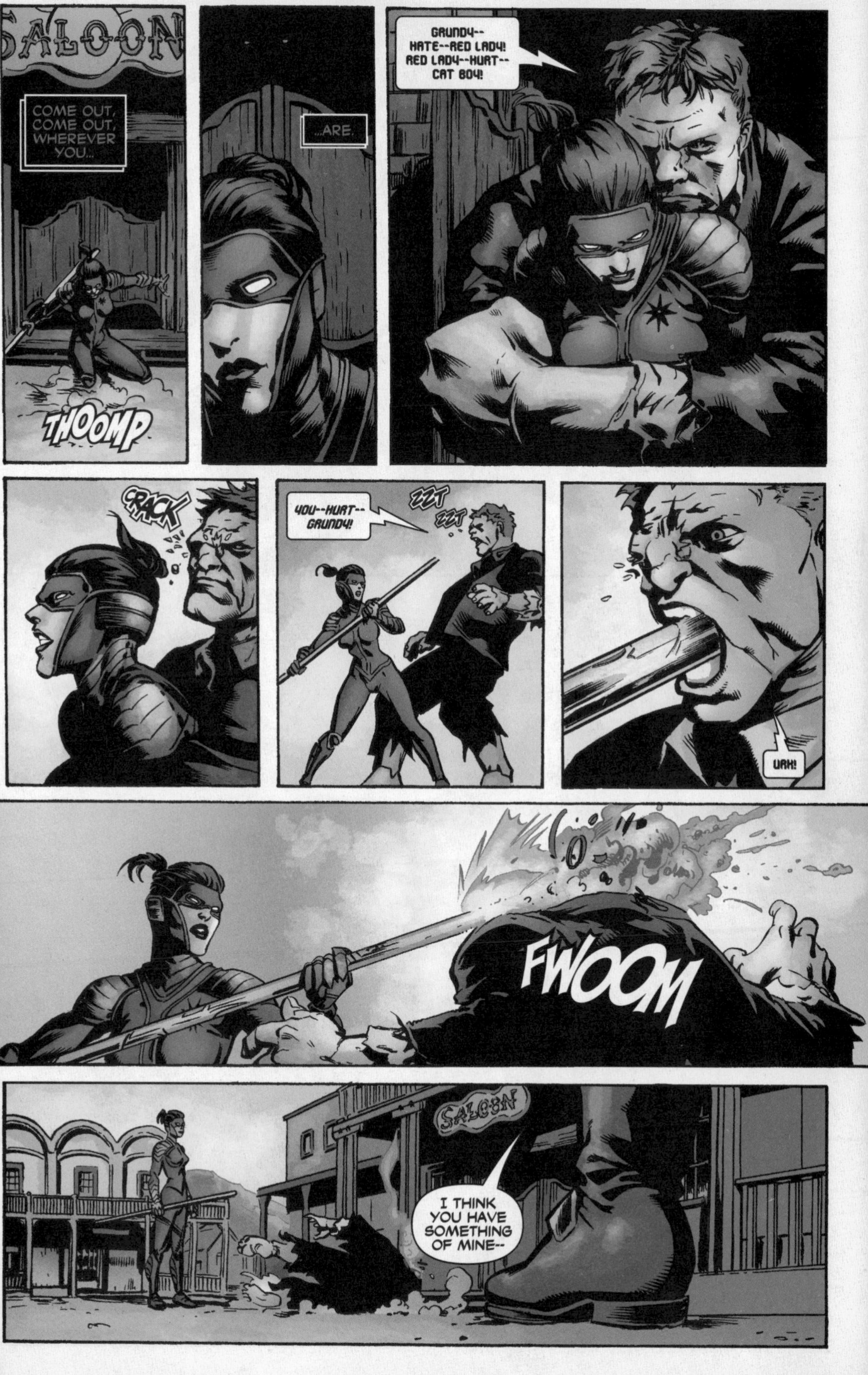
SALOON
COME OUT, COME OUT, WHEREVER YOU...
THOOMP
...ARE.
GRUNDY-- HATE--RED LADY! RED LADY--HURT-- CAT BOY!
CRACK
YOU--HURT-- GRUNDY!
ZZT
ZZT
URK!
FWOOM
SALOON
I THINK YOU HAVE SOMETHING OF MINE--

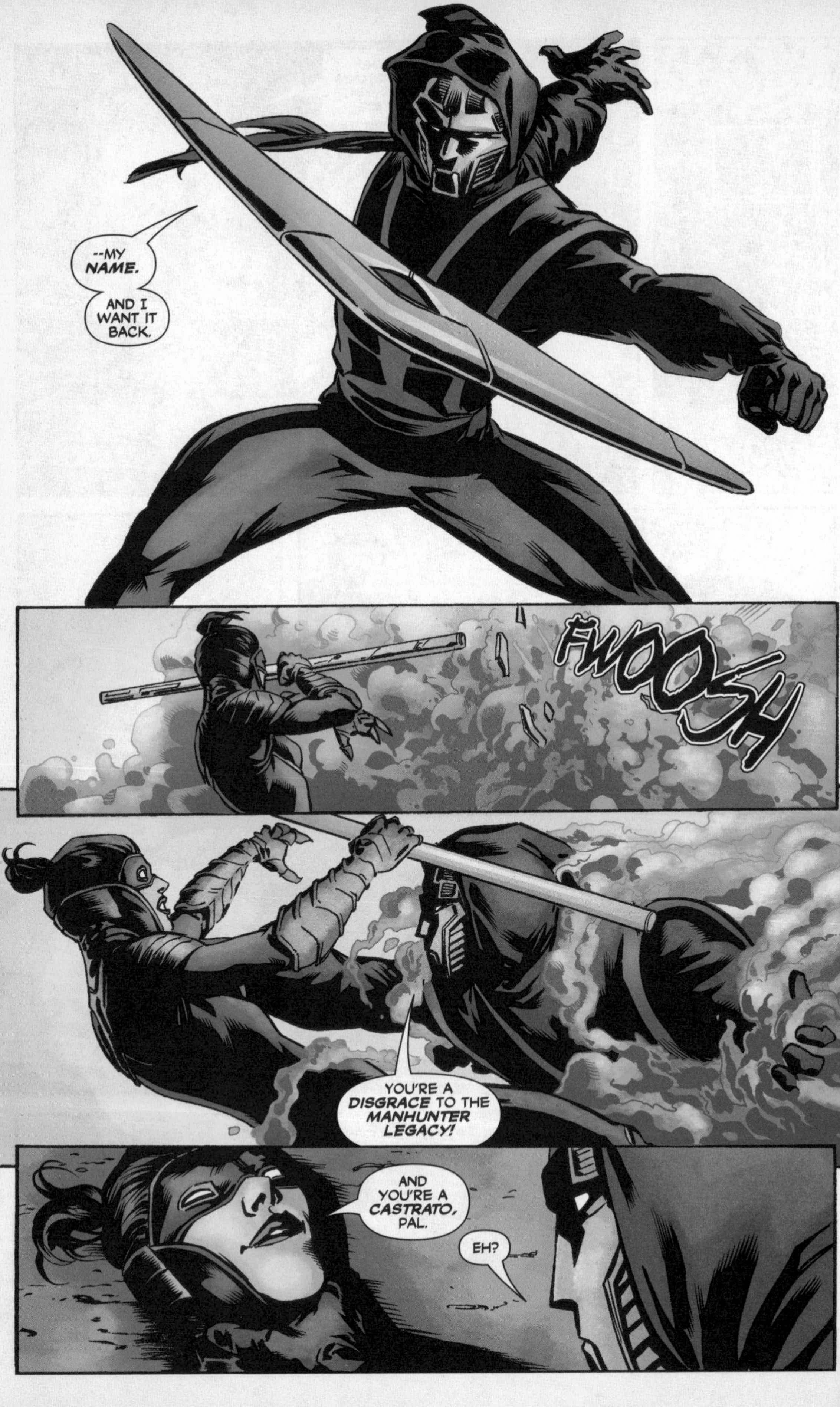
--MY NAME.
AND I WANT IT BACK.
FWOOSH
YOU'RE A DISGRACE TO THE MANHUNTER LEGACY!
AND YOU'RE A CASTRATO, PAL.
EH?

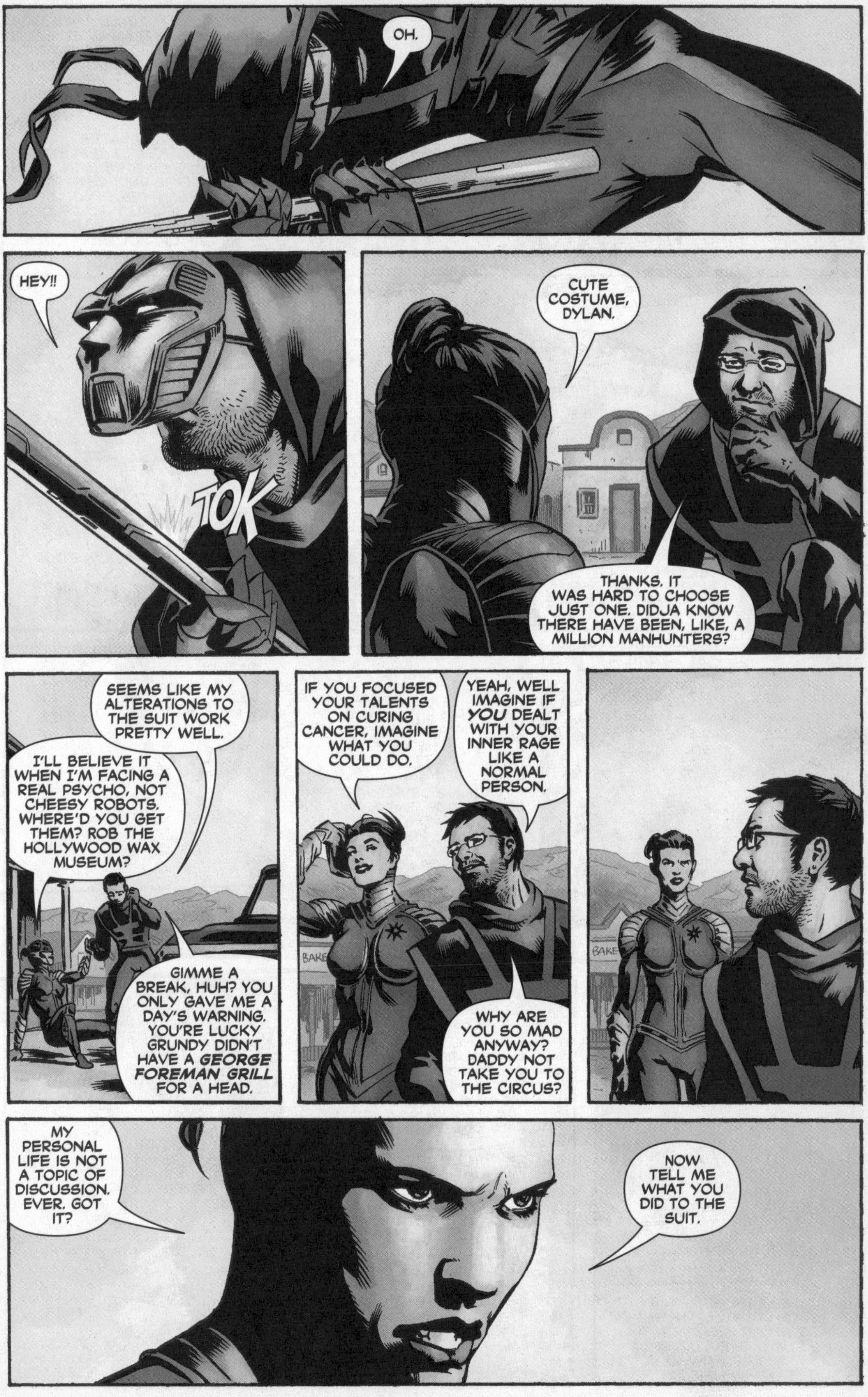
OH.
HEY!!
TOK
CUTE COSTUME, DYLAN.
THANKS. IT WAS HARD TO CHOOSE JUST ONE. DIDJA KNOW THERE HAVE BEEN, LIKE, A MILLION MANHUNTERS?
SEEMS LIKE MY ALTERATIONS TO THE SUIT WORK PRETTY WELL.
I'LL BELIEVE IT WHEN I'M FACING A REAL PSYCHO, NOT CHEESY ROBOTS. WHERE'D YOU GET THEM? ROB THE HOLLYWOOD WAX MUSEUM?
GIMME A BREAK, HUH? YOU ONLY GAVE ME A DAY'S WARNING. YOU'RE LUCKY GRUNDY DIDN'T HAVE A *GEORGE FOREMAN GRILL* FOR A HEAD.
IF YOU FOCUSED YOUR TALENTS ON CURING CANCER, IMAGINE WHAT YOU COULD DO.
YEAH, WELL IMAGINE IF *YOU* DEALT WITH YOUR INNER RAGE LIKE A NORMAL PERSON.
WHY ARE YOU SO MAD ANYWAY? DADDY NOT TAKE YOU TO THE CIRCUS?
MY PERSONAL LIFE IS NOT A TOPIC OF DISCUSSION. EVER. GOT IT?
NOW TELL ME WHAT YOU DID TO THE SUIT.

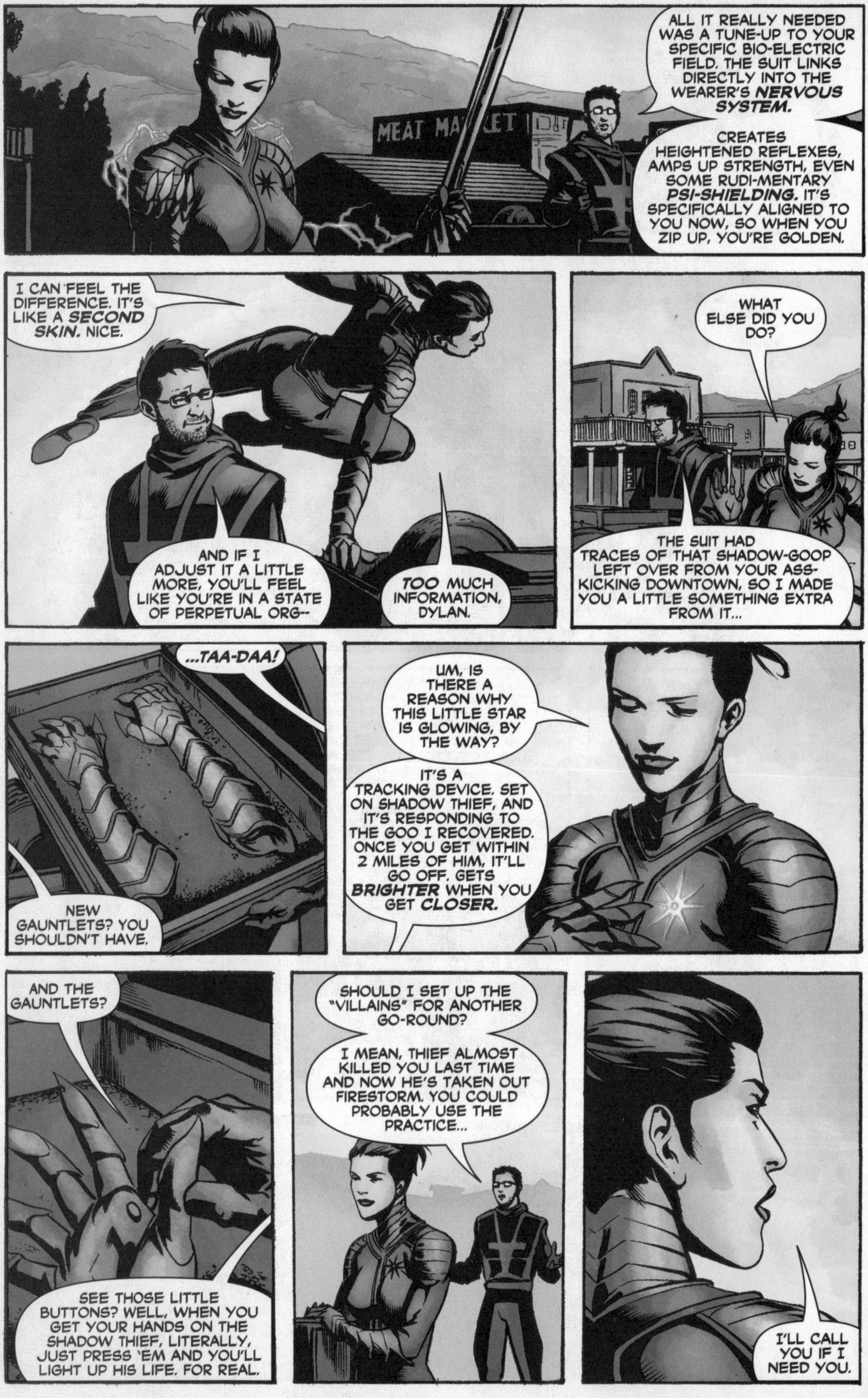
ALL IT REALLY NEEDED WAS A TUNE-UP TO YOUR SPECIFIC BIO-ELECTRIC FIELD. THE SUIT LINKS DIRECTLY INTO THE WEARER'S NERVOUS SYSTEM.
CREATES HEIGHTENED REFLEXES, AMPS UP STRENGTH, EVEN SOME RUDI-MENTARY PSI-SHIELDING. IT'S SPECIFICALLY ALIGNED TO YOU NOW, SO WHEN YOU ZIP UP, YOU'RE GOLDEN.
MEAT MA KET
I CAN FEEL THE DIFFERENCE. IT'S LIKE A SECOND SKIN. NICE.
AND IF I ADJUST IT A LITTLE MORE, YOU'LL FEEL LIKE YOU'RE IN A STATE OF PERPETUAL ORG--
TOO MUCH INFORMATION, DYLAN.
WHAT ELSE DID YOU DO?
THE SUIT HAD TRACES OF THAT SHADOW-GOOP LEFT OVER FROM YOUR ASS-KICKING DOWNTOWN, SO I MADE YOU A LITTLE SOMETHING EXTRA FROM IT...
...TAA-DAA!
NEW GAUNTLETS? YOU SHOULDN'T HAVE.
UM, IS THERE A REASON WHY THIS LITTLE STAR IS GLOWING, BY THE WAY?
IT'S A TRACKING DEVICE. SET ON SHADOW THIEF, AND IT'S RESPONDING TO THE GOO I RECOVERED. ONCE YOU GET WITHIN 2 MILES OF HIM, IT'LL GO OFF. GETS BRIGHTER WHEN YOU GET CLOSER.
AND THE GAUNTLETS?
SEE THOSE LITTLE BUTTONS? WELL, WHEN YOU GET YOUR HANDS ON THE SHADOW THIEF, LITERALLY, JUST PRESS 'EM AND YOU'LL LIGHT UP HIS LIFE. FOR REAL.
SHOULD I SET UP THE "VILLAINS" FOR ANOTHER GO-ROUND?
I MEAN, THIEF ALMOST KILLED YOU LAST TIME AND NOW HE'S TAKEN OUT FIRESTORM. YOU COULD PROBABLY USE THE PRACTICE...
I'LL CALL YOU IF I NEED YOU.

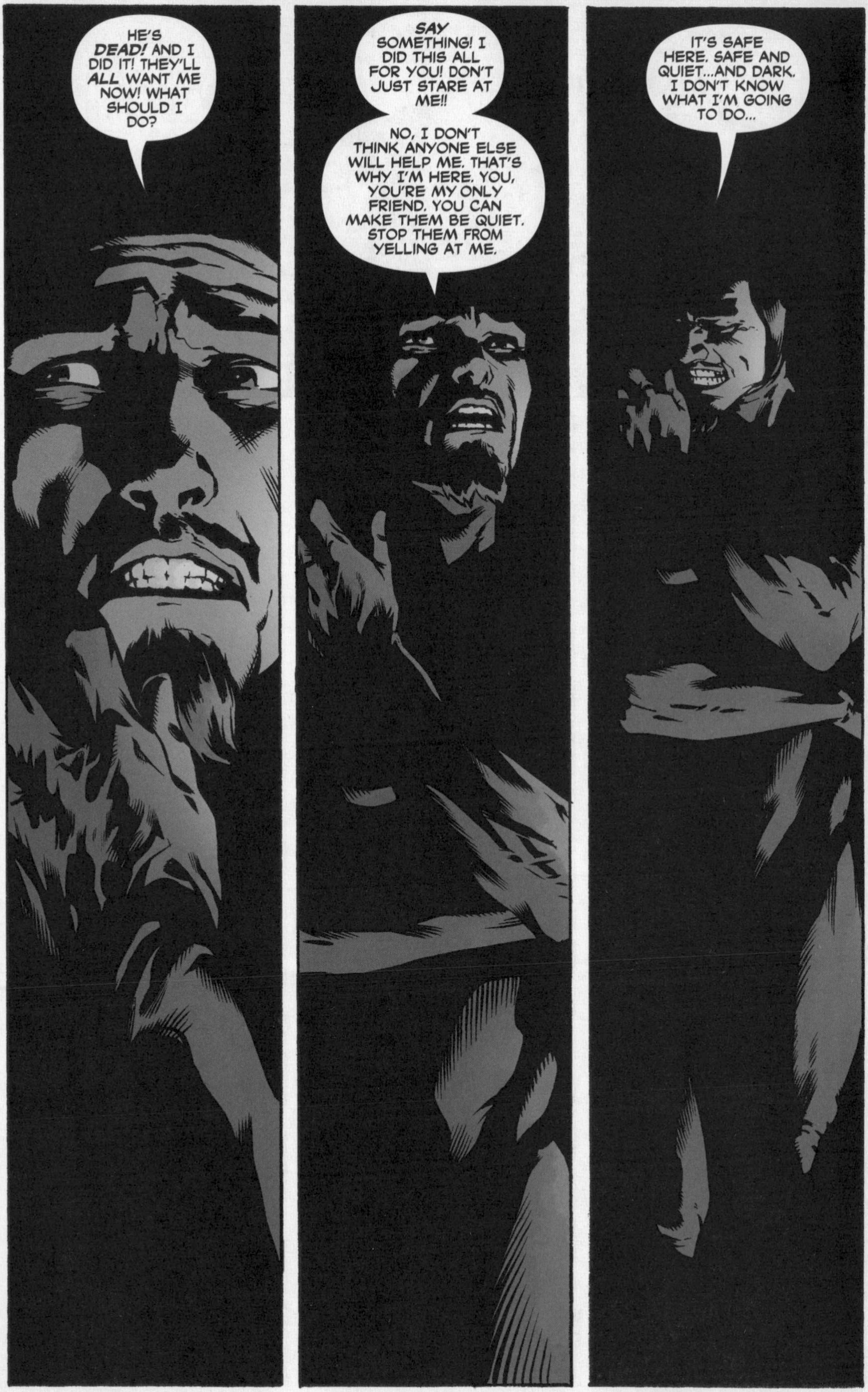
HE'S *DEAD!* AND I DID IT! THEY'LL *ALL* WANT ME NOW! WHAT SHOULD I DO?
SAY SOMETHING! I DID THIS ALL FOR YOU! DON'T JUST STARE AT ME!!
NO, I DON'T THINK ANYONE ELSE WILL HELP ME. THAT'S WHY I'M HERE. YOU, YOU'RE MY ONLY FRIEND. YOU CAN MAKE THEM BE QUIET. STOP THEM FROM YELLING AT ME.
IT'S SAFE HERE. SAFE AND QUIET...AND DARK. I DON'T KNOW WHAT I'M GOING TO DO...

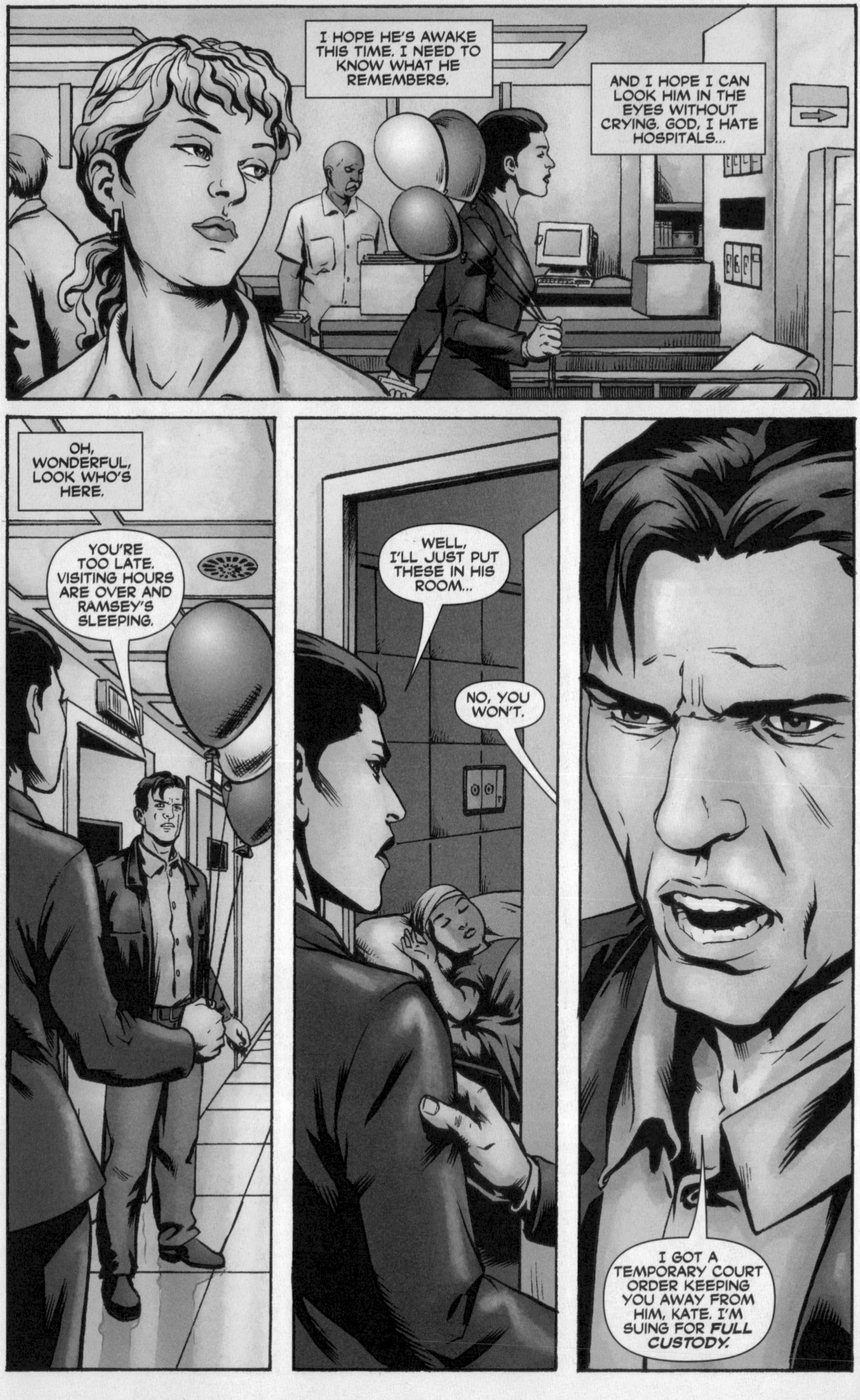
I HOPE HE'S AWAKE THIS TIME. I NEED TO KNOW WHAT HE REMEMBERS.
AND I HOPE I CAN LOOK HIM IN THE EYES WITHOUT CRYING. GOD, I HATE HOSPITALS...
OH, WONDERFUL, LOOK WHO'S HERE.
YOU'RE TOO LATE. VISITING HOURS ARE OVER AND RAMSEY'S SLEEPING.
WELL, I'LL JUST PUT THESE IN HIS ROOM...
NO, YOU WON'T.
I GOT A TEMPORARY COURT ORDER KEEPING YOU AWAY FROM HIM, KATE. I'M SUING FOR *FULL CUSTODY.*

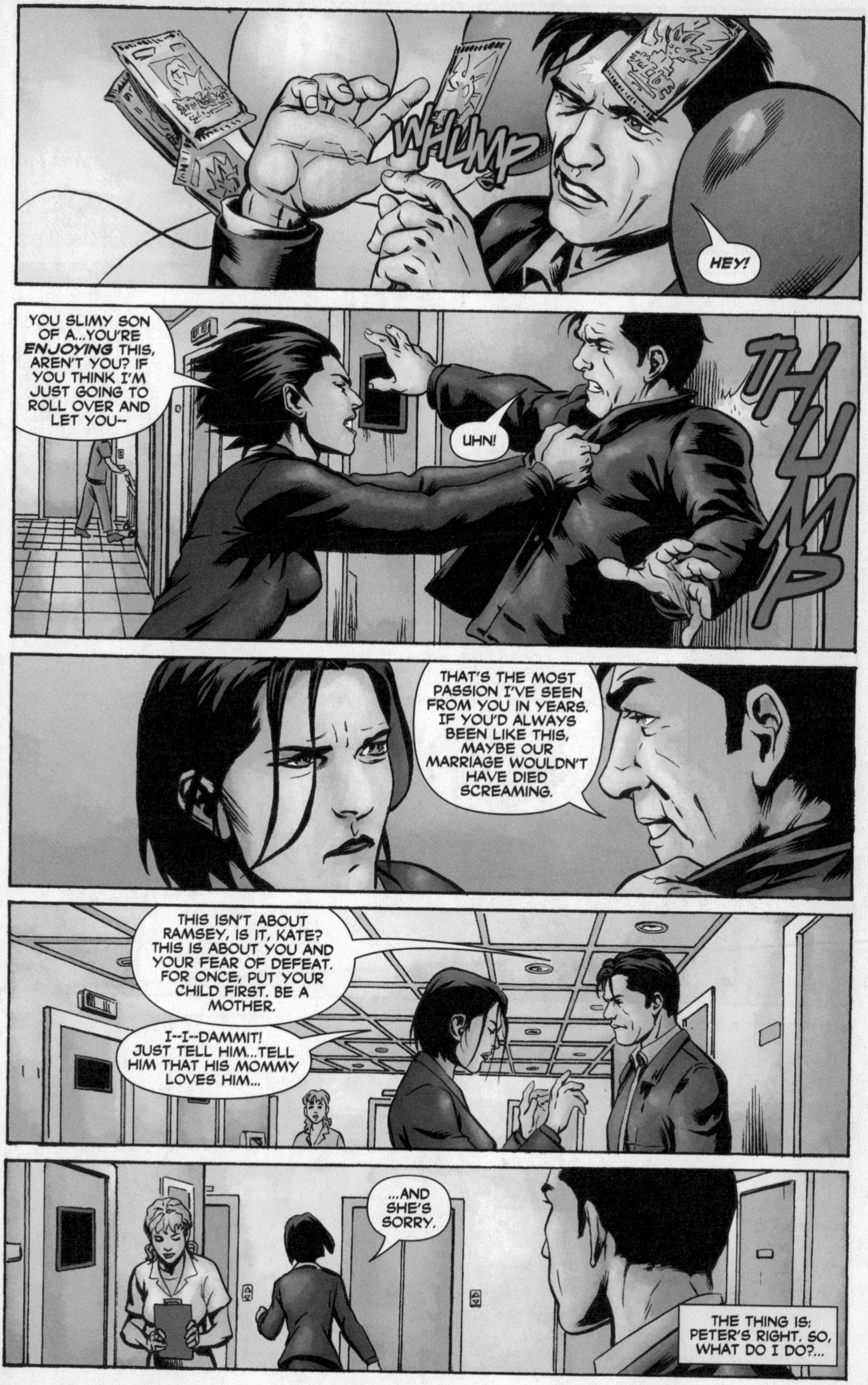
WHUMP
HEY!
YOU SLIMY SON OF A...YOU'RE *ENJOYING* THIS, AREN'T YOU? IF YOU THINK I'M JUST GOING TO ROLL OVER AND LET YOU--
UHN!
THUMP
THAT'S THE MOST PASSION I'VE SEEN FROM YOU IN YEARS. IF YOU'D ALWAYS BEEN LIKE THIS, MAYBE OUR MARRIAGE WOULDN'T HAVE DIED SCREAMING.
THIS ISN'T ABOUT RAMSEY, IS IT, KATE? THIS IS ABOUT YOU AND YOUR FEAR OF DEFEAT. FOR ONCE, PUT YOUR CHILD FIRST. BE A MOTHER.
I--I--DAMMIT! JUST TELL HIM...TELL HIM THAT HIS MOMMY LOVES HIM...
...AND SHE'S SORRY.
THE THING IS: PETER'S RIGHT. SO, WHAT DO I DO?...

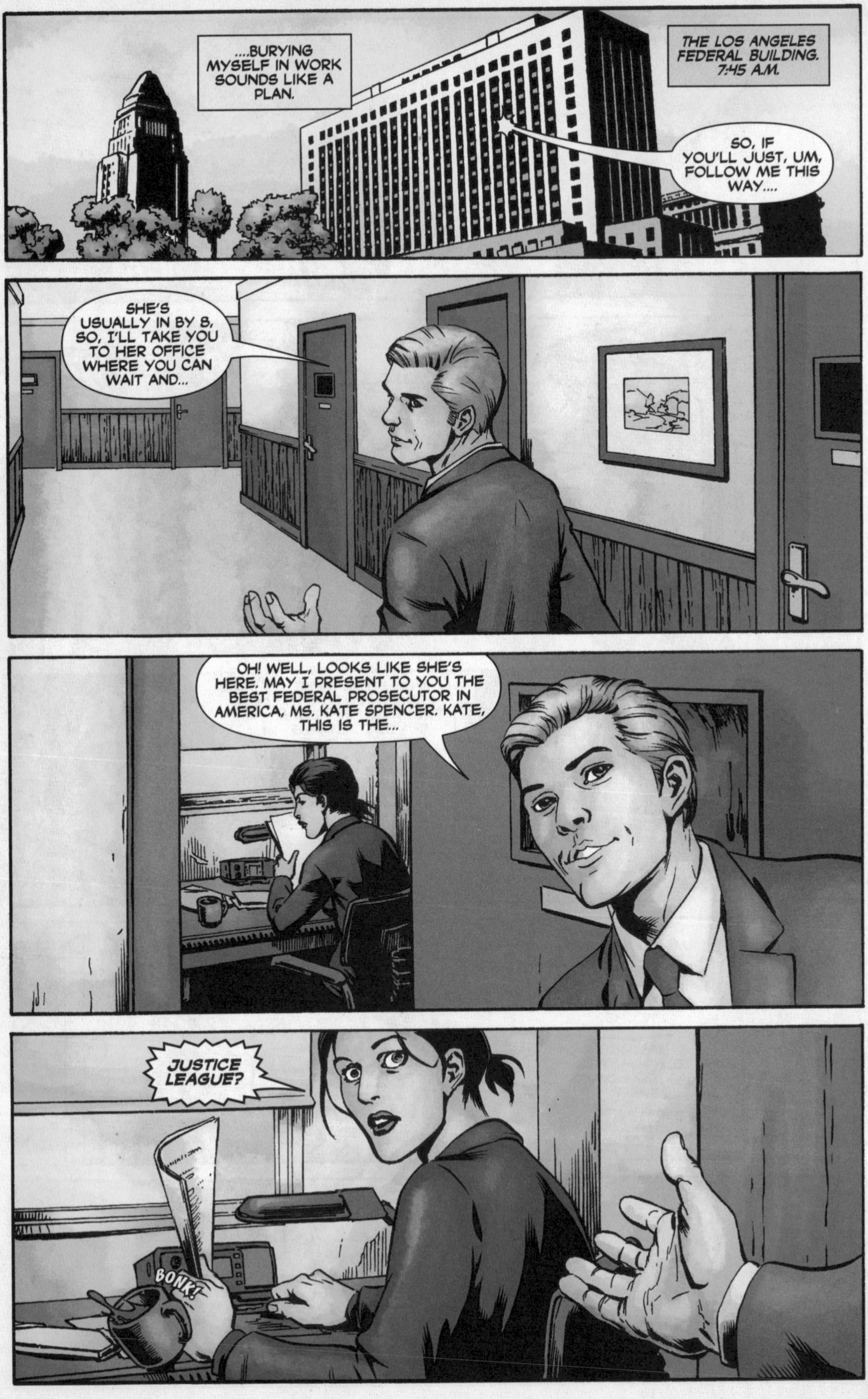
....BURYING MYSELF IN WORK SOUNDS LIKE A PLAN.
THE LOS ANGELES FEDERAL BUILDING. 7:45 A.M.
SO, IF YOU'LL JUST, UM, FOLLOW ME THIS WAY....
SHE'S USUALLY IN BY 8, SO, I'LL TAKE YOU TO HER OFFICE WHERE YOU CAN WAIT AND...
OH! WELL, LOOKS LIKE SHE'S HERE. MAY I PRESENT TO YOU THE BEST FEDERAL PROSECUTOR IN AMERICA, MS. KATE SPENCER. KATE, THIS IS THE...
JUSTICE LEAGUE?
BONK!

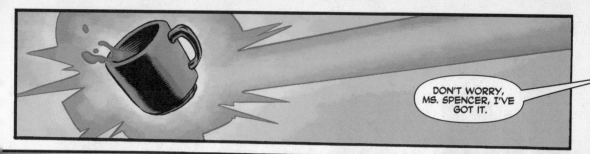

DON'T WORRY, MS. SPENCER, I'VE GOT IT.

I KNOW HOW EXPENSIVE THOSE LATTES CAN BE.

SO, HOW LONG ARE YOU IN TOWN? I KNOW A GREAT SUSHI PLACE IN WEHO AND...

MS. SPENCER, WE ARE HERE TO DISCUSS RECENT EVENTS CONCERNING FIRESTORM.

DAMON, I CAN HANDLE THINGS FROM HERE. THANKS.

OK, BUT--

SORRY. HE'S A LITTLE STARSTRUCK. WE DON'T GET MANY SUPERHEROES AROUND HERE.

SHALL I HAVE SOME MORE CHAIRS SENT IN?

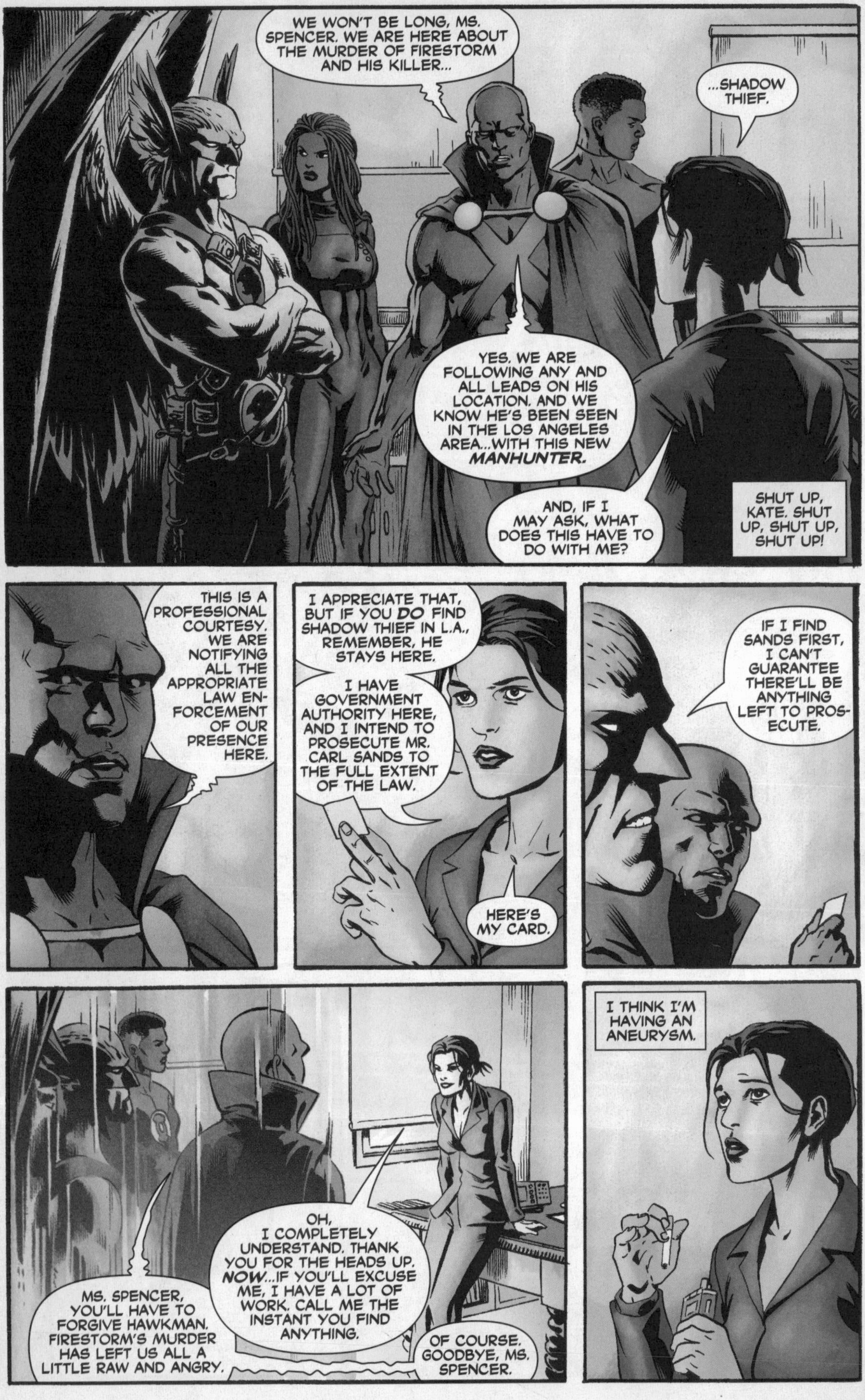
WE WON'T BE LONG, MS. SPENCER. WE ARE HERE ABOUT THE MURDER OF FIRESTORM AND HIS KILLER...
...SHADOW THIEF.
YES. WE ARE FOLLOWING ANY AND ALL LEADS ON HIS LOCATION. AND WE KNOW HE'S BEEN SEEN IN THE LOS ANGELES AREA...WITH THIS NEW MANHUNTER.
AND, IF I MAY ASK, WHAT DOES THIS HAVE TO DO WITH ME?
SHUT UP, KATE. SHUT UP, SHUT UP, SHUT UP!
THIS IS A PROFESSIONAL COURTESY. WE ARE NOTIFYING ALL THE APPROPRIATE LAW ENFORCEMENT OF OUR PRESENCE HERE.
I APPRECIATE THAT, BUT IF YOU DO FIND SHADOW THIEF IN L.A., REMEMBER, HE STAYS HERE.
I HAVE GOVERNMENT AUTHORITY HERE, AND I INTEND TO PROSECUTE MR. CARL SANDS TO THE FULL EXTENT OF THE LAW.
HERE'S MY CARD.
IF I FIND SANDS FIRST, I CAN'T GUARANTEE THERE'LL BE ANYTHING LEFT TO PROSECUTE.
MS. SPENCER, YOU'LL HAVE TO FORGIVE HAWKMAN. FIRESTORM'S MURDER HAS LEFT US ALL A LITTLE RAW AND ANGRY.
OH, I COMPLETELY UNDERSTAND. THANK YOU FOR THE HEADS UP. NOW...IF YOU'LL EXCUSE ME, I HAVE A LOT OF WORK. CALL ME THE INSTANT YOU FIND ANYTHING.
OF COURSE. GOODBYE, MS. SPENCER.
I THINK I'M HAVING AN ANEURYSM.

NOW I KNOW WHY THERE ARE SO FEW ACTIVE METAHUMANS IN L.A.

EVERYTHING IS SO DAMN SPREAD OUT. IT'S NOT LIKE I CAN SWING FROM SKYSCRAPER TO SKYSCRAPER.

CONTACT!

BING BING BING

LET'S SEE HOW GOOD THIS TRACKING STAR REALLY IS, DYLAN.

THIS IS PATHETIC. I NEED A JETPACK OR SOMETHING.

EVENIN', LADY. LIKE THE SUIT.

THANKS.

AT LEAST I WON'T HAVE TO GO FAR TO BURY HIM....

HOLLYWOOD FOREVER
CEMETERY

CLOSED

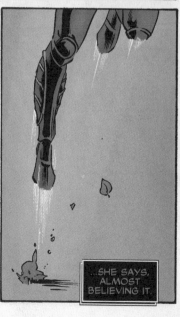

...SHE SAYS, ALMOST BELIEVING IT.

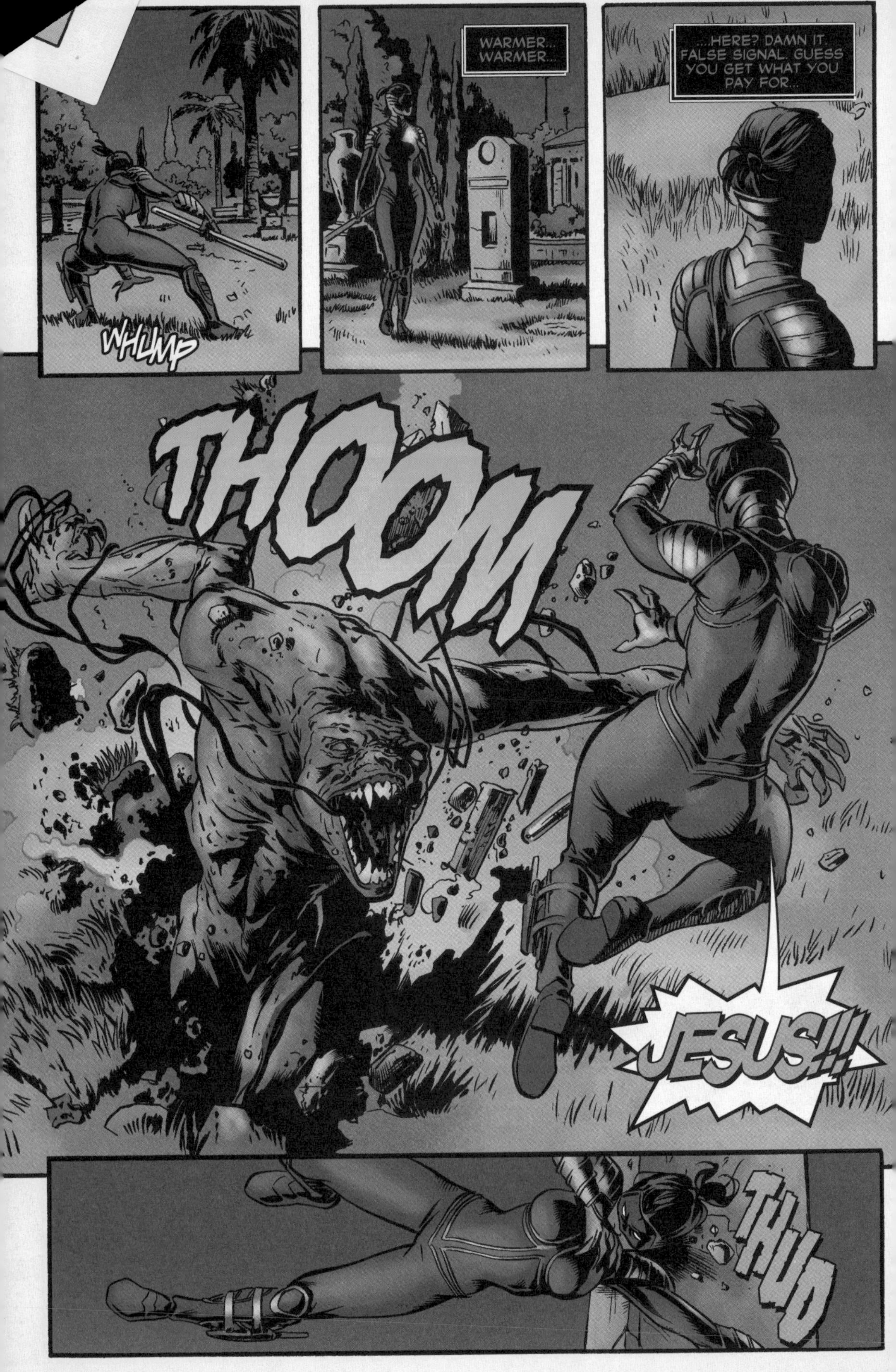
WHUMP
WARMER... WARMER...
...HERE? DAMN IT. FALSE SIGNAL. GUESS YOU GET WHAT YOU PAY FOR...
THOOM
JESUS!!
THUD

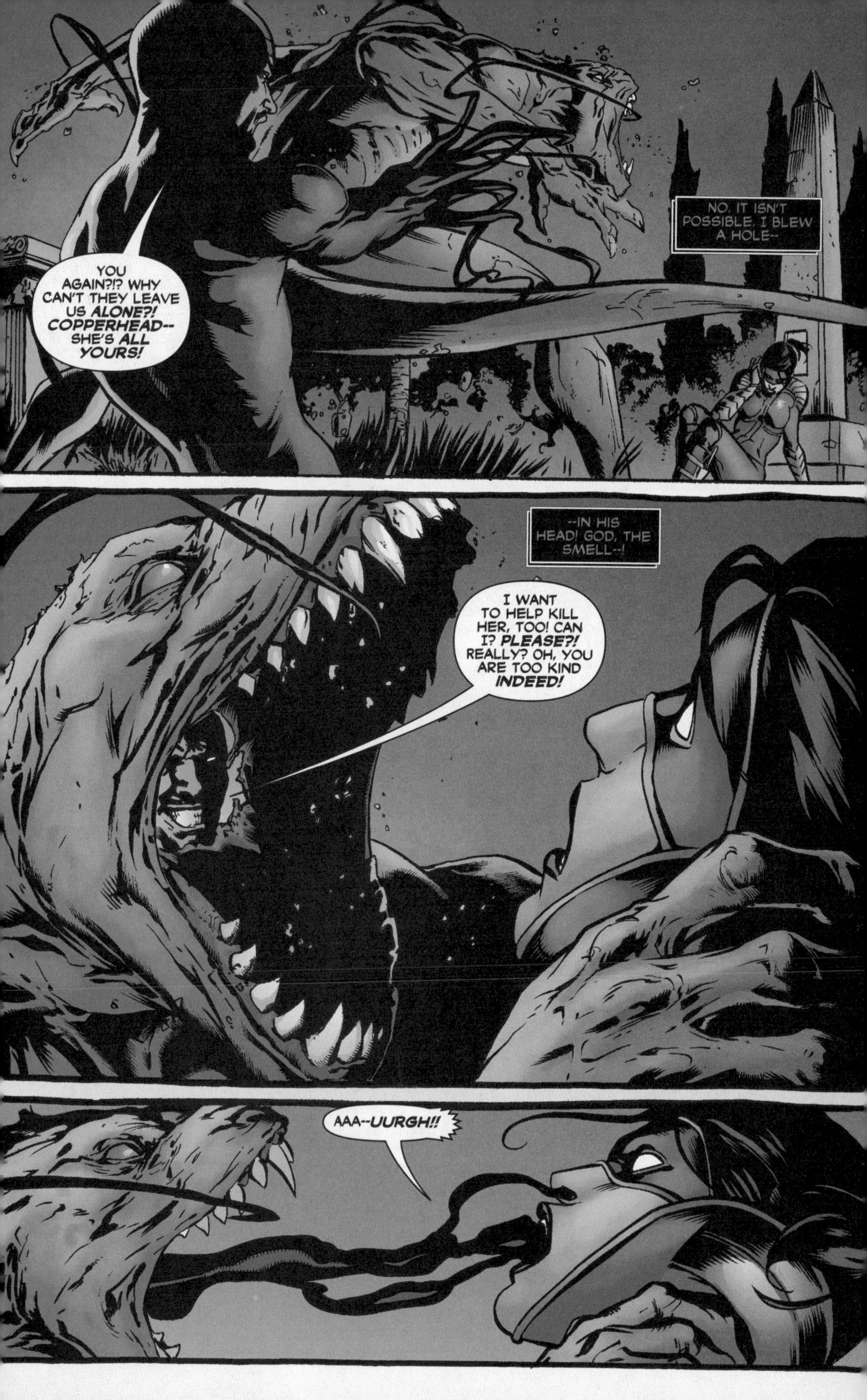
NO. IT ISN'T POSSIBLE. I BLEW A HOLE--
YOU AGAIN?!? WHY CAN'T THEY LEAVE US ALONE?! COPPERHEAD-- SHE'S ALL YOURS!
--IN HIS HEAD! GOD, THE SMELL--!
I WANT TO HELP KILL HER, TOO! CAN I? PLEASE?! REALLY? OH, YOU ARE TOO KIND INDEED!
AAA--UURGH!!

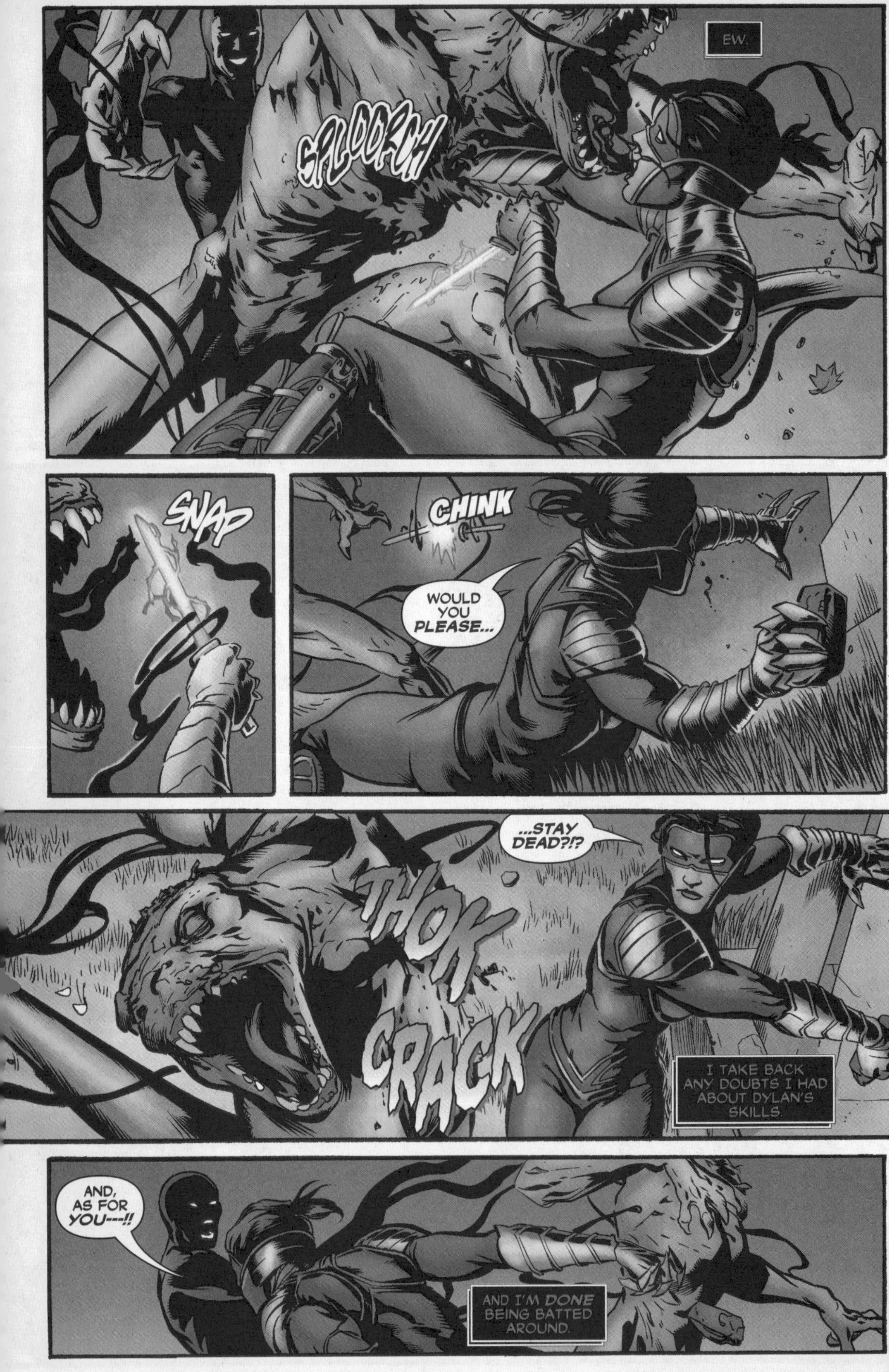
EW.
SPLOORCH
SNAP
CHINK
WOULD YOU PLEASE...
...STAY DEAD?!?
THOK
CRACK
I TAKE BACK ANY DOUBTS I HAD ABOUT DYLAN'S SKILLS.
AND, AS FOR YOU---!!
AND I'M DONE BEING BATTED AROUND.

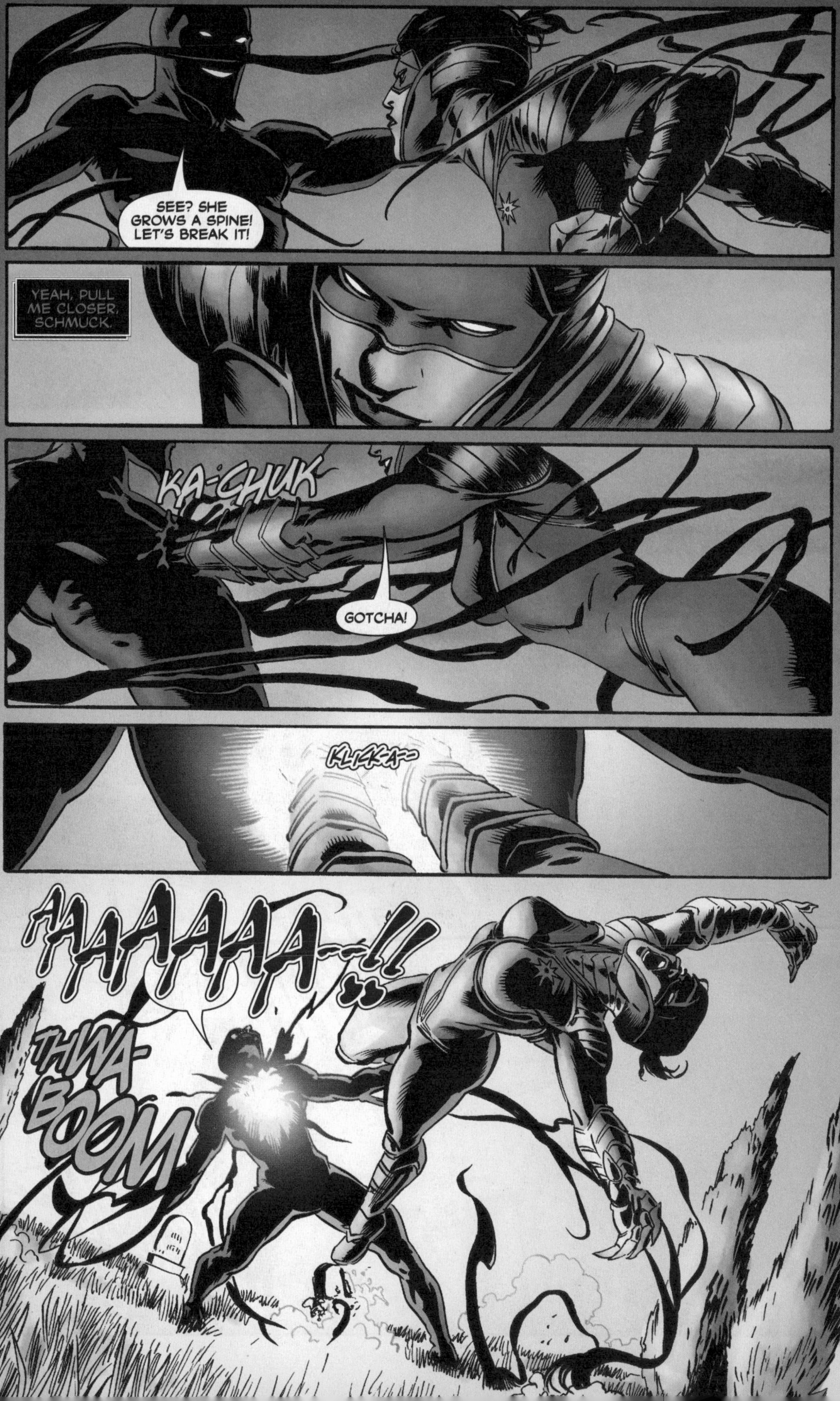
SEE? SHE GROWS A SPINE! LET'S BREAK IT!
YEAH, PULL ME CLOSER, SCHMUCK.
KA-CHUK
GOTCHA!
KLICK-A--
AAAAAAA--!!
THWA-BOOM

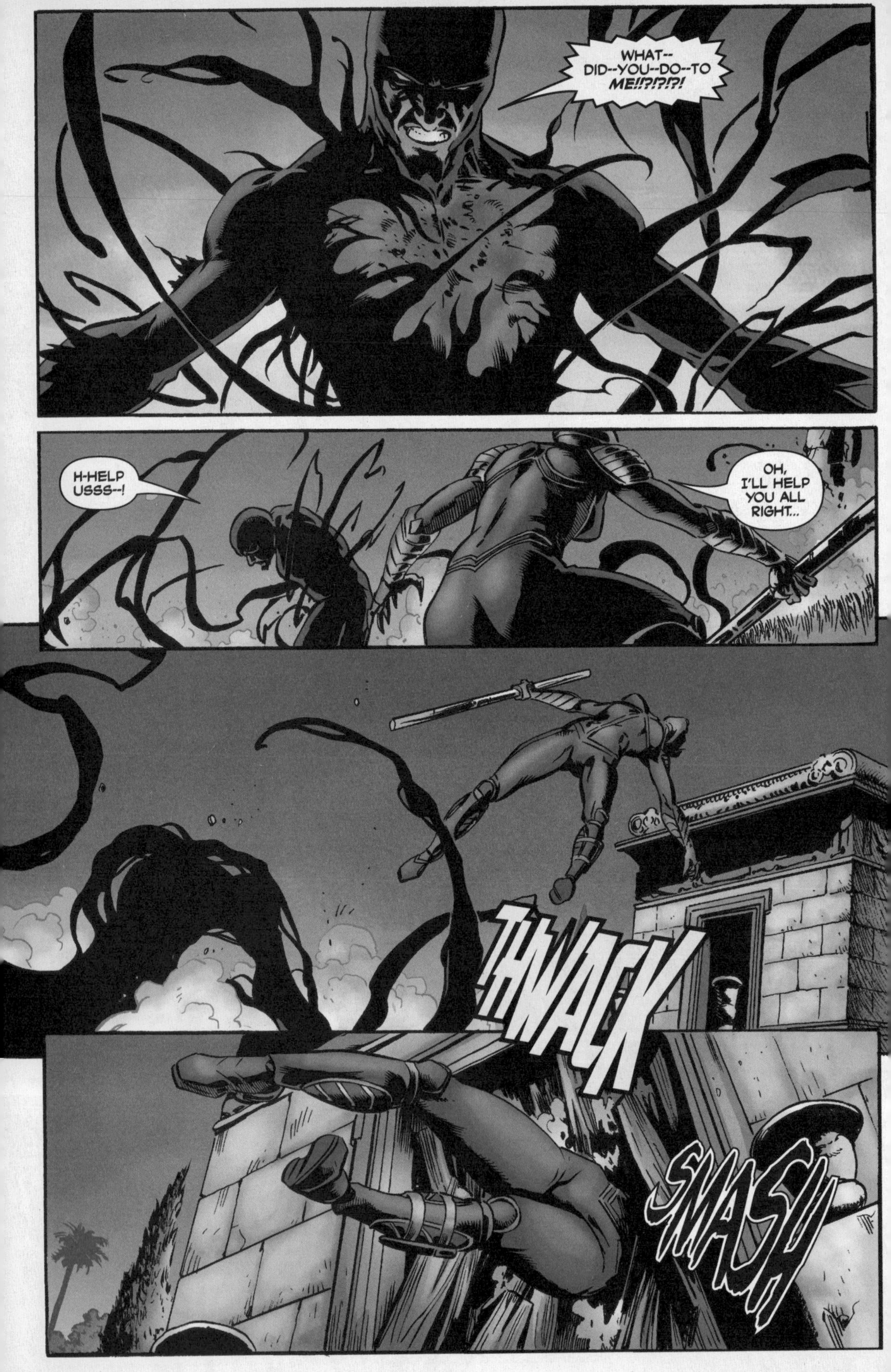
WHAT--
DID--YOU--DO--TO
ME!!?!?!?!
H-HELP
USSS--!
OH,
I'LL HELP
YOU ALL
RIGHT...
THWACK
SMASH

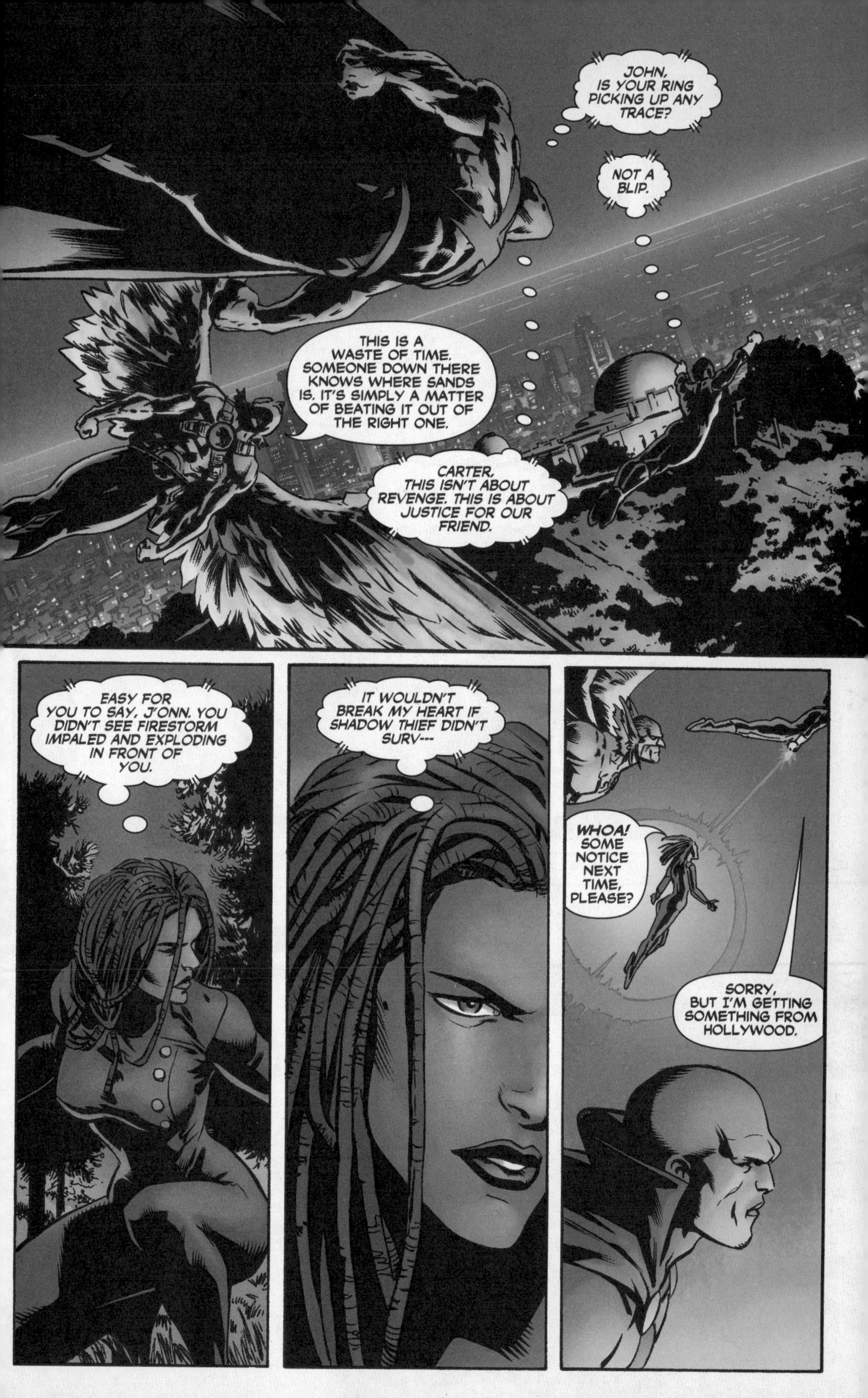
JOHN, IS YOUR RING PICKING UP ANY TRACE?
NOT A BLIP.
THIS IS A WASTE OF TIME. SOMEONE DOWN THERE KNOWS WHERE SANDS IS. IT'S SIMPLY A MATTER OF BEATING IT OUT OF THE RIGHT ONE.
CARTER, THIS ISN'T ABOUT REVENGE. THIS IS ABOUT JUSTICE FOR OUR FRIEND.
EASY FOR YOU TO SAY, J'ONN. YOU DIDN'T SEE FIRESTORM IMPALED AND EXPLODING IN FRONT OF YOU.
IT WOULDN'T BREAK MY HEART IF SHADOW THIEF DIDN'T SURV---
WHOA! SOME NOTICE NEXT TIME, PLEASE?
SORRY, BUT I'M GETTING SOMETHING FROM HOLLYWOOD.

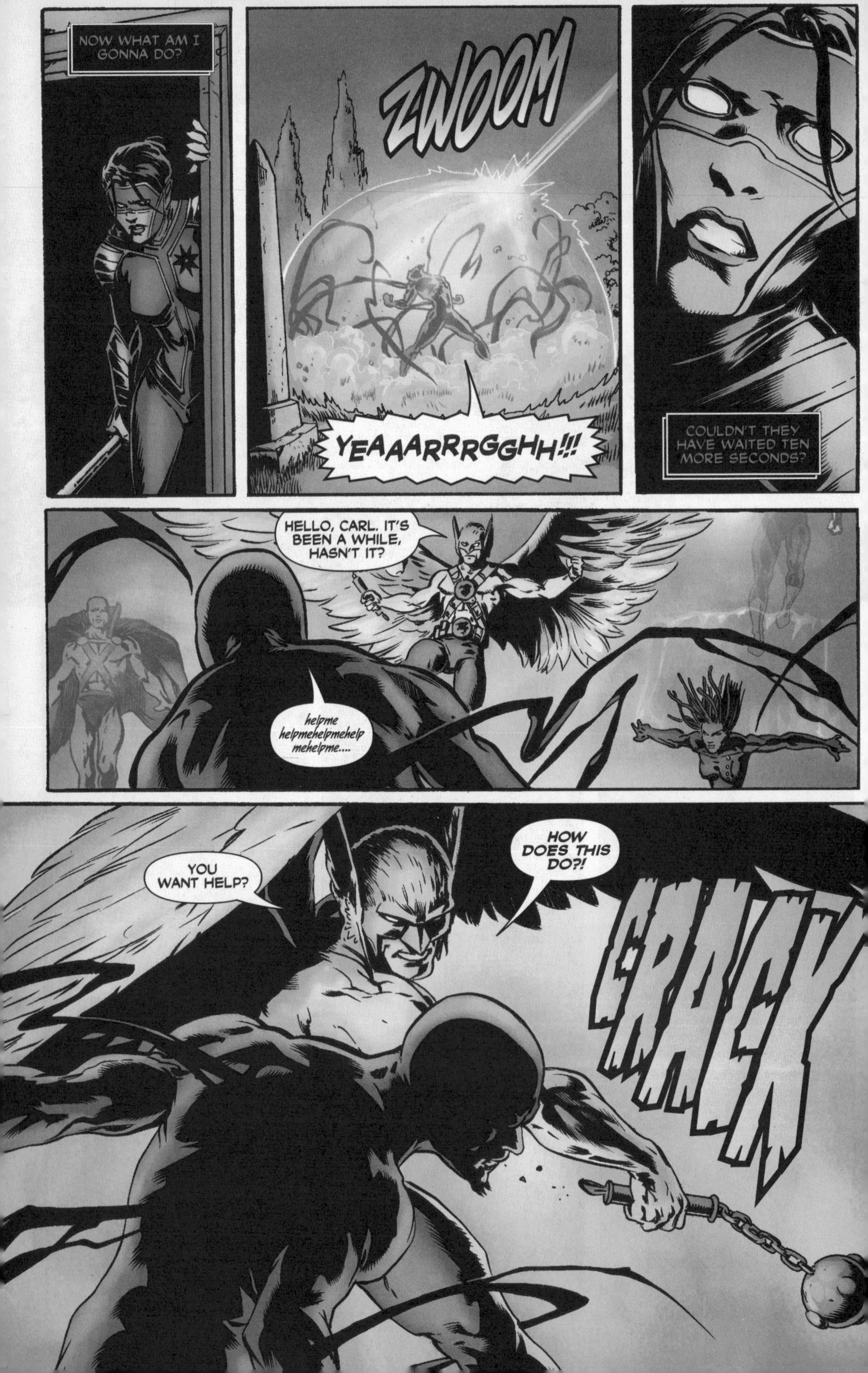
NOW WHAT AM I GONNA DO?
ZWOOM
YEAAARRRGGHH!!!
COULDN'T THEY HAVE WAITED TEN MORE SECONDS?
HELLO, CARL. IT'S BEEN A WHILE, HASN'T IT?
helpme helpmehelpmehelp mehelpme....
YOU WANT HELP?
HOW DOES THIS DO?!
CRACK

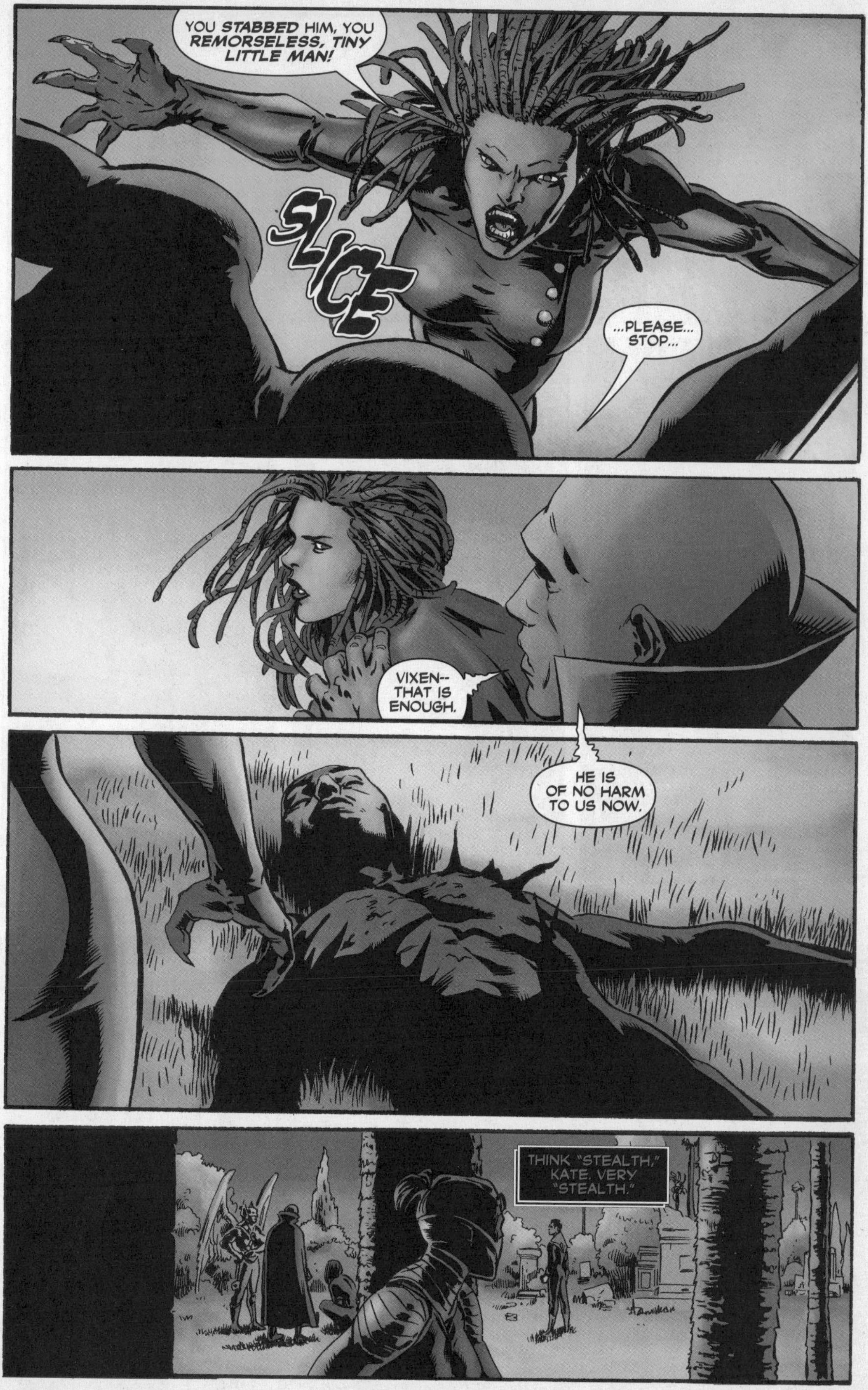
YOU **STABBED** HIM, YOU **REMORSELESS, TINY LITTLE MAN!**
SLICE
...PLEASE... STOP...
VIXEN-- THAT IS ENOUGH.
HE IS OF NO HARM TO US NOW.
THINK "STEALTH," KATE. VERY "STEALTH."

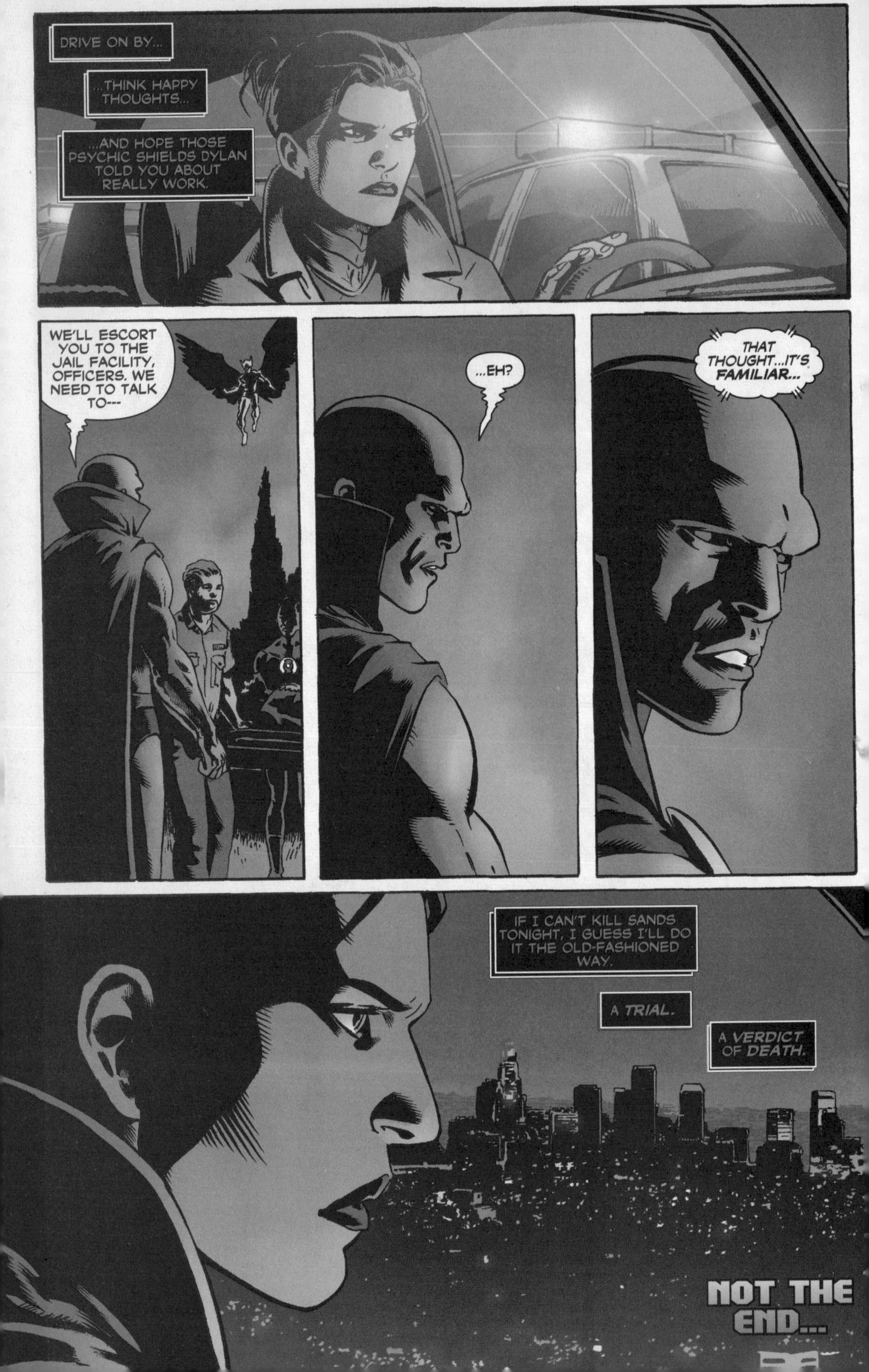
DRIVE ON BY...
...THINK HAPPY THOUGHTS...
...AND HOPE THOSE PSYCHIC SHIELDS DYLAN TOLD YOU ABOUT REALLY WORK.
WE'LL ESCORT YOU TO THE JAIL FACILITY, OFFICERS. WE NEED TO TALK TO---
...EH?
THAT THOUGHT...IT'S FAMILIAR...
IF I CAN'T KILL SANDS TONIGHT, I GUESS I'LL DO IT THE OLD-FASHIONED WAY.
A TRIAL.
A VERDICT OF DEATH.
NOT THE END...